HUMANITARIAN VIOLENCE

DIFFERENCE INCORPORATED

Roderick A. Ferguson and Grace Kyungwon Hong, Series Editors

HUMANITARIAN VIOLENCE

The U.S. Deployment of Diversity

NEDA ATANASOSKI

Difference Incorporated

University of Minnesota Press

Minneapolis

London

Portions of chapter 1 were previously published as "'Race' toward Freedom: Post–Cold War U.S. Multiculturalism and the Reconstruction of Eastern Europe," *Journal of American Culture* 29, no. 2 (June 2006): 219–29. Portions of chapter 4 were previously published as "*Dracula* as Ethnic Conflict: The Technologies of 'Humanitarian Intervention' in the Balkans during the 1999 NATO Bombing of Serbia and Kosovo," in *Monsters and the Monstrous: Myths and Metaphors of Enduring Evil,* ed. Niall Scott (New York: Rodopi, 2007), 61–79.

Published by the University of Minnesota Press
111 Third Avenue South, Suite 290
Minneapolis, MN 55401-2520
http://www.upress.umn.edu

Library of Congress Cataloging-in-Publication Data
Atanasoski, Neda.
Humanitarian violence : the U.S. deployment of diversity / Neda Atanasoski.
(Difference incorporated)
Includes bibliographical references and index.
ISBN 978-0-8166-8093-1 (hc)
ISBN 978-0-8166-8094-8 (pb)
1. United States—Foreign relations. 2. United States—Military policy—Social aspects. 3. Imperialism—Social aspects. 4. Humanitarianism—United States. 5. War and society—United States. I. Title.
E183.7.A83 2013
327.73—dc23   2013030773

Printed in the United States of America on acid-free paper

The University of Minnesota is an equal-opportunity educator and employer.

20 19 18 17 16 15 14 13   10 9 8 7 6 5 4 3 2 1

CONTENTS

INTRODUCTION

The Racial Reorientations of U.S. Humanitarian Imperialism

IN 2012 the International Criminal Tribunal for the Former Yugoslavia (ICTY), which was founded by the United Nations Security Council in 1993 to adjudicate war crimes and crimes against humanity committed during the 1990s wars of secession, announced its plans for completion in 2016. The existence of the Tribunal as an institutional site for advancing international humanitarian and human rights law for two decades now has made it, alongside the International Criminal Tribunal for Rwanda, a permanent fixture of the postsocialist world. In contrast to the relatively brief duration of the Nuremberg and Tokyo Tribunals after the Second World War, the longevity of the ICTY and other tribunals institutionally inscribes spaces of atrocity, ethnic cleansing, and sectarian conflict as the undeviating feature of the post–Cold War geopolitical landscape. In the words of former ICTY president Antonio Cassese, the Tribunal is necessary for the "restoration of peaceful and normal relations between people who have lived under a *reign of terror*."[1] Cassese's casting of ethnic and religious violence as "terror" that must be overcome through the operations of the perpetual Tribunal echoes uneasily with the perpetual "war on terror" waged by the United States and its Western European allies in the Middle East. Although the Tribunal, as a site of juridical humanization and international human rights law, might seem opposed to the post-9/11 U.S. bypassing of international governing bodies in its wars and treatment of prisoners in Afghanistan and Iraq, it is important to ask: How have ideas about terror, humanity, war, and justice resonated across such distinct modes of geopolitical power? How does the evocation of ethnoreligious conflict in the 1990s figure into contemporary conceptions of terror? What is the relationship between perpetual warfare, humanitarianism, and human rights in the envisaging of freedom after the demise of communism? How does human difference (racial, religious, and gendered) become the mode through which the conditions of possibility for human redemption and atrocity become coarticulated? How do certain parts of the world become legible as landscapes of atrocity, while others become spaces of humaneness and humanization?

Like the contemporary war on terror, the humanitarian military interventions that led to the rise of the Tribunal were not framed in traditional terms as wars for territorial gain or against nation-states. Rather, these wars have been fought in the name of democracy and against illiberal beliefs and modes of governance, such as religious fundamentalism and ethnic nationalism, which are seen to perpetuate atrocity through racism, sexism, and religious and political persecution. The popularization of the term "collateral damage" to describe the loss of civilian lives in instances of U.S. militarism in the 1990s aptly encapsulates this shift. Since the United States and its allies portray themselves as waging wars against tyrannical creeds, and not against the peoples of a particular nation, culture, or racial or religious group, humanitarian militarism prohibits attention to its own death dealing. It is, instead, represented as a struggle to restore human dignity by protecting diversity (though not material equality), made sacred in the rule of law. Moreover, targeted regimes, including those headed by rogue dictators, extragovernmental insurgents, and religious "extremists," are imagined to have already made the lives of civilians killable. The concept of "collateral damage" illustrates how certain acts of violence become intelligible as acts of atrocity, while other modes of killing are comprehensible solely as acts of redemption. With the advent of twenty-four-hour news networks and the Internet in the post–Cold War world, and through the ongoing impact of photojournalism and documentaries, images of atrocity circulate in real time, eliciting Euro-America's humanitarian gaze and calling for the military and juridical humanization of barbarous geographies. Making spaces of atrocity transparent and accessible to our interventionism, visual, military, and legal technologies work in concert to affirm "our" humanity by saving those suffering under a "reign of terror." These technologies conceal instances of "our" brutality, enacted in the name of peace, reconciliation, and the rule of law, while paradoxically reinscribing violence and injury through the process of humanizing the other.

Focusing on the consolidation of the humanitarian gaze in instances of U.S. militarism during the Vietnam War, the Soviet–Afghan War, and the 1990s wars of secession in the former Yugoslavia, *Humanitarian Violence* explores the wartime political, media, and juridical frames of visibility and transparency that justify the ongoing need for imperial rule in the post-socialist era. While existing studies of U.S. imperial ascendancy in the aftermath of 9/11 do not, for the most part, consider the postsocialist global condition as relevant to the nation's repertoire of dominance, this book contends that U.S. militarism—as well as other forms of interventionism—in the present is in fact an instantiation of a *postsocialist imperialism* based in humanitarian ethics. The predominant fiction of the United States as a multicultural haven, which morally underwrites the nation's equally brutal war waging and peacemaking meant to facilitate the spread of liberal democracy and free markets after the fall of communism, conceives parts of the world that are still subject to the violence of U.S. power as being permanently in need of reform because they are homogeneous and racially, religiously, and sexually intolerant. The ensuing entangled notions of humanity and atrocity that follow from such mediations of war and crisis have resignified the struggle for freedom in the post–Cold War era, so that what is at stake is no longer the making of a world free from communism but rather the making of a world in which all can enjoy racial and religious freedom, as exemplified by the principles of U.S. liberal democracy. Cultural narratives supporting U.S. militarism increasingly participate in racializing religious and ideological differences depicted as illiberal, thus supplementing the racialization of bodies under previous imperial formations. Even as media and political discourses surrounding humanitarian militarism reference and build on a history of European racial imperialism, U.S. settler colonialism, and pre–civil rights racial formations in which racial difference was associated with the exclusion of nonwhite bodies from the civic life of the nation, an emergent discourse of race targeting religious and ideological difference makes postsocialist and Islamic nations the potential objects of U.S. disciplining violence.

In order to apprehend the cultural, political, and historical contours of contemporary U.S. racial logics undergirding postsocialist imperialism, it is crucial to bring together the imperial and Cold War histories of U.S. interests in and fantasy of Eastern Europe, Asia, and the Middle East that continue to shape present-day imaginaries of freedom. Assessing Eastern Europe as a neglected but constitutive region in the American (trans)-national imaginary, I argue that in spite of the differences between twentieth century U.S. imperial ventures in Vietnam, postsocialist Central and Eastern Europe, and Afghanistan from the 1980s to the present day, juxtaposing them enables a novel perspective on the imbrications of war, race, and cultural production. A relational analysis of these distinct instances of

U.S. humanitarian intervention brings to the fore how in each case European racial and imperial projects were recast to produce the U.S. fantasy of militarism as morally multicultural. In this regard, U.S. cultural reworkings of the tropes of racialized difference organizing Western Europe's imperial past, through which the nation narrates itself as an empire working on behalf of individual and minority rights, complement the historical tenet of American exceptionalism that casts U.S. interventionism as the anti-imperial engine of liberation. This historicization of postsocialist modes of racialization that has accompanied and justified the shifting terrains of U.S. imperial domination in the second half of the twentieth century brings into relief the ways in which cultural production provides the armature for framing U.S. militarism as humanitarian, defining morality itself in racialized terms through the enactment of U.S. power. The inherent instability of dominant cultural frames, however, also leads to alternate accountings.

The fiction of the United States as a nation that is morally suited to humanize landscapes of atrocity through imperial military and juridical rule presupposes that, in contrast to the racism of previous European empires and the narrow-mindedness and fanaticism of contemporary ideological foes, with the advent of civil rights, America became an exemplary racial democracy for democratizing nations. The sanctifying of human diversity through humanitarian warfare and the rule of law produces a temporal frame of humanization in which previously excluded others' inclusion into racial and religious modernity marks their moment of arrival. Meanwhile, social worlds and modes of governance that do not align with humanitarian and human rights regimes are considered out of time. Visions of justice and human potential in which liberal rights are not the mechanism of salvation, such as those espoused by socialist revolutionaries or communities of faith, are thus often critiqued as being monocultural and inhumane. Since the end of the Second World War, the association between U.S. racial and religious pluralism and tolerance, national development, and freedom has been marshaled to distinguish the United States from contemporary ideological and religious enemies as diverse as communism and Islam, whose regimes and beliefs are conceived of as anachronistic because they do not accept or nurture individual and group differences. The merging of racial and religious multiculturalism and postsocialist imperial intervention as a mechanism of historical and economic development, though it was spurred by Cold War geopolitics, first came to a head in the 1990s with the hypervisibility of the Balkans as a site of ethnoreligious strife in the U.S. imaginary. Contrasted with American racial and religious multiculturalism, the Balkans became a tableau of "ethnic cleansing" and genocide against which U.S. humanitarian militarism was consolidated and articulated as an ethical interventionist project protecting diversity in the region. Even as the United States continues the violent civilizing legacies of European imperialism, postsocialist modes of imperial rule in effect in the Balkans and, more recently, in the Middle East are depicted as fundamentally different from the older powers, the dead and defunct empires, because of America's embodiment of diversity and belief in liberal rights (racial, religious, and sexual).

In this sense, the U.S. postsocialist imperial project can be thought of as a project of converting humanity to liberal personhood through the enactment of humanitarian violence. As a humanizing mode of governance, postsocialist imperialism is contingent on multiculturalism as a value system and mode of knowledge about the world that demands that individuals declare their faith in a global humanity made manifest in normative articulations of racial, religious, and cultural diversity enshrined as individual juridical rights. Because it authorizes ongoing imperial violence, multiculturalism can be characterized not simply as a new racial technology but rather as the *afterlife of previous racial forms* that relies on modern racial epistemes to apprehend and eliminate illiberal ways of inhabiting ethnic, religious, and sexual difference. Conceiving of multiculturalism as a global ideal through which the sanctity of human diversity is declared, humanitarian projects have subsumed and supplanted the civilizing and humanizing aspirations of European racial imperialism. By justifying contemporary U.S. imperialism through its disarticulation from European imperialism, multiculturalism has ironically become the language of global salvation from white supremacy and illiberal regimes.

Of course, the Enlightenment narrative of human progress conceived through Western European racial imperialism and civilizing mission is the scaffolding on which subsequent aspirations to humanize not-yet-modern others have been built. In this sense, European imperialism has an afterlife in U.S. postsocialist imperialism that continues to make relevant its core notions of moral development and humanizing ambitions. At the same time, postsocialism marks the emergence of novel modes of interpreting the imperatives of the world map set in place by European imperial rule. In the nineteenth century, Western European imperial supremacy mapped the globe through narratives of racial hierarchy. European nations conceived of their preeminence by representing the imperial metropoles as racially pure, while portraying non-European bodies as geographically and morally distant from European modernity.

In contrast, at the start of the Cold War, imperial Europe's racial map of the colonies was subsumed into an ideological cartography that divided the free world and the unfree world. Unlike the notions of racial purity and superiority that accompanied European imperialism, late twentieth-century U.S. geopolitical ascendancy has utilized the nation's racial pluralism to rationalize its militarism and interventionism as a technology of freedom. Developing in response to the juridical gains of the civil rights movement, the liberation struggles in the Global South, and the threat of communism, racial multiculturalism isolated the possibility of human uplift within the boundaries of the U.S.-led "free world," while homogeneity became associated with the suppression of human difference in the Communist "unfree world." Coding the U.S.S.R. and the Eastern Bloc as ethnically homogeneous, even if only ambiguously European, enabled U.S. foreign policy to portray Soviet foreign interests as expansionist and "imperialist." In contrast, the United States' self-understanding as a racially diverse nation, with the paradigm of multiculturalism taking the place of early Cold War civil rights, buttressed its logic of "containing" the Communist threat in the Third World by distancing U.S. military interventionism from an association with European colonialism.

Though most critiques of multiculturalism emphasize only racial formations, I am interested in the ways in which multiculturalism categorizes, normalizes, and pathologizes religious as well as racial differences. Secularism, generally understood to be the commitment of U.S. and Western European nations to protect religious freedom from the tyranny of the state, has in recent years become globalized as a project of redeeming humanity from conditions of religious "unfreedom." Meanwhile, within the United States, the coexistence of multiple and varied faiths, each allowed freedom of conscience and practice for its followers under the auspices of the liberal nation-state, is the sign of religious freedom. The collapsing of religious plurality with religious freedom can be thought of as a mode of religious multiculturalism. As such, religious multiculturalism is a discourse that with racial multiculturalism is coconstitutive of normative notions of a converted, reformed, and emancipated humanity in the postsocialist era.

Building on Cold War legacies, U.S. postsocialist imperial logics make meaning of geopolitical, economic, and social transformations in which the yet-to-be-humanized other is no longer marked *only* by a *visible difference*, legible on the skin, but *also* by an *interior difference of belief*. Indeed, U.S. geopolitical ascendancy has been justified through the racialization of ideologies and illiberal religiosity as a logical extension and justification of the racialization of bodies and continents underlying European imperialism. For instance, during the Cold War, the Soviet Union was conflated with "Russianness," and therefore whiteness, in the U.S. imaginary. Meanwhile, communism emerged as the (ideological) difference that could not be assimilated into the U.S. worldview. In this sense, U.S. orientation against communism after the Second World War can be thought of as a *racial reorientation* on both foreign and domestic fronts. With the advent of the Cold War, the most important difference dividing the globe was thus no longer just racial/biological, as it had been in the eighteenth and nineteenth centuries, but also cultural/ideological.[2] In other words, Cold War geopolitical imaginaries that conceived of the United States as the sole protector of the global landscapes of freedom reconfigured the European imperial *spatialization of race relations* as the *racialization of belief and ideology* mapped onto those previous spatializations.

Through the racialization of ideological and religious formations conceived of as antithetical to the flourishing of human diversity, proliferating "regimes of terror" that have replaced communism at once reaffirm older notions of humanity and introduce new ones. The need to render interiorized difference visible has necessitated the merging of military, media, and juridical technologies that make instances of atrocity, stemming from supposedly anachronistic belief systems, ever more transparent to U.S. and Western publics. The unprecedented focus on revealing hidden human rights abuses produces a geopolitical counterpart to the assumed openness (and visible racial diversity) of U.S. democracy. Images of barbarism rooted in intolerance, condensed in figurations such as the mass graves of the Rwanda and Bosnia genocides, ethnic rape/death camps in Bosnia and Kosovo, and, in the post-9/11 era, the veiled woman allegedly oppressed by Islamic patriarchy, make distant landscapes of persecution accessible to moral outrage. "Our" feelings of shock and military action are, in turn, framed as bringing these places into the fold of historical progress. Understanding how technologies of visuality and transparency reaffirm Euro-American humanity requires more than an exploration of the kinds of lives that are given value and those lives that are made/let to die in the present. It is equally important to draw attention to how and why certain ideologies and belief systems are given life, while others are displaced, suppressed, and forgotten in the making of new world orders and epistemes. As the sites through which the tension between crisis and normality is articulated, resolved, and framed, political, media, literary, and visual cultures create and re-create appropriate fantasies of the good, producing the condition of possibility for the conversion of ideology and belief.[3] As U.S. media and political rhetorics generate and engulf ever-new geographies of horror within the nation's moral imaginary, national (and global) populations declare their faith in a common humanity through their capacity to feel for the subjugated and violated other, and through military–humanitarian intervention.

The military, media, and juridical technologies of U.S. humanitarian ethics as a moral and visual language of racial, religious, and historical redemption have engendered a dual temporality of postsocialist imperialism that is both sacred (a moment of global arrival to a state of freedom) and secular (part of a broader narrative of juridical human progress). The victory of liberal capitalist democracy and the defeat of other possible lifeworlds, including socialism, seem to affirm the universality of the United States and Western Europe at "the end of history." At the same time, with ongoing wars, the perpetuation of human progress is made manifest through violence, as the United States and its European allies seek to make life in their own image in parts of the world where vestiges of atrocity remain. Military interventionism and the emergent international juridical regime, enshrined in tribunals set up to counter the effects of atrocity, displace modes of governance and sociality seen as illiberal, becoming the twin engines of human and historical deliverance from states of unfreedom. Humanitarian violence is thus justified through cultural narratives about creating an afterlife for those lives freed through rights and recognition, so that they may participate in and emerge as properly human through the liberal rule of law and free-market development (of which the United States is a harbinger). In this sense, postsocialist imperial expansion cannot be understood purely in terms of territorial gain and exploitation but as the enfolding of humanity into a global account of racial, religious, and sexual self-realization.

Secularism, Multiculturalism, and the Racialization of Religion

Following the demise of the Soviet Union, the United States, now the only superpower, for the first time openly articulated its global interests as imperialist.[4] Through developments in political, media, and juridical modes of racialization in the second half of the twentieth century, however, the nation continues to assert its exceptional status, this time as an empire. Jodi Melamed has usefully defined racialization as the "process that constitutes differential relations of human value and valuelessness" through distinct racial categorizations of bodies and spaces.[5] Building on Melamed's definition, this book connects the value and valuelessness of bodies to the value and valuelessness of belief systems and social worlds. Indeed, contemporary U.S. imperialism deploys military and juridical violence as twin mechanisms for converting individuals and supplanting ideological systems out of sync with liberal modernity. The formerly Communist subject can thus become a participant in neoliberal capitalism, the racist can come to embrace difference, and the Muslim can be a proper secular citizen. As the expression of America's national, racial, and religious transcendence of its past of slavery, exclusion, and segregation, multiculturalism assumes that the United States has fulfilled the promise of universal inclusion through juridical rights (if not material equality) for its own citizens. Framed as an emancipatory ideology, multiculturalism is transnationalized through U.S. imperialist militarism in the rest of the world. The racial multiculturalism and religious multiculturalism that inform contemporary understandings of secularism and humanitarianism in the United States have produced a normative value system through which U.S. citizens, as subjects individuated through their differences, demonstrate their tolerance and ability to recognize landscapes of atrocity, intolerance, and homogeneity. In other words, U.S. citizens place their faith in multiculturalism as a mode of secular morality through which they apprehend what needs to happen in order for the rest of the world to be free.

Since the nation's founding, conceptions of Americans' access to rights and freedoms have been anchored in both religion and race. Talal Asad notes that the two origin narratives in American rights language are, first, "the Puritan escape to religious freedom from persecution in England; and second, the story of the constitution of thirteen American colonies in a new sovereign state, signifying a repudiation of English despotism."[6] Although, as Asad points out, the United States' initial definition of humanity was based on the exclusion of English tyranny, Native American paganism, and African slaves' subhumanity, America's formative prophetic story of captivity and deliverance (of the Puritans and colonists from English despotism) "always demands the redemption of subjects if they are to vindicate their human status and join the universe of free, equal, and sovereign individuals."[7] Because of the histories of slavery and genocide, portraits of the United States as a beacon of freedom begin with accounts of religious rather than racial liberty. Moreover, that the advancement of the United States as a nation is now associated with the structures of secular citizenship and modern statecraft on a global scale speaks to the power of the origin story detailing how different religious groups escaping Old World discrimination came to live side by side, practicing their own faiths and allowing others to worship in their own way.[8] In this sense, the ideal of religious freedom is the cornerstone for formulations of America's "exceptional liberty."[9]

The imbrication of race and religion in contemporary geopolitics represents the transnationalization of U.S. secular conceptions of liberty and rights.[10] Yet the commonplace linking of America's origins to the Puritans' arrival and the nation's subsequent progress toward democratic inclusivity depends on Protestant understandings of faith based in an individual relationship with God.[11] Protestant notions of religious liberty, experienced as one's own freedom of conscience leading to self-realization, cast tolerance for others' personal convictions as paramount to secular development. Secularism, more than just the separation of church and state, is a framing device for the United States' self-conception as a nation *built on* and *productive of* diverse faiths, cultures, and peoples. In short, secularism can be understood as an ideology of human difference and its transcendence in this world.[12] Within the structures of liberal citizenship, the human rights regime, and international humanitarian law—the supposed guarantors of secular redemption—certain nations, such as the United States, are vested with the moral authority to recognize those spaces in need of emancipation. Although the very possibility of religious freedom in the United States clearly depended on a series of racial exclusions, it also laid the groundwork for the subsequent incorporation of bodily and normative religious difference into a national mythology of religious and racial advancement that redeems not just domestic but global humanity. This was evident even in older U.S. imperial formations, though it has come into crisis in present-day humanitarian imperialism.[13]

What the ideal of religious tolerance does to perpetuate the nationalist narrative of the United States as a unique nation in the colonial era, multicultural pluralism does in the current period. After the Second World War, liberal antiracism, adding to existing accounts of the United States as an exemplary incarnation of religious freedom, refigured human ethnoracial diversity as sacred in this world. After the juridical accomplishments of the civil rights movement, racial diversity now supplements religious multiplicity as a badge of American liberty, defining the United States as a *secular racial democracy*. The advent of de jure racial equality is considered the moment of national conversion from intolerance to tolerance, marking the nation's transcendence of previous systems of racial and gender hierarchies and authorizing U.S. geopolitical ascendance in terms of its moral supremacy. Of course, though civil rights were granted to nonwhite

Americans in the 1950s and 1960s, U.S. capitalism continued to depend on racialized labor, reproducing material inequalities. Remarkably, the fact that the United States could portray itself as a nation committed to racial democracy by the mid-twentieth century reveals the extent to which the chronicling of capitalist development buries the very injustices it produces.[14]

The remembrance of a racist and unjust past, emphasized only to the extent that it reaffirms what we have overcome, was advanced and sustained by the official and institutional narrativizing of state-sanctioned antiracism in the United States throughout the Cold War period, and in opposition to other visions of human equality, particularly the socialist one. According to Mary Dudziak, at the height of anti-Communist sentiment, "in addressing civil rights reform from 1946 through the mid-1960s, the federal government engaged in a sustained effort to tell a particular story about race and American democracy: a story of progress, a story of the triumph of good over evil, a story of U.S. *moral superiority*."[15] Similarly, Nikhil Pal Singh argues that the American "civic mythology of racial progress" has been shaped by an abbreviated periodization of the civil rights era beginning with the 1954 *Brown v. Board of Education* Supreme Court desegregation decision and culminating in the 1965 Voting Rights Act.[16] Through this reperiodization and appropriation of civil rights history, "civic myths about the triumph over racial injustice have become central to the resuscitation of a vigorous and strident form of American exceptionalism—the idea of the United States as both a unique and universal nation."[17] The myth of racial progress, dependent as it was on the juridical humanization of the racial other, was consolidated not just through the civil rights history of black–white relations but, as Asian American scholars have argued, through the mobilization of the "model minority" discourse that emphasized ethnic minorities' potential for assimilation and upward mobility in U.S. democracy after the lifting of the immigration exclusion acts.[18] The advent of civil rights, representing more than the legal recognition of nonwhite Americans and women, stands for the redemption of the United States and its citizenry from its past of slavery, exclusion, and white supremacy. As accounts of racial progress produced nationally legitimated histories of racial forgetting, civil rights and multiculturalism became the foremost juridical and moral frames through which the United States described itself as the leader of the free world. Because individual and minority rights, enshrined in civil rights laws, are held up as the actualization of America's anti-Communist, messianic promise of freeing the world from totalitarianism during the Cold War, the United States still positions itself as the protector and enforcer of rights, now on a global scale. In this sense, humanitarian militarism and recent developments in international law are coconstitutive.

The geopolitical reorganization that demanded and resulted in civil and political rights domestically in turn racialized intolerance, illiberalism, and homogeneity as inhuman states, obstructing the spread of democracy, individualism, free expression, and, importantly, free markets. While secular multiculturalism presumes that beliefs are something that each individual chooses, and that can therefore change, the racial and, to an extent, cultural differences into which one is born are increasingly singled out as needing special protection from the tyranny of monoculturalism. Like Melamed's incisive genealogy of state-sanctioned antiracism in the United States in *Represent and Destroy,* this book is also interested in "how liberal terms of difference have depoliticized economic arrangements by decisively integrating the knowledge-architecture that has structured global capitalism's postwar development . . . into what racial equality may signify or what may signify as racial equality."[19] The changes Melamed traces in multicultural modes of racialization through neoliberalism I route through the lens of postsocialism and the advent of humanitarian violence in the new world order. Whereas as an analytic, neoliberalism enables an exploration of liberalism's historical formations and refigurations of racial capitalism in the contemporary period, a postsocialist analytic shifts the frame of inquiry to center on the social, political, and cultural legacies and displacements of socialism as an ethical limit to liberal capitalism as the only organizing principle of human good. Centering on socialism as a worldview that destabilized and denaturalized the association between capitalism and human emancipation, moreover, enables an analysis of why U.S. racial thinking needed to racialize beliefs and not just bodies. The U.S. Cold War conflation of socialism with false consciousness, or ideology, that demanded that the U.S. convert hearts and minds has in the present day been displaced onto emergent illiberal modes of existence, governance, and religiosity, which are figured as being in need of reform just as the Communist world had once been. These displacements authorize the United States' violent disciplining of dissonant lives, aspirations, and temporalities as a humanitarian struggle for global racial, sexual, and religious rights.

Since 1989, the contrasting of the United States as a site of freedom with a growing number of geopolitical enemies who ostensibly require the nation's ongoing vigilance has thus evolved through the imbrication of juridical technologies with the racializing technologies of perpetual warfare. U.S. military violence is repositioned as humanitarian against terrorism and religious fundamentalism. The emergence of the "new world order" that has rapidly taken shape through neoliberal restructuring is in many ways still entrenched in the Cold War racial narratives that divided and categorized the globe as being either free or unfree. Therefore, even as the racial and geopolitical ideologies associated with European imperialism, the Cold War era, and the postsocialist transition of Eastern European nations appear to be no longer relevant and bound to their distinct historical moments, emphasizing their cultural entanglements and ongoing legacies enables a relational and transnational theoretical frame through which to grasp emergent racial and imperial formations. Since 9/11, for instance, U.S. culture has homogenized Muslims as potential terrorists or as religious fanatics in spite of their national, racial, ethnic, and cultural diversity. The current racialization of Muslims fits uneasily into the predominant racial analytics of American cultural studies that are largely based on domestic race relations and historically racialized groups, such as African Americans, Asian Americans, and Latinos. It is not enough to simply posit that Muslims are a new racial group within the United States, since systems of belief and entire social worlds, rather than just individual bodies, are racialized to uphold U.S. militarism in the Middle East.

The routing of American morality through narratives of racial and religious transcendence and tolerance in the Cold War era and through militarized humanitarianism and multiculturalism in the 1990s laid the groundwork for the contemporary racialization of Islam. Islam is conceived of as a religion that is antithetical to U.S. principles because, like communism before it, it cannot accommodate difference and individuation.[20] "The present discourse about the roots of 'Islamic terrorism' in Islamic text [assumes] . . . that the Qur'anic text will force Muslims to be guided by it."[21] The univocality presumed of Islam as a religious dogma racializes it as a mode of faith precluding free will or individual agency. Islam is positioned in opposition to U.S. faith in secular diversity and justified through racialized narratives of unfreedom that are already familiar. These available racial narratives were constructed and adjusted throughout the second half of the twentieth century in relation to communism, making homogenized depictions of Islamic intolerance recognizable as morally unacceptable and threatening to American humanitarian projects on behalf of global freedom and democracy.

The Imperial Technologies of Postsocialist Humanity

Contemporary notions of human rights, upheld through the technologies of perpetual warfare and an international juridical regime, what I am calling "postsocialist imperialism," increasingly divide the world between locales in need of humanizing intervention and those that are morally empowered to enact the violent humanization of the other. Within postsocialist geopolitics, then, while some nations, such as the United States, come to exemplify universal humanity, having supposedly achieved the promise of racial and religious inclusion, other regions become sites of atrocity and terror that must be redeemed through the disciplining technologies of the United States' humanitarianism. Although inhuman acts, such as ethnic cleansing, genocide, suicide bombing, and the like, are represented as exceptional, they are in fact woven into the everyday texture of how residents of the Global North experience their own transcendent universality in the new world order. Landscapes of atrocity and terror have become the paramount geographic and temporal fantasies through which the Global North knows and affirms its humanity. As one region defined by monstrous violence is replaced by the next in global imaginary—Rwanda, Bosnia, Kosovo, Afghanistan, Iraq, and Syria—media and political circuits produce a structure of crisis and resolution. Foregrounding the need for U.S.-Western moral condemnation and intervention, postsocialist visual rhetorics of inhumanity elide vast economic and material inequalities that are perpetuated by the enactment of constant humanitarian warfare. Killing because of religion, race, and ethnicity is considered an anachronistic remainder of previous social worlds, out of the frame of historical progress (thus the language of "ancient" or "primordial" ethnic, racial, and religious hatred is often used to characterize conflict in some parts of the world). North American and Western European nations, meanwhile, conceive of their own killing as necessary to advance liberal reform and rights (women's rights, the rights of religious minorities, etc.). Fighting to bring inhuman geographies into the fold of historical progress, humanitarian wars against terror, or atrocity, are regarded as a sacrifice necessary to humanize the world.

The humanitarian gaze, through which U.S. audiences look upon the pain, suffering, brutality, and violence of the other, has led to the development of a humanitarian affect that aligns "our" feelings for the victims of illiberalism, monoculturalism, and intolerance with the military and juridical technologies working to save those subject to inhuman atrocities. Ironically, it was the U.S. military failure in Vietnam that became the occasion for humanitarianism to emerge as a global ethic. The public opposition to the war as an instance of U.S. imperialism in an era when the United States positioned itself as stridently anti-imperialist took shape as a humanitarian critique. Refusing to see the Vietnam War as a war against Soviet expansionism, through mass demonstrations and opposition to national policy U.S. citizens declared their humanity by their capacity to feel outrage on behalf of the Vietnamese. In spite of the viciousness of the war waged by their nation, photojournalistic images that captured the horrors of combat as experienced by the Vietnamese population made American violence appear transparent to U.S. audiences. In subsequent histories of the Vietnam War, the evolution and maturation of American humanity are told as a story of moral shock resulting from the televised and journalistic documentation of the war, which led to change. The rejection of the Cold War framing of U.S. interventionism, as well as the embracement of humanitarian affect, in some sense marks the Vietnam War as the first instance of postsocialist sentiment in the United States.

In spite of the revival of Cold War militarism in the 1980s, the United States' covert support for the mujahideen during the Soviet–Afghan War consolidated the humanitarian framework that would become the condition of possibility for future wars. The Soviet invasion of Afghanistan and subsequent media coverage led to the shift in the United States' geopolitical focus from racial to religious prejudice as the manifestation of intolerance and inhumanity that had to be defeated. The "godless" Communists' suppression of Islam in Afghanistan constructed the mujahideen as worthy subjects of aid. The humanitarian imagery and language developed in the media during the Vietnam War and the Soviet–Afghan War merged in the postsocialist era through the conflation of ethnic and religious strife in portraits of the wars of secession that engulfed the former Yugoslavia. While the new media and military technologies of the 1990s figured U.S. humanitarianism and multiculturalism as forces of progress, technological premodernity was ascribed to ethnoreligious conflict in the Balkans. Furthermore, the unprecedented merging of media and military operations in the postsocialist period facilitates the association between humanitarian multicultural ethics and U.S. imperial sovereignty.[22]

Emergent political fantasies, constituted through innovations in visual and media technologies, define the scope of life/humanity after socialism by opposing the arbitrary violence of the other (atrocity) with the benevolent violence of "just" humanitarian militarism. With the collapsing of humanitarianism and warfare, notions of the human can emerge only through images and discourses about violence, degradation, and dehumanization. Wendy Hesford's concept of the "human rights spectacle," which refers to "the incorporation of subjects (individuals, communities, nations) through imaging technologies and discourses of vision and violation into the normative market of human rights internationalism," is useful in this regard.[23] Hesford argues that through human rights spectacles, which increasingly emphasize humanitarian and faith-based initiatives as opposed to international law, victims are integrated into "the global morality market that privileges Westerners as world citizens."[24] Thus human rights rhetorics produce a "moral vision" through which Western audiences emerge as properly moral subjects of sight. As the other is frozen in a media and political fantasy that reproduces the spectacular moment of death, devastation, and destruction, landscapes of atrocity become fossilized as geographies of inhumanity—reminders of what is good and what is evil. This fixing of atrocity and terror as permanent also becomes the permanent justification for military intervention.

Just as the terror of inhuman atrocity is removed from the temporal frame of the humanitarian present (racism, religious fundamentalism, and intolerance are viewed as out of our time), so too postsocialist imperialism distances itself from previous instances of imperial governance through narratives of multicultural inclusion. Defined temporally and spatially in relation to atrocity, postsocialist imperialism reaffirms the capacity for human progress through the incorporation and accommodation of normative human difference. Even as multicultural humanitarian ethics privilege human difference as the grounds for universality, they reaffirm secular and liberal conceptions of difference conducive to the operations of capital over other modes of inhabiting difference that could lead to a progressive politics of alliance. As Julietta Hua notes, the "paradoxical operation [of universality in human rights aspirations] is evident in claims to global diversity that desire to recognize and protect difference and particularity, even as they advocate that these particularities subordinate to a broader order of universality."[25] In fact, she argues, there is no end to the individual voices and experiences to be heard, accommodated, and accounted for within the frame of universal human rights. Thus certain voices and experiences become favored as representative or authentic.

This critique speaks not only to how very particular figurations of victimization and abuse form the basis of universalizing articulations of justice but also to how, for certain visions of universality to become dominant, others must give way. Analogous to how contemporary human rights and humanitarian projects have laid claim to universality, previous imperial projects did so as well through "civilizing" and "humanizing" missions in the colonies. Indeed, the contemporary collusion between postsocialist imperialism and human rights is not new. Whereas postsocialist imperialism is the contemporary condition of possibility for the consolidation of a new human rights regime enabled by humanitarian militarism, earlier articulations of human rights were an outgrowth of previous imperial modes of governance and rule. Randall Williams points out that "in order to gain an adequate account of what U.S. monopolistic military power means for international law, we have to shift our analytic perspective from one that assumes imperialism is a problem *for* international law, to one that grasps their mutually constitutive relationship."[26] He explains, from the inception and signing of the Universal Declaration of Human Rights (UDHR) in 1948, the international notion of human rights espoused an anti-anticolonialist stance. A new ideological iteration of the Rights of Man, the Declaration could not but reproduce "an already existing international division of humanity."[27] It did so, in part, through the displacement of "alternative forms of universality present at the moment of the inception of the UDHR. Counter and contrary to the lofty, abstract juridical ideals of international human rights, such alternative conceptions and practices of freedom were much more deeply rooted in the actualities of struggle."[28] Postsocialist imperialism, utilizing the aspirational notion of universal humanity enshrined in the Declaration, which already entailed a disarticulation of the notion of human rights from decolonizing visions of freedom, justice, and struggle, evolved through a further series of displacements.

Following the demise of most socialist nations, which during the Cold War insisted on the importance of social and economic rights as a counterpart to the civil and political rights championed by the U.S. state, a global human rights regime based in liberal law increasingly monopolized notions of justice and facilitated the spread of free-market economies. U.S. ideas about the good life are ascribed universal value, having supposedly demonstrated their superiority over Communist lifeworlds. As other visions of emancipation and virtue are consigned to the realm of historical failure, human rights appear as the only possible ethical politics in the world today. Meanwhile, the global postsocialist condition has been shaped by U.S. imperialism as the military muscle enforcing humanitarian justice. Contrary to earlier eras in U.S. history, including the Cold War era, when U.S. exceptionalism was conceived through the nation's disavowal of its imperial ambitions, postsocialist imperialism is embraced as part of the United States' universal promise of redeeming the world from conditions of racial and religious unfreedom.

Addressing the configurations of the contemporary U.S. empire, a number of excellent works have analyzed the post-9/11 state of exception in national politics and culture in relation to the older histories of American exceptionalism and imperialism.[29] Most studies emphasize that U.S. militarism during the decade-long occupation of Afghanistan and Iraq represents a new form of imperial domination.[30] However, post-9/11 cultural and political justifications of U.S. imperialism are, I contend, connected to and have developed from the secular moral language underlying the racial, juridical, and military projects of late twentieth-century American multicultural humanitarianism. For instance, in a post-9/11 opinion piece in the *New York Times Magazine*, the political scientist and public intellectual Michael Ignatieff wrote about Thomas Jefferson's "exceptional" dream of spreading self-government and freedom to the whole world as the "last imperial ideology left standing in the world, the sole survivor of national claims to universal significance."[31] While Ignatieff acknowledges that the American ideal of freedom was forged out of the contradiction that the United States "is the only modern democratic experiment that began in slavery," he also argues that the "exceptional character of American liberty" proclaimed by every American president has inspired "Americans to do the hard work of reducing the gap between dream and reality. . . . First white working men, then women, then blacks, then the disabled, then gay Americans."[32] In his assessment that contemporary U.S. imperialism has the potential to bring democracy and self-rule, Ignatieff replicates the same developmental narrative he details in this brief history of the U.S. march toward granting universal rights. Ignatieff's thoughts on U.S. imperialism are representative of how contemporary claims to U.S. imperial sovereignty are necessarily based in the U.S. narrative of racial and sexual progress, which is a story of redemption. This account of moral development allows Ignatieff and other proponents of U.S. imperialism to claim that the United States is the only nation "with the resourcefulness and the energy . . . for the task" of "encouraging freedom."[33] Only by continually retelling the domestic narrative of multicultural progress and thereby burying the origins of U.S. capitalist growth in slavery and racial exploitation can the new imperialists uphold the United States' potential for universality, humanitarianism, and justice.

The Racial Reorientations of Cold War Geopolitics

Analytic modes required to grasp the racializing logics of contemporary empire necessitate an elaboration of the Cold War context and its relation to earlier racial categorizations. Notions of racial and religious difference that emphasize incorporation and inclusion into the U.S. national body as a way of concealing ongoing inequities and exclusions developed against the threat of Eastern Europe during the Cold War. This history buttresses the current U.S. opposition to religious intolerance (imagined as "terrorism," "antifeminism," or theocracy) that has replaced the ideological evil embodied by the former Eastern Bloc as a foremost site of struggle for American democracy. With the end of the Second World War, communism was racialized as a homogenizing totalitarian ideology that destroys human difference and individualism. Linked through their opposition, communism and freedom became the two rival racialized ideologies dividing the world between morality and immorality, and good and evil. At the historical juncture when the United States superseded the Western European nations as the foremost world power, U.S. cultural works reconceptualized "freedom" to deemphasize histories of domestic racial unfreedom and Western European imperialism, both of which were foundational to the making of U.S. dominance. Meanwhile, ongoing U.S. racial troubles were displaced and projected onto Eastern Europe, associating the Communist "evil empire" with the legacy of European racial imperialism. Emphasizing domestic racial progress, U.S. militarism aligned itself with a defense of global postcoloniality and the "free world" against the specter of Communist terror. In the United States, communism was associated with terror because Communist difference was not visibly marked on the body. As FBI director J. Edgar Hoover warned in 1950, Communists "operate under a cloak of deceit," making them "not always easy to identify."[34] Hoover's cloak metaphor explained that Communists' interiority and beliefs, rather than their exteriority and skin color, distinguished them from free, ideologically unburdened Americans. Reformulating older conceptions of threatening difference, American culture and politics conceived of Communist ideology as a perpetual threat because it was imperceptible, requiring ongoing national vigilance at home and abroad.

Beginning with the Cold War, the association between human diversity, freedom, and America's moral obligation to military intervention was solidified. The map of the "free world," whose contours were determined through

U.S. politics, culture, and militarism, profoundly refigured the European imperial racial map of the globe. Whereas European imperialism anxiously emphasized the racial supremacy and whiteness of the imperial metropoles over the racialized space of the colonies, with the start of the Cold War the United States drew attention to its domestic racial diversity as a sign of the nation's anti-imperialism and universality.[35] Scholars of race and imperialism have emphasized the connection between race thinking and spatial orientations that molds geopolitical imaginaries.[36] As Denise Ferreira da Silva has shown, in modernity, a "particular strategy of power—the *analytics of raciality*—has produced *race difference* as a category connecting place (continent) of 'origin,' bodies, and forms of consciousness. The primary effect of this mechanism has been to produce *race difference* as a strategy of engulfment . . . used in the mapping of modern global and social spaces."[37] In other words, with European modernity, race difference was apprehended in visual terms through bodies, and bodies were imagined to signify particular places of origin. This meant that both bodies and continents were racialized.[38]

In the second half of the twentieth century, the racial categorization of bodies and spaces consolidated through European modernity and imperialism persisted, even as the meaning and value assigned to these categories shifted in how the "free world" was mapped. Mary Dudziak, Thomas Borstelmann, and others have demonstrated that at the historical juncture when national liberation movements in the Third World began to successfully overthrow Western European colonial powers, institutionalized segregation and racism in the United States proved to be an insurmountable contradiction to the United States' claims of being a true democracy.[39] Racialized bodies, which had been distanced from the European and American nations' self-conceptions, now became incorporated into national core ideals.[40] Producing racial diversity as a sign of democracy, development, and modernization with the advent of the Cold War, the United States fashioned a racial mapping of the world that subsumed older racial imaginaries into a narrative of potential progress for the decolonizing nations in the so-called Third World through its leadership. The Three Worlds ideology through which knowledge about the globe was organized produced three domains: "a 'free' First World that is modern, scientific, [and] rational; . . . a 'communist' Second World controlled by ideology and propaganda; . . . and a Third World that is 'traditional,' irrational, overpopulated, religious, and economically backward."[41]

While the obstacles that the Second and the Third Worlds had to overcome to become properly free differed in the U.S. geopolitical and cultural
imaginary—with the Second World having to shed ideology and the Third
World having to shed premodernity and tradition—the racialization of both
"worlds" no longer solely emphasized bodily difference but, rather, ideological, cultural, and religious states of oppression. Justifying its militarism
in the name of a democratic postsocialist future, the United States' conceptions of the free world simultaneously used and disavowed older imperial
and racial fantasies.[42] Jodi Kim, Christina Klein, Melani McAlister, and others have elaborated on the reinterpretation of European Orientalism in
U.S. Cold War culture. Their concern, however, has been primarily with the
development of twentieth-century racial and imperial logics in the nonwhite Third World rather than in Eastern Europe.[43] Studies that have
focused on Eastern Europe, including Kate Baldwin's and Penny Von
Eschen's, provide valuable insights into the relationship between domestic
racial ideologies and nonwhite U.S. citizens who traveled to the Soviet
Union.[44] Thus far, however, scholarship in the field of American Studies has
not connected an analysis of the transnational production of U.S. racial
logics to Eastern Europe as the constitutive outside, through, and against
which conceptions of difference and diversity were reformulated in the service of humanitarian militarism. While earlier research demonstrates that
U.S. culture produced narratives about domestic racial pluralism to justify
the nation's geopolitical ambitions in the nonwhite world, foregrounding
how Orientalist and imperial tropes were reworked vis-à-vis communism
in Eastern Europe enables a retheorizing of racialization as a transnational
process for the differential valuation of ideological formations and social
worlds.

In contrast to American cultural perceptions of the Middle East and East
Asia, in which U.S. military interventionism was represented as a benevolent defense of nonwhite natives against the terror of communism, the
"Communist East" emerged as a racialized negative reflection onto which
the nation could project imperialist tendencies and a racist past. Appre-
hending Eastern Europeans as white in the U.S. racial frame facilitated the
movement in the modes of racialization that authorize contemporary U.S.
imperial rule.[45] Amid the shift in domestic racial formations, Communist
systems (more so than Eastern European bodies) were racialized as nonmodern and unfree. Even though, as Jodi Kim has pointed out, early Cold
War documents described the U.S.S.R. in Orientalizing terms as Asiatic, in
the wake of the civil rights movement in the United States, Soviet global

influence was associated with the maintenance of white supremacy.[46] Soviet totalitarianism was described in racializing terms that U.S. citizens could recognize through allusions to America's own record of racism. For instance, in the early years of the Cold War, the U.S. history of slavery was projected onto the U.S.S.R. A 1950 National Security Council document explained that "there is a basic conflict between the idea of freedom under a government of laws, and the idea of slavery under the grim oligarchy of the Kremlin."[47] In the United States, the process of "Sovietization" was perceived as "rigorous enough to threaten 'an end to diversity.'"[48] The racialized specter of Communist unfreedom became a repository for anxieties surrounding the limitations of liberal reforms to account for ongoing inequality in the nation.

The predominant characterization of Soviet communism as an anachronistic racial and political ideology that sought to end diversity was paramount for portrayals of the Soviet Union as a twentieth-century imperial power opposed by the United States. Hugh Seton-Watson's 1961 book, *The New Imperialism*, proposed that even within the Eastern Bloc, the Soviet Union acted as an imperial force in the so-called satellite nations because the latter were subordinate, dependent, and unwilling conscripts to Soviet power.[49] In this formulation, "the Soviet Bloc constituted the largest land empire in history."[50] Supporting the view that the Soviet Union was a manifestation of Russian imperialism, numerous scholars of postsocialist transition have argued that the economic and social changes in the aftermath of communism should be viewed as processes of decolonization.[51] Yet, as Francine Hirsch notes, "in creating a postcolonial narrative, these leaders and scholars drew on *Western* works from the height of the Cold War that characterized the Soviet Union as a colonial empire and a 'breaker of nations.'"[52] Quite the opposite, the Soviet version of "empire," as centralized rule, developed *in contrast to* European imperialism (which Soviet policy condemned).[53]

Casting Soviet expansionism as a form of domination that Western Europe gave up at midcentury and that the United States eschewed altogether, U.S. political and military interests in the Third World were, in contrast, represented as the anti-imperialist defense of non-Western nations' independence from the encroachment of Soviet imperialist rule. Through the misperception that the Soviet Union was ethnically homogeneous, U.S. militarism itself functioned as a racializing technology, justifying the nation's interventionism in the name of a global struggle against imperial racial domination. For example, in both the Korean and the Vietnamese civil wars, the United States characterized its warfare as a defense of non-white "native" democratic regimes in the face of Soviet "puppet" regimes. Since 1989, even as American political and cultural representations about postsocialism interpreted the demise of the Soviet "evil empire" as a victory for Western ideals of freedom based in democracy, pluralism, and free markets over totalitarianism and repression, intensifying nationalisms and violent conflict in the former Yugoslavia seemed to contradict the promises of tolerance and diversity envisioned in the spread of liberal capitalist democracy. However, the seeming incongruence between the postsocialist celebratory discourse of global redemption from Communist unfreedom and instances of ethnic conflict that resulted from the violent destruction of previous modes of governance was resolved in the emergence of a multiculturalist humanitarian ethic as the new rationalization of military interventionism and U.S. imperialism. The racial epistemes developed during the Cold War buttress contemporary acknowledgments that the United States is an imperial power, even as the nation maintains its distance and difference from European racial imperialism and Soviet imperialism. The by-now entrenched geopolitical figuration of U.S. militarism as antiracist facilitated an understanding of America's postsocialist empire as the first moral empire founded on the belief in the sacredness of human diversity rather than on territorial or economic exploitative ambitions.

Postsocialist Conditions

To date, scholarship in the United States has primarily addressed postsocialism as a historically and regionally bound concept to describe the state of economic and political transition in nations that were formally socialist during the Cold War. As an analytic lens, postsocialism is thus only considered relevant to Eastern and Central Europe and, occasionally, to China and Vietnam. The premise of this book, however, is that postsocialism is a global condition that produces a social, economic, and cultural ethic that builds on and disavows previous racial and imperial formations.[54] As a conceptual frame denoting the displacement as well as the ongoing significance of socialism, postsocialism indicates that the contemporary geopolitical formations, such as the perpetual war on terror, are best understood not by positing a historical break with the past but, rather, by exploring the ongoing inheritances of previous fantasies about the global good. I thus emphasize the imbrication of the European imperial legacy, as well as the legacy of the Cold War, in the postsocialist era.

Within the cultural, political, and academic tendency to showcase and grapple with the new, the past comes to be remembered as bound and fleeting, even though it continues to provide the foundation for the present. This perception of the past is especially evident in the dominant usage of twentieth-century temporal markers of transition in which the "post" of postcoloniality, postsocialism, and postmodernity is equated with the new. The "post" in this sense is meant to signal a transitional time period that constructs itself through an understanding of being unlike an earlier geopolitical or ideological formation. The notion of the postcolonial state, for instance, references imperial histories to understand national independence and development as moving out of and overcoming colonial histories.[55] Meanwhile, the "post" in postsocialism references a bygone era of "unfreedom" under communism in order to describe Eastern European nations' embracement of democracy and free-market capitalism. Still other theorizations of postsocialism focus on transition, which, as scholars have noted, freezes former Soviet Bloc nations between the past and the future rather than seeing them as integral to the development of contemporary modes of governance and personhood.[56] Indeed, the self-proclaimed role of the United States as the protector and harbinger of freedom, helping nations through postcolonial and postsocialist transitions in the second half of the twentieth century, has also relegated European imperialism and communism to the past, thus framing U.S. liberal democracy and "protective" intervention as essential for future development.

In contrast, the postsocialist analytics that inform this book's methodology do not conflate the "post" with the "after," opening up a complex engagement with the temporal and spatial intersections and dissonances between past and current ideological and geopolitical formations that resist both the accounts of progress and redemption in the post–Cold War world. Conceiving of current U.S. imperialism as a postsocialist imperialism is not just about naming a form of domination that arose after the demise of the Eastern Bloc but also about the analytics of empire that are mindful of temporal and spatial relationality. Reconsidering racial and imperial formations relationally, across spatial and historical boundaries, this book traces the afterlife of the European imperial imaginary in the twentieth-century U.S. cultural tableau. I emphasize that one important cultural mode through which post–World War II U.S. imperial ambitions were obscured was the reworking of the very same nineteenth-century European texts that had unabashedly participated in promoting empire. By foregrounding the circulation of older Western European narratives and genres in U.S. culture, however, I do not mean to propose that they served to promote the same kind of imperial structures, what Edward Said calls "a unique coherence" between the British, French, and American experiences.[57] Instead, I insist on the breaks that occurred through the repetition, in particular the resignification of race through multiculturalism, which enabled the expression of what I call a racial secular morality that has justified U.S. global violence since the end of World War II. To this end, chapters 1, 2, and 4 trace how U.S. media, political rhetoric, and creative works revisited Western European imperialist cultural tropes in order to constitute an exceptionalist narrative of U.S. power for the postsocialist era. Chapter 3 also addresses the recycling of previous tropes, though rather than turning to the recycling of European imperial culture I address how the 1980s U.S. support for the mujahideen was re-narrated in the post-9/11 period. Finally, chapter 5, through its focus on the ICTY, explores how warfare, once past, is remembered and normalized in institutional narratives producing authoritative historical and juridical accountings.

The social, economic, and ethical contours of postsocialism, in this sense, are much broader than what is encompassed by the governmental and structural reforms in formerly socialist nations that occurred after the fall of the Berlin Wall in 1989 (that is, the "transition"). Rather, as I am suggesting, postsocialism has produced a distinct historical and aspirational narrative that builds on previous imperial formations and notions of humanity. A postsocialist analytic, referencing as it does previous ethical systems as well as other modes of geopolitical restructuring (for instance, postcolonialism), offers an opportunity for a historically and regionally relational critique that explodes the universalizing teleology of the U.S. progress narrative. Chad Thompson argues, for instance, that because the twin Enlightenment ideologies of capitalism and communism share a sense of colonized peoples as historically static, postsocialism, rather than signaling the end of history, is an opportunity to reconceptualize history as nonteleological.[58] While Thompson takes the postsocialist era as a chance to rethink historical narratives, Shu-mei Shih writes that as a conceptual frame, postsocialism allows for a more complex engagement with time and space. She explains, "If we understand the 'post' in postsocialism in its polysemous implications not only of 'after,' 'against,' and 'in reaction to' but also of 'ineluctably connected to' and 'as a consequence of,' we approach a generally inclusive understanding of the post-socialist human."[59] For Shih, this multifaceted understanding of, and engagement with, postsocialism supports the study of "the relational and mutually constitutive dynamics of these [postsocialist, postcolonial, and posthumanist] 'post' conditions in different parts of the world."[60] For instance, while postcolonial studies have privileged the British and French Empires and their legacies, attention to postsocialism "demands the study of the Soviet Empire as well as other non-European empires and colonialisms."[61] Moreover, the "relationship between postcoloniality and postsocialism needs much greater unpacking," for if "postsocialism is resoundingly not postcolonial," it is necessary to ask whether the postsocialist moment is a post-postcolonial moment (and whether the two "posts" in post-postcolonial cancel each other out).[62] Shih's insights about the relationship between postsocialism and postcoloniality suggest not only the need to expand the analyses of previous imperial forms but also that the study of postsocialism is one of contemporary forms of colonialism and imperialism.

Arguing that the United States is a part of a postsocialist global condition particularizes and situates the universal claims of humanitarianism and human rights that morally underwrite U.S. global violence. Yet this opportunity is lost if postsocialism is relegated to periodizing a particular moment of regional transition that at once affirms the death of socialism and consigns it to an ideological formation representing distance from U.S. and Western modernity and universality. As Sharad Chari and Katherine Verdery argue, the predominant usage of postsocialism as a temporal designation in the U.S. academe is quite different from understandings of postcoloniality that developed with the rise of postcolonial theory in the 1980s and 1990s.[63] While the gap between the height of the decolonizing movements and the theoretical writing on postcoloniality produced a critical reflection on colonialism's ongoing legacies and the pitfalls of postcolonial nationalisms, because postsocialism is understood to describe a particular geopolitical transformation it has had no similar critical edge or traffic as an idea and a theory.[64] In contrast, Chari and Verdery posit that thinking between postcolonialism and postsocialism, both of which, as analytics, theorize political change and the process of "becoming something other than," allows for fresh perspectives on empire, Cold War knowledge formations, and state-sanctioned racism.[65]

Many of the theorizations of postsocialist change, to date, have utilized ethnography to assess the ways in which formerly socialist citizens have reinvented themselves as postsocialist subjects.[66] Yet just as crucial as understanding the "becoming other than" through ethnography, postcolonialism and postsocialism invite analyses of the representational and juridical processes by which previous lifeworlds, systems of governance, and their notions of humanity, history, and the global good are displaced and made irrelevant. To grasp this latter shift, a cultural studies approach focusing on the intertextual and transnational imaginaries produced by new and old media, political rhetoric, academic and activist discourses, and literary and visual texts is needed.[67] In this cultural assemblage, the past figures into new historical and redemptive narratives, and novel normative aspirations are articulated. Prevailing national and global notions of common humanity and morality are never unchallenged, and paying attention to how dominant historical and spatial narratives of good and evil are taking shape enables cultural critique to unearth and foreground those temporalities, spaces, and social worlds that have been displaced or suppressed.

If postsocialist imperialism produces a global ethic of humanitarianism that asserts its universality through a series of displacements (such as those of previous racial imperial forms and ethical systems), then a postsocialist analytic that hones in on those modes of living and ideologies that have been cast aside also provincializes contemporary visions of justice that are monopolizing. Foregrounding complex temporal and spatial nodes, a postsocialist analytic punctures the seamless narrative of historical progress evident in the culture and politics of postsocialist imperialism, which tells a linear story about the passing of European racial imperialism and communism in order to conceive of racial and religious redemption as the fulfillment of America's global messianic promise. Moreover, in attending to the relationality of multiple imperialisms and geopolitical regimes, a postsocialist analytic attends to and refuses commonplace conflations (for instance, the conflation between communism and totalitarianism or between "illiberal" social worlds, such as communism and Islam).[68] At the same time, it underscores the imbrications between, for instance, European racial imperialism and postsocialist imperialism or between communism and capitalism in the development of the contemporary global economy.[69] Addressing change, becoming, and transition will thus necessitate foregrounding links, displacements, and inheritances. As this book maintains, to grasp the delinking of race, racism (or intolerance), and racialization in postsocialist imperial rule, including the racialization of religious difference, it is crucial to dwell on the relationship of current racial logics to those of the Cold War era and the moment of European imperialism.

Chapters

Humanitarian Violence addresses the historical, political, and cultural field in which the consolidation of a multiculturalist humanitarian ethic—the moral condition of possibility for the enactment of postsocialist imperialism— took shape. Each chapter foregrounds the racialization and displacement of socialist and Communist social worlds and the recuperation and reformulation of European imperial racial logics and representational frames taking place in late twentieth-century U.S. culture. To contextualize the advent of postsocialist imperialism, chapter 1 engages the dual racial temporalities framing the geopolitical reorganization of the 1990s: the racial progress narrative of multiculturalism, on the one hand, and the cyclical violence narrative framing ethnoreligious conflicts, on the other. Charting the relationship between the U.S. post–civil rights racial ideology of color blindness, which quickly gave way to liberal multiculturalism, and the postsocialist-era racialization of religious difference that was enabled through the multicultural normalizing of racial difference, this chapter analyzes the temporalizing fictions of spatial and ideological distance popularized by contemporary travelogues about Central and Eastern Europe. As an imperial, visual, and narrative technology, U.S. late Cold War and post–Cold War travelogues can be read as perpetuating the afterlife of eighteenth- and nineteenth-century European imperial culture, engendering the landscape of late twentieth-century U.S. humanitarian dominance. Andrea Lee's *Russian Journal* (1981), Yelena Khanga's *Soul to Soul: The Story of a Black Russian American Family, 1865–1992* (1992), and Robert Kaplan's *Balkan Ghosts* (1993) exemplify the evolution of the postsocialist geopolitical imaginary from the 1970s to the 1990s, through which it is possible to trace how notions of U.S. racial progress depended on portraits of Eastern European anachronism.

The next three chapters focus on distinct cultural dynamics undergirding postsocialist imperialism and humanitarianism in instances of U.S. militarism. Chapter 2 analyzes the visual dynamics of imperial critique in photojournalistic and documentary representations of the U.S. military defeat in the Vietnam War (1954–1975). Arguing that cultural criticisms of imperial brutality and excess are not distinct from but, rather, foundational to future imperial projects, I examine the discourses surrounding transparency, visuality, and the Vietnam War as central to the late Cold War emergence of humanitarian feeling as a moral mode of framing wartime violence. Locating the materialization of humanitarian affect in a moment of loss in U.S. Cold War history, I read Joseph Conrad's *Heart of Darkness*

(1899, 1902) as a delimiting narrative for portraits of U.S. atrocities committed during the war. Rather than looking to post-Vietnam adaptations of
Heart of Darkness, this chapter studies Conrad's narrative more broadly as
the imperial referent for a domestic critique of imperial violence.[70] I argue
that the racial contradictions and imperial "horror" that structured Conrad's rendering of atrocity and humanity in *Heart of Darkness* resurfaced
after the war in cultural works that sought to ethically represent U.S. brutality in Vietnam. The chapter foregrounds the irony that humanitarian feeling emerged as the moral victory of a military defeat, an irony that would
eventually underlie conceptions of humanitarianism as the justification for
war in the postsocialist period.

The third chapter continues to develop the relationship between moral
shock and humanitarian feeling by assessing the U.S. political and media
exposés of the Soviet–Afghan War (1979–1989). Exploring the dynamic of
imperial projection, I argue that the roots of the contemporary racialization
of religious difference in the United States lie in the merging of moralizing and humanitarian languages framing that war. The Reagan Doctrine
encouraged covert military aid to guerilla fighters opposing the Soviet "evil
empire" as part of the nation's divinely ordained duty. Accounts of the
mujahideen fighters' piousness and stubborn opposition to atheistic communism in 1980s political rhetoric and news stories represented a nascent
articulation of humanitarian militarism that reflected a religious reordering of the U.S. worldview. Chronicles of Soviet human rights abuses in
Afghanistan, which were contrasted with the mujahideens' enduring faith
in God, called for Americans to revive their own faith in the morality of U.S.
militarism enacted on behalf of freedom and democracy, ideals that had
come into question with the Vietnam War. However, unlike early Cold War
ideology that proposed saving the racial other from Communist imperialism, in Afghanistan the victim of religious persecution became the foremost figure around which the call to intercede on another's behalf was
organized. Political and media investment in the Soviet–Afghan War thus
laid the groundwork for postsocialist notions of religious persecution justifying military intervention.

Chapter 4 addresses the merging of humanitarian militarism and postsocialist imperialism during the 1999 North Atlantic Treaty Organization
(NATO) bombing of Serbia and Kosovo, Operation Allied Force. With Operation Allied Force, new media and military technologies worked in tandem
to refigure the Balkans as a region whose ethnoreligious barbarity could be
redeemed through developments in U.S. weapons technologies and new

systems of communication, such as twenty-four-hour news coverage and the Internet. Resolving the contradictions inherent in humanitarian warfare, postsocialist imperial notions of U.S. racial progress worked alongside visual and rhetorical emphases on Balkan religious and ethnic premodernity to contrast human and inhuman forms of violence. As I argue, America's humanitarian duty to end religious and ethnic strife in 1999 resuscitated a Gothic frame to apprehend "undead" ethnoreligious conflict, authorizing postsocialist modes of imperialism, and to contrast postsocialist humanity from ongoing states of inhumanity. However, the Gothic appropriations in U.S. political rhetoric, televised news formats, and the Internet also revealed ongoing anxieties about undead racial troubles in the United States, even as they continued to perpetuate the late twentieth-century racialization of Eastern Europe.

The final chapter turns from an analysis of imperial warfare to imperial juridical redemption. Building on the previous chapters' elaboration of the production of postsocialist humanitarian imperialism and the racialization of religious difference since the end of the Cold War, I investigate the gendered discourses surrounding secular redemption and human rights. Since the signing of the Dayton Peace Accords in 1995, which ended a three-year war in Bosnia and Herzegovina, "Bosnia" has become a conceptual referent for a global feminist ethics, anchored in Euro-American principles of multicultural tolerance and human rights, that has redefined the boundaries of the free world. Utilizing the adjudication of rape warfare as a site of feminist jurisprudence in the ICTY, the chapter assesses the interconnection between the progress narrative of Euro-American feminism concerned with human rights and the discursive production of faith and redemption in international institutions of justice. I argue that in the postsocialist world, institutional sites (such as the ICTY) that administer and produce humanitarian law demand faith in a notion of common humanity that is based on ideas of tolerance and justice founded in the law. The ongoing production of bodies and landscapes of devastation, dehumanization, and death, like that of Bosnia and its inhabitants, is necessary insofar as it authorizes unequal sovereignties through the institutionalization of human rights regimes.

In the contemporary moment, as the religious intolerance attributed to atheistic communism is projected onto fundamentalist Islam, what counts as a human rights abuse against which the United States is morally compelled to act has shifted. In the immediate aftermath of 9/11, the cultural memory of U.S. aid to the mujahideen and Bosnian Muslim victims of Serbian aggression suggested that the failure of previous instances of humanitarian aid to

•

"discipline" Islam justified a larger-scale U.S. military intervention in the Middle East in the present. After nearly a decade of U.S. warfare in Afghanistan and Iraq, humanitarianism is again being conjured up, this time as an impossible undertaking, butting heads with an Islamic people hopelessly steeped in religious and ideological backwardness. Throughout the book, I stress the need to historicize the contemporary conflation of ethnic, racial, and religious intransigence that authorizes U.S. warfare. Even though post-9/11 U.S. interventionism no longer conceals its imperial intentions as it did during the Cold War, the racial discourses about "freedom" developed in the United States during the second half of the twentieth century continue to inform the racialization of religious difference against which American democracy is figured.

1   RACIAL TIME AND THE OTHER

Mapping the Postsocialist Transition

IN 1991 THE HISTORIAN ARTHUR SCHLESINGER JR., who rose to fame at the height of the Cold War as the chronicler of the Kennedy administration's days in the White House, published a controversial book on multiculturalism, *The Disuniting of America: Reflections on a Multicultural Society*.[1] Presenting a dystopic vision of America's future, in which multiculturalism exceeds the desire for national unity among distinct cultures and turns to separatist aspirations, Schlesinger warns that "at the end of the Cold War, [when] we have an explosion of long repressed ethnic, racial, religious, national antagonisms . . . Yugoslavia is a murderous portent of the future."[2] As a major Cold War liberal thinker, Schlesinger's concerns in the early 1990s, articulated through his fears of global ethnic, racial, and religious conflict in "murderous" places like Yugoslavia, encapsulate the postsocialist predicament faced by the United States: how to characterize the potential for U.S. national progress and a new moral imperative in the absence of the Soviet enemy. Debates about racial, religious, cultural, and civilizational difference were at the center of the crisis. In the vacuum left by the passing of the Three Worlds geopolitical and developmental episteme, the United States' racial present and its racist history were reframed in relation to the story of the postsocialist world and its possible futures.[3] Certainly the consolidation of multiculturalism in the 1980s and 1990s came, for some, to symbolize the fulfillment of the promises of U.S. democracy and its commitment to the ideals of equality and liberty enshrined in the nation's founding documents. As multiculturalism emerged as the national racial ideology that had the potential to resolve the contradictions that slavery, segregation, and racism posed in U.S. history, the nation portrayed itself as a beacon of racial progress, pluralism, and coexistence in the face of global horrors stemming from ethnic and religious violence. Beginning in the

1990s, therefore, one crucial task of U.S. nationalist, liberal multiculturalism was to distinguish normative modes of inhabiting and representing diversity from aberrant ones, which could lead to "tribalism" and separatism of the kind witnessed in the former Yugoslavia, Chechnya, and Rwanda.

The fall of the Berlin Wall in 1989 brought about two competing figurations of racial and historical development and the postsocialist future. On the one hand, the demise of communism was seen as a triumph of American liberalism and the fulfillment of the promises of civil rights and the Cold War struggle for global freedom, individualism, and diversity. On the other hand, ethnic and religious conflicts, often dubbed primordial and natural in certain parts of the world, came to represent the rejection of liberal democratic values and racial and economic modernity. For Schlesinger, "The fading away of the Cold War has brought an era of ideological conflict to an end. But it has not, as forecast, brought an end to history. One set of hatreds gives way to the next."[4] In his refutation that we are seeing the "end of history," Schlesinger refers to Francis Fukuyama's by now well-rehearsed 1989 prediction that "what we may be witnessing is not just the end of the Cold War, or the passing of a particular period of postwar history, but the end of history as such: that is, the end point of mankind's ideological evolution and the universalization of Western liberal democracy as the final form of human government."[5] For Fukuyama, as for Schlesinger, the end of the Cold War signaled the need to reconceptualize the narratives of history and futurity as a way of refiguring the meaning of U.S. national projects and geopolitical interests. However, Fukuyama's perspective represented a celebratory vision of communism's demise, one in which no new ideological alternative to parliamentary liberal democracy threatened U.S. values as communism once did.[6] Fukuyama's critics, meanwhile, including most famously Benjamin Barber, Samuel Huntington, and Arthur Schlesinger, emphasized that the ethnic and religious conflicts that came to the fore after communism, displacing the older ideological battle between communism and capitalism, were just as dangerous to the principles of liberal democracy as the previous threat of totalitarianism.[7] The problem, according to U.S. media, political, and cultural discourses, was not just that people in the Balkans, Africa, and the Middle East were premodern but, rather, that their view of history was stagnant, cyclical, and incongruous with democratic development. These regions' and religions' perverse conception of history, it was implied, represented the greatest threat to American values since the dissolution of the Communist empire.[8]

By way of contextualizing the advent of humanitarian imperialism and its attendant racial imaginaries, this chapter addresses the shifting conceptions of historical and national development that shaped postsocialist moral geography in the United States. As cultural documents invested in mapping spatial, as well as temporal, fault lines, travelogues were crucial in fashioning new political, journalistic, and popular racial fantasies of the postsocialist Eastern European landscape. For instance, Robert Kaplan's travelogue *Balkan Ghosts*, which portrays Balkan geographies through the trope of ancient and unceasing religious hatreds, is infamously the text that most influenced Bill Clinton's views on the former Yugoslavia throughout the 1990s.[9] Producing temporalizing narratives about totalitarianism and transition, travelogues gave life to two complementary yet opposing racial and historical narratives: the first, liberal multiculturalism and the fulfillment of America's racial progress narrative; the second, ethnoreligious violence as the manifestation of ahistorical hatreds and cyclical time. Certainly, since the age of Western European imperialism, travel has served as a vehicle for Western knowledge of the historical present and "self-realization" through portraits of distant temporalities and spaces.[10] Thus as spectacular accounts of ethnic and religious violence in the Balkans replaced images of the Communist threat, travelogues were a foremost genre through which U.S. citizens came to experience and envision the spatial–temporal reorganization of previous geopolitical epistemes and imagine the new ideological clashes dividing the globe. These new fictions of self and other defined and shaped U.S. imperial aspirations. Against vivid accounts of ethnic cleansing and religious hatred rooted in the failures of the socialist experiment, multiculturalism emerged as an emblem of national unity and liberal democracy, and as a sign of the end of racial and racist history in the West.

As an imperial, visual, and narrative technology, U.S. late Cold War and post–Cold War travel can be read as perpetuating the afterlife of eighteenth- and nineteenth-century European imperial culture, engendering a new fantasy of late twentieth-century U.S. humanitarian dominance. Like European imperial travelogues, U.S. travel literature about Eastern Europe in the 1980s and 1990s produced an image of the (American national) self in contrast to the (Communist and postsocialist) other through techniques of spatial, temporal, and racial distancing. European imperial geographies, which were most vividly experienced and imagined by the metropoles' readership through travelogues, were fundamentally connected to vision as a modern technology of power through which space was apprehended, classified, and commanded. Scholars of nineteenth-century travel writing, including Inderpal Grewal, Caren Kaplan, and Mary Louise Pratt, have shown that as a technology of modernity, travel, which contributed to the consolidation of the European self against the other, was as much about mobilizing the gaze as it was about physical mobility.[11]

As part of the mythology of U.S. racial progress, American travelogues portraying Eastern Europe often substituted the multicultural gaze for the primacy of the "white male" gaze mobilized in earlier travelogues, constructing novel racializing discourses of spatial and temporal distance through the rubric of Communist and postsocialist totalitarianism and intolerance. As U.S. multiculturalism was aligned with freedom, mobility, and rights, the U.S. media's focus on growing ethnoreligious nationalism and conflict in postsocialist Eastern Europe portrayed the region as an anachronistic reflection of a pre–civil rights era U.S. racist past. In travelogues that located intolerance as a constitutive ideological element in Eastern European landscapes, U.S. racial dynamics emerged as the standard by which to judge postsocialist democratization. The myth of U.S. racial progress, which had since the 1950s been narrated as *domestic* racial advancement, was resignified following the demise of state socialism as an *evolutionary model* for the former Eastern Bloc nations.

By transnationalizing U.S. domestic racial logics, late Cold War and post–Cold War travelogues produced cultural and political knowledge about Eastern Europe as a spatial embodiment of a Euro-American racist past.[12] Charting the relationship between the U.S. post–civil rights racial ideology of color blindness, which quickly gave way to liberal multiculturalism, and the postsocialist era racialization of religious difference that was enabled through the multicultural normalizing of racial difference, this chapter contends with the novel temporalizing fictions of spatial and ideological distance that supported and facilitated the burgeoning of American postsocialist humanitarian imperialism. The first section addresses racial time as constitutive of how travelers' accounts of Communist alterity and postsocialist futurity took shape in the U.S. imaginary. I underscore the imbrication of the post–civil rights mythology of domestic racial progress and conceptions of Eastern European belatedness and failure in the late twentieth century. The rest of the chapter analyzes three popular travelogues that racialized the postsocialist landscape, implicitly and explicitly contrasting U.S. racial progress with Eastern European anachronism. Black American journalist Andrea Lee's 1981 travelogue, *Russian Journal*, attempts to resolve the contradictions inherent in the post–civil rights logic of color blindness by envisaging the Soviet Union in the late Cold War years as a space in which the United States could reflect on its own history of racism. Published a decade later, in 1992, Afro-Russian journalist Yelena Khanga's *Soul to Soul: The Story of a Black Russian American Family, 1865–1992* creates a multicultural fantasy of postsocialist democracy, reconciliation, and futurity. As multiculturalism became the condition of possibility for conceiving of Eastern European enlightenment, tolerance, and incorporation into Europe and the West after the fall of communism, religious fundamentalism displaced communism as the obstacle to the U.S.-led West's humanization of the East. In this regard, I read Robert Kaplan's 1993 travelogue, *Balkan Ghosts*, which portrays the Balkans as a space of ancient ethnoreligious conflict, as the dystopic counterpoint to the multicultural progress narrative of democratization and assimilation into liberal democratic modes of governance. As I show, multiculturalism and the racialization of religious difference, as the racial frameworks through which postsocialist space has been apprehended, are the coconstitutive temporalizing narratives underwriting the consolidation of humanitarian imperialism.

The "Chronopolitics" of Travel and the Free World

Since the Cold War era, the trope of travel in the United States has not only invoked temporalizing narratives of spatial distance to produce historically and geopolitically contextualized knowledges of self and other, but also connected these framings of time and space to chart the contours of the free world. Because Communist countries limited their citizens' right to go abroad, during the Cold War prohibitions on travel became emblematic of the Eastern Bloc's unfreedom and imprisonment behind the Iron Curtain.[13] Consequently, travel was one of the major ways through which U.S. citizens realized their freedom as workers in a capitalist system, enjoying their hard-earned money and leisure time while developing firsthand knowledge of the rest of the world.[14] Henry Luce perhaps most famously formulated the association between travel, mobility, and capitalist free markets in the context of Cold War geopolitics when he deployed travel as a metaphor for U.S. commerce and global economic interests. In his famous "American Century" article, Luce wrote, "Americans—Midwestern Americans—are today the least provincial people in the world. They have traveled the most and they know more about the world than any other people of any other country. America's worldwide experience in commerce is also far greater than most of us realize."[15] Luce thus linked the possibility of travel in the

American Century with U.S. citizens' economic and epistemic command of the globe.

The Cold War association between capitalism, mobility, and U.S. freedom made travel a readily accessible frame through which to recount the demise of communism. Travelogues circulated intertextually alongside political and media figurations of transition to reorder American knowledge about Eastern Europe and, consequently, about the "free" and "unfree" parts of the world. Additionally, the correspondence between travel and the temporal imaginaries necessary to apprehend the phenomenon of Eastern Europe's "transition" in regional and global terms also made recourse to a longer history of travel as a metaphor for time (past, present, and future) and temporality (whether as progress, development, or degeneration). As Johannes Fabian argues, since the eighteenth century, the idea of travel in Western European culture has produced a "temporalizing ethos."[16] Writing from the era, for instance, imagined " 'the philosophical traveller, sailing to the ends of the earth, [as] in fact travelling in time; he is exploring the past; every step he makes is the passage of an age.' "[17] Referencing these early portrayals of travel, Fabian makes the case that although travelogues' primary preoccupation is, of course, with "the description of movements and relations in *space*," the preoccupation with time was a precondition for portraits of spatial distance in modernity. As travel became a source of Western secular knowledge about the world, it led to a reconceptualization of time itself. Travelers' "radically immanent vision of humanity at home in the entire world and at all time" crystallized the shift from sacred to secular time, in which "relationships between parts of the world [could] . . . be understood as temporal relations. Dispersal in space reflects directly . . . sequence in time."[18]

Distinguishing secular from sacred time, Fabian notes that in the Judeo-Christian tradition, "Time was . . . celebrated as a sequence of specific events that befall a chosen people."[19] During the Middle Ages, "the Time of Salvation was conceived as inclusive or incorporative: The Others, pagans and infidels (rather than savages and primitives), were viewed as candidates for salvation. Even the conquista, certainly a form of spatial expansion, needed to be propped up by an ideology of conversion."[20] In contrast, modern secular conceptions of time are both expansive and exclusive:

> The pagan was always *already* marked for salvation, the savage is *not yet* ready for civilization. . . . Evolutionary sequences and their concomitant political practice of colonialism and imperialism may *look* incorporative;

after all, they create a universal frame of reference able to accommodate all societies. But being based on the episteme of natural history, they are founded on distancing and separation.[21]

In European imperial knowledge about the world, the "savage . . . lives in another Time" even as "secularized time [became] a means to occupy space, a title conferring on its holders the right to 'save' the expanse of the world for history."[22] With the advent of postsocialism, U.S. conceptions of saving the world for history (and historical progress) refigured the Cold War paradigm of saving the world from communism to that of saving the world from humanitarian atrocities. The temporal association of difference as distance played out in the Euro-American imaginary through a new geopolitical demarcation of successful and failed democratization and, concurrently, through the mapping of spaces of human rights, the universal frame of reference for freedom, and spaces of atrocity. Even as the demise of the U.S.S.R. signaled the potential for the global expansion of liberal democracy without opposition, travelogues continued to produce the universality of liberal and humanitarian principles through exclusions—places "not yet ready for civilization" and mired in ethnoreligious conflict. As racial freedom and liberal democracy came to represent the fulfillment of secular progress, religious zealotry displaced Communist oppression as the sign of Eastern European backwardness. Spaces where the transition from communism to capitalism appeared to fail were portrayed as outside of a secular as well as a Western Judeo-Christian (linear) conception of time. The commonplace understanding of ancient hatreds, resurging in the absence of Communist management of difference, produced places like the Balkans and Chechnya as current-day examples of a pagan, cyclical vision of time that was completely antithetical to the time of progress.

Fabian's insight that "geopolitics has its ideological foundations in chronopolitics" is crucial for thinking through the temporal and spatial distancing of postsocialist Eastern Europe through the political and academic languages of "transition."[23] The conceptual device of "transition" uses temporal change (as a marker of national progress or regression) to produce new knowledge about the world in the absence of communism as an ideological and ethical limit to capitalist expansion. According to Anita Starosta,

re-imagining Eastern Europe in the present [entails] the double question of exchange value (on the market of ideas) and of timeliness. For, just as in the economic and political registers reforms have been directed at drawing Eastern Europe out of its imputed backwardness and isolation from the West, so on the discursive and epistemological registers the manifest task has been to update the terms in which we think about this object in transition. But successful inscription into the global, which is the ostensible goal of any such updating, also contains an irreducible ambivalence: it signals liberation and finally grants the region visibility by forging—in the double sense of establishing *and* simulating—its continuity with the rest of the world, while at the same time it subsumes it to an order not of its own making.[24]

Starosta's insights about Eastern Europe's perpetual belatedness underscore the epistemological and temporal crisis that followed the fall of the Berlin Wall, not just for Eastern Europe but for the United States and the West. If the terms by which the free world was defined in the Cold War years took shape through and against the Communist other, then after 1989 the subsumption of Eastern Europe into such a "free world" not of its own making would also entail the redefining of freedom itself in a new historical frame. At this time, ethnic, racial, and religious conflict emerged as the prevalent way in which Eastern European refusal of U.S. promises of freedom reaffirmed its backwardness and ideological distance from the West—a belated racism reemerging. That the U.S. nationalist mythology of racial progress, and the association of racial freedom with free markets and democracy, was already well established during the Cold War facilitated the racializing of failed transition in terms of religious conflict. In other words, the time of transition has been narrated dually as the progressive expansive racial time of U.S. liberalism and the regressive, cyclical racial time of the other.

Whereas during the early years of the Cold War the United States had to address the inherent contradictions between legally sanctioned racial segregation and discrimination and its international stance as leader of the "free" world—including the nonwhite Third World—by the late 1970s and in the 1980s, the apparent fulfillment of civil rights in the law increasingly worked to authorize U.S. claims to defending freedom globally, connecting the mythology of domestic racial progress to the aspiration of global interventionism. The Carter administration, for instance, explicitly prioritized international human rights over the earlier Cold War model of "containment." Having supposedly achieved racial equality at home, the nation could turn its attention to pursuing rights for the racially oppressed throughout the world, as was evident in the rigorous critique of South African apartheid.[25] Although Reagan's 1980 election brought about a decidedly more conservative rhetoric that linked U.S. foreign policy with nationalist interests, it nevertheless built on the associations between U.S. militarism and international justice to mask U.S. neoimperialist ambitions.[26]

The rise of multiculturalism as the prevalent mode of understanding U.S. race relations as the enlightened counterpoint to ethnic violence must be contextualized within the regressive economic and social policies of the 1980s.[27] The rearticulation of racial meaning that took place in the United States at this time marked a shift from the rhetoric of civil rights, which demanded institutional inclusion, to the rhetoric of multiculturalism, which flattened out ongoing racial disparities through the compensatory language that celebrated diversity for its own sake. Numerous scholars have pointed out that the ideological appeal of multiculturalism was based in abandoning the promises of the civil rights movement. According to James Lee, multiculturalism as an ideology attempted to "reorganize the heretofore unequal representation of American life"; however, it failed to correct the material disparities based in the effects of racial difference and, in fact, exacerbated them.[28] In the 1990s, multicultural ideology masked the incoherence between investing in free markets and promoting substantive equality against racial discrimination. As Peter McLaren notes, liberal multiculturalism in the context of free markets is based on the assumption that the "cognitive equivalence or the rationality imminent in all races . . . permits them to compete equally in a capitalist society."[29] The 1990s U.S. appeals for ethnic and racial equality in Eastern Europe reveal that recourse to multiculturalism as a narrative of transition ultimately subordinated the material effects of racial discrimination to the ideal of capitalist development. Turning to an analysis of travelogues, the sections that follow trace the transnationalization of U.S. racial ideologies, particularly multiculturalism, in portrayals of capitalist progress toward freedom, and the coconstitutive racialization of religious difference as a signal of spatial and temporal distance from freedom in the postsocialist world.

"Double Lives": Color Blindness and the Racial Past

In the winter of 1990 the New York Public Library presented a lecture series entitled "The Art and Craft of Travel Writing." One of the invited speakers was Andrea Lee, a black American journalist and fiction writer, who spoke about her book, *Russian Journal*, a collection of entries written during the ten months Lee spent in the U.S.S.R. between 1978 and 1979. At the time of its original publication in 1981, U.S. critics were particularly interested in gaining insight into a black American's perspective on the characters and landscapes of the U.S.S.R.[30] In her 1990 New York Public Library lecture, however, Lee concluded that "given what has happened in Eastern Europe since then, I might as well have written a book about dynastic Egypt, or about Beirut in its palmy days as 'little Paris.' "[31] Lee's description of her travelogue as a "period piece"—a fossilized vision of "that past Russia that's frozen in . . . *Russian Journal*"—framed her Russian writings as part of "an epoch that has vanished."[32] Lee's portrait of the Soviet Union as a land from long ago, akin to ancient Egypt, might seem surprising considering that the U.S.S.R. did not officially cease to exist until 1991. Nevertheless, her discussion is representative of the way in which in the years immediately following the fall of the Berlin Wall, the United States redefined and asserted its political and symbolic leadership in the postsocialist region by demonstrating the irrelevance of Soviet political and cultural formations to present-day politics, in which new Eastern European nations were imagined as fledgling democracies to be molded in the U.S. image.

In contrast to Lee's 1990 portrayal of the Soviet Union as "frozen" in the past and immaterial to present-day U.S. culture and politics, her travelogue, *Russian Journal*, dramatized the importance of the Soviet Union in the American imaginary in the years preceding the Reagan-era reescalation of Cold War tensions. Rather than reading Lee's travelogue as a historically isolated "period piece," as she suggests, her narrative invites a more complex analysis of the tremendous racial, geopolitical, and cultural reorganizations that linked the late Cold War years to the postsocialist era through the trope of travel. Upon Lee's publication of *Russian Journal*, cultural critics' interest in her racialized perspective on the U.S.S.R. foreshadowed the rise of multiculturalism as the predominant U.S. racial ideology in the 1980s and, in the 1990s, as an important evaluative lens through which the United States and Western Europe judged the successes and failures of Eastern European nations' transition to liberal democracy. Thus in spite of the way in which U.S. political and cultural discourses proclaimed the extinction of the Soviet Union, travelogues encapsulated the ways in which the United States' conceptions of Eastern Europe throughout the 1990s continued to be informed by the political and racial dynamics of Cold War history. In particular, the displacement of a U.S. racist past onto the construct of Soviet totalitarianism during the Cold War, exemplified in Lee's travelogue, was foundational to the subsequent postsocialist racialization of Eastern European transition.

Lee's Soviet travelogue first appeared in two consecutive installments of the *New Yorker* in the summer of 1980, which coincided with the reescalation of Cold War tensions in the United States to a level unprecedented since the 1950s.[33] American concerns that a new Cold War was afoot began following the Soviet invasion of Afghanistan in 1979, an action that was interpreted as overtly imperialist and seen as a direct threat to the United States. In the words of William Pfaff, a regular contributor to the "Reflections" column in the *New Yorker*, this Soviet act was seen as the start of a "Second Cold War."[34] Soon thereafter, George Kennan, the original architect of the Cold War "containment" policy, stated that this moment in U.S. history marked the "greatest 'militarization of thought and discourse' since the Second World War."[35] By the time Lee's work was published as a collection of essays in 1981, the United States had already boycotted the 1980 summer Olympic Games in Moscow. Then California governor Ronald Reagan, who was waging an intense campaign for the presidency, urged the nation to discontinue diplomatic initiatives and to cut off all communication with the U.S.S.R.[36] In the *New Yorker*, Pfaff argued that U.S. and Soviet interests in the "Second Cold War" were "substantial rather than symbolic" because Middle Eastern oil was at stake. He urged that U.S. policy address the Soviets' new and aggressive imperialist position in the Third World with a military stance.[37] Though Pfaff described U.S. foreign policy in the Third World as a stabilizing presence in contrast to the Soviets' militant threats in the region, he contended that the new Soviet expansionism pushed the limits of the American "virtues of liberalism, [which] are not warlike."[38] In this perspective, the Soviet invasion of Afghanistan exceeded the bounds of liberal tolerance, not because of U.S. political and economic interest in Middle Eastern oil but, rather, because Soviet imperialist expansion into the Third World threatened the just and liberal ambitions of the United States in the region.

The post–civil rights reordering of U.S. racial ideologies, occurring as it did in the context of the Cold War, was worked out in part through cultural and political knowledge produced about the U.S.S.R. This association between U.S. racial thinking and the U.S.S.R. had its roots in an earlier moment in U.S. history. In her work on radical African American thinkers who traveled to the U.S.S.R. during the first half of the twentieth century, Kate Baldwin argues that

> the conceptual aid of internationalism enabled an exposure of the ways in
> which the major antagonisms with which the early Cold War period was

associated—a fear of Soviet imperialism—had a genealogy in U.S. attitudes towards race. A fear of blacks transgressing the racial status quo of white supremacy characterized by Jim Crow was restated as a fear of outside infiltration and contamination of the national polity during the 1950s.[39]

In contrast to the politics of racial segregation that motivated Claude McKay's, Langston Hughes's, W. E. B. Du Bois's, and Paul Robeson's interest in Russia and the Communist experiment, the racial ideologies contextualizing the revival of U.S. fears about Soviet imperialism in the period between 1979 and 1980, which framed Andrea Lee's Russian journey, stressed that domestic racial equality had been achieved. Building on Baldwin's insightful connection between the fear of Soviet imperialism and the color line in the early part of the century, it is suggestive to consider the resurgence of U.S. anxieties about Soviet imperialism in the Middle East alongside changing racial paradigms in the United States at this time.

Andrea Lee's *Russian Journal*, though well received by the reviewers, troubled most critics who expected a uniquely black look at Russia. Of the journal entries spanning the ten months she spent in Russia with her husband, who was a student of Russian history, only one of Lee's entries reveals that she is a black American. The disjuncture between the critics' obsession with Lee's absent racial point of view and Lee's narrative effacement of her racial difference in the Soviet Union parallels the tension between the official policies of the post–civil rights ideal of integration and color blindness and the emergence of multiculturalism in the 1980s. My reading of *Russian Journal* and its critical reception concentrates on how these two racial paradigms worked in tandem to write African Americans into citizenship over and against the Cold War construct of Soviet illiberalism. With the resurgence of the Cold War in the 1980s, cultural depictions of the United States as democratic and racially just rationalized U.S. militarization and interventionism in the Middle East, particularly Afghanistan, as democratic and anti-imperialist in contrast to Soviet imperialism in the region.

Returning to Lee's 1990 lecture, in which she reflected back on the now-spent global imaginary of which *Russian Journal* was a part, it is striking that she calls on the numerous conventions of the European imperial travel narrative to explain her fascination with the U.S.S.R., "a culture theoretically alien to her own."[40] Lee confesses, "Russia all my life represented the farthest possible psychological and cultural distance from home."[41] Her acknowledgment that being brought up in the United States determined the contours of how she perceived Communist Russia's difference before she ever set foot there in 1978 provides the context for her conscious acceptance, and rejection, of particular European modes of travel. Lee provides a dramatic example of an entry that she eventually chose to exclude from *Russian Journal*:

> European and European-American artists have so often been drawn to the exoticism of darker-skinned, simpler cultures and warmer climates. The exposure to something so clearly defined as alien, as the furthest limits of "other," gives a jolt of energy that propels inspiration many steps along. It's logical that an artist should feel like a foreigner. As for me, a writer with mixed African and European blood, I find that I am interested in primitivism but uninterested in Africa or the warm countries. My own impulse toward what is alien has attracted me instead to an exotic northern country of white-skinned barbarians.[42]

While "primitivism," limits of otherness, exoticism, and "barbarians" represent the tropes and characters that have structured European imperial travel writing, as Lee points out, her point of entry as a traveler lies in her experience of racial difference in the United States. Refiguring conventional European travelogues' language of racial otherness as savagery and whiteness as civilization, Lee's interest is in "white-skinned barbarians," the exotics from the north. The rejection of this "embarrass[ing]" passage from the final manuscript, while it is indicative of *Russian Journal*'s refusal to directly reproduce the European imperialist vocabulary, nevertheless points to the traces of the racial reordering of these temporalizing conventions in the *Journal*'s frame for sketching Russian characters and places.

Lee's self-consciousness about the conventions of travel writing leads her to speculate that her attraction to Russia as the place most psychologically and culturally distant from home was, in fact, an attraction to the similarity between herself and Russians under Communist rule—both led "double lives." In the lecture, Lee offers certain biographical details that she had excluded from the book itself. She reveals that she grew up in a "middle class Afro-American family," who, in spite of their deep commitment to the civil rights movement and integration, felt separate from both the poorer African Americans and the white Americans. "Double lives," Lee notes, meant both "double knowledge and double insecurity." She explains that in a racially divided society, "we grew up adept at assimilation without absorption . . . and developed an esprit de corps of a tiny garrison of spies."[43] The metaphor of the spy, one that has inspired so many depictions of the Soviet Union in Cold War culture, refigures Lee's position as a traveler in the U.S.S.R. in terms of reporting her findings on the "Other" to U.S. audiences. She implies that her experience of growing up as an African American in the United States directly prepared her for her role as a spy and traveler, for she was able to recognize that "the Soviet Union at that time specialized in double lives. Almost everyone we met had a public persona and a radically different private one."[44] She thus concludes, "the psychological effects of a totalitarian system and of racism in a democratic country have a certain amount of overlap."[45] Lee's explanation figures Russia's story as one that Americans can best understand through the U.S. national experience and history of racism. Yet the overlap between U.S. racism and Soviet totalitarianism was not a coeval one, since Lee projects an earlier civil rights U.S. history onto the Soviet Union's present in 1979.

Lee's perspective on the affinity between totalitarianism and racism inspired her 1984 autobiographical novel, *Sarah Phillips*, which explores the difficulties of growing up middle class and black in the U.S. civil rights era. In her 1990 lecture, Lee suggests that she now sees "*Russian Journal* and *Sarah Phillips* as a diptych, complementary variations on the same theme."[46] For her, "it was this kind of glimpse, this momentary flash of understanding, that had always made traveling worthwhile . . . [as a way of] seeing oneself in another person, and comprehending that person."[47] In other words, it is by conjuring up a U.S. racial past that readers can experience a "momentary flash of understanding." The recognition that Americans and Soviets share common experiences can only be imagined through temporal distancing. Thus although Lee decided not to write " 'a black look at Russia,' " she understood the process of writing *Russian Journal* as enabling her to consider the racial history of the United States while in the U.S.S.R.[48] Ironically, even though Lee reads her own work in *Russian Journal* as the inspiration for critically considering U.S. racial history, her lack of racial transparency as the narrator of the *Journal* and the absence of biographical details within its narrative led critics of the book to claim that these were flaws in an otherwise well-constructed travelogue.

Russian Journal's critical reception, which both praised Lee's representation of Soviet difference and demanded full disclosure of her experience as a black American in Russia, is indicative of the extent to which (presumably) white Americans continued to be troubled by not having been granted access to Lee's racial perspective on the U.S.S.R. In his "Books of The Times" review, John Leonard was mystified as to why it is only two-thirds of the way into Lee's *Journal* that we find out she is black. Leonard laments:

> She says she is black, and drops the subject. It is a daring strategy, because we want to know more: was it better or worse for her, being black? Does it help

account for her critical intelligence, her wait-and-see skepticism, her lyrical exactitude, as though Henry James had gone to St. Basil's?—Not a word. Miss Lee has been to Harvard and to Paris. She will leave Moscow for the Aegean. In "the logical light," she will miss her dark tower and despise the clumsy spies. Only a remarkable writer could throw away such a badge of identity and insist on our seeing, anyway, precisely what she saw, on her austere terms.[49]

While Leonard can praise Lee as a "remarkable writer" and recognize the "daring strategy" of not mentioning her blackness, his introduction of these few lines of praise is framed by his exploration of how readers have been if not misled at least kept in the dark about Lee's true identity. His obvious discomfort with "seeing . . . precisely what she saw" without knowing ahead of time that he is seeing from a "black perspective," indeed, without being granted access to knowing the black subject as fully as the Russian subject of her travelogues, indicates that Lee's observations in the U.S.S.R. cannot stand for an American perspective without referencing her racial perspective. In fact, Leonard reviewed Lee's book alongside a book by Elizabeth Pond, a white American who had written *From the Yaroslavsky Station: Russia Perceived*; not once does Leonard mention Pond's race or the lack of biographical information in her exploration of contemporary Soviet society. If the "self-effacing producer of information is associated with the panoptic apparatuses of the bureaucratic state," Leonard's review suggests that a black American's perspective, in spite of Lee's narrative strategy of racial effacement, cannot be a proper apparatus of the U.S. state without announcing and making transparent her blackness to a presumed white audience.[50]

In another review, Susan Jacoby, herself an expert on Russia and Yelena Khanga's coauthor in *Soul to Soul*, found *Russian Journal* "subtly crafted" and perceptive, though she also described Lee's decision to not discuss her black perspective on Russia as a serious "omission."[51] While Jacoby suggests that merchandising the book as an "ethnic curio piece" would limit the scope and audience of the work, she also speculates that Lee, who is "so light skinned," with "a freckle-spattered, sand-toned complexion," would not have needed to identify herself in Russia as a black American and would thus be able to avoid the "extremely rigid racial and ethnic stereotypes" most Russians held. Jacoby goes on to propose that "the sight of a black person immediately arouses fear of the dark" in Russian people. Jacoby's emphasis on Lee's light skin relies on the familiar American trope of racial "passing" to explain Lee's narrative strategy. Even then, Jacoby speculates that Lee's perspective must have been skewed, for though she does not foreground being black in the *Journal*, Lee's exposure to Russian prejudice must have "affected [her] . . . in some way." Jacoby's figuration of the Russians' literal state of being unenlightened—of being afraid of the dark when they see a dark-skinned person—draws attention away from the more immediately obvious discomfort with racial ambiguity on the part of a U.S. readership. Her emphasis on Russian racism in relation to black Americans suggests that while Lee's racial difference might only be coincidental in the United States, in the U.S.S.R. it affected every aspect of daily life—a proposition that *Russian Journal* does not bear out.[52]

Reviews of *Russian Journal* can be read as expressing a tension between the ideal of "color blindness" in the United States and the desire to project a narrative of U.S. racial progress onto an imagined landscape of Soviet intolerance. According to legal scholar Patricia Williams, "the liberal ideal of color blindness is too often confounded. . . . The very notion of blindness about color constitutes an ideological confusion at best, and denial at its very worst."[53] In the reviews, Lee's decision to not provide a black perspective on Russia was read as a refusal made possible by her light skin, which supposedly allowed her to "pass" as white in the U.S.S.R. This reading implied that in the United States, Lee could be both a black American and have a choice about whether she wanted her race to matter in her writing; meanwhile, Russia was imagined as a space where race matters a priori, and thus, where if she had been darker, Lee would have inevitably faced prejudice. By implying that color blindness might work in the United States but that it certainly could not be possible in the unenlightened and racist U.S.S.R., where people were still afraid of the dark, Lee's critics reproduced the "ideological confusion" of color blindness in a transnational context. At the same time, the *New York Times* review of *Russian Journal*, with its emphasis on Lee's Harvard education, her mobility across Russia and Europe, and her middle-class background, casts Lee as a success story of the civil rights struggle and affirmative action era. That Lee is made to embody U.S. racial progress implies that she should have acted more explicitly as an ambassador of U.S. liberalism in the U.S.S.R. Regrets that Lee did not analyze the conditions of racial prejudice in the U.S.S.R. by explicitly addressing Russia's backwardness in relation to the United States in matters of racial equality suggest a desire for Lee to stand along the East–West divide as a model for the success of U.S. civil rights and democracy—to provide a look at Russia that at once celebrates U.S. "diversity" and participates, through a representation of racial difference, in the refueling of 1980s Cold War tensions.

Though Lee did not write a black American perspective on the U.S.S.R., her *Journal* constructs a racialized and temporalizing opposition between freedom and unfreedom. Her Russian landscape is a dark frontier at the edge of Europe from which one might assess the East–West divide. In the chapter "Running," Lee traverses the whole of Moscow.[54] After reaching the top of the Lenin hills, she observes the city's expanse:

> From a distance, Moscow gives most of all an impression of denseness—not height—and industrial vigor. Barges and riverboats move constantly up and down the broad, dull waters of the Moskva; watching them, I thought of the historical importance of this river, which from medieval times has linked Moscow to trade routes leading to Central Asia and the Baltic. Back then, the city must have been scarcely visible from these bluffs about the river. This was true even in 1914, when Baedecker described the same view. . . . Well, the vegetable fields, the churches, and the poorhouse have vanished, and many-towered Moscow has spread to the other side of the river.[55]

From the Lenin hills, Lee takes in the architectural layout of Moscow and dwells on the historical importance of this city that links Europe to Central Asia. The prerevolutionary Baedecker guide, with its mention of churches and poorhouses as points of orientation, functions as a signpost of the pre–Communist past, for now the landscape is darkened with industrial and Stalinist Gothic towers, which appear "sinister."[56] In Lee's description, Communist industrialization does not lead Russia toward the West, but it orients it toward the East. Whereas in earlier times the Moskva River represented trade routes, Lee's topographic view portrays the city's literal eastward expansion across the river. The passage foreshadows the Soviet invasion of Afghanistan in 1979 and seems to gesture to Soviet imperialist ambitions.

Later in the book, Lee contrasts the Moskva with the Mississippi, which stands for the United States as a space of freedom. Lee recalls the Mississippi as it was described in *Huckleberry Finn*, a book that has made her "painfully homesick, not for family and friends, but for the entire country, as if it were something I could embrace with a single thought."[57] In this passage, homesickness for the United States from the U.S.S.R. figures the meaning of nation within the Cold War context as subordinating the binding ties of blood and community to that of ideology—a nation can be embraced "with a single thought." Lee writes:

> What I like about America is amazingly simple: that I can talk there without stopping to censor my thoughts, and that I can wander freely without passport or identification, without concern for entering a *zapretnaya zonai* (forbidden zone). Minor-sounding things, but they bear on the most important

liberations in life: from confinement and fear. It's impossible to imagine Huck Finn and Nigger Jim floating down the Neva, the Volga, or the Moskva—difficult to think of a great Russian work that so directly celebrates freedom.[58]

Lee's vision of freedom and of liberation from her perspective as a traveler in the Soviet Union draws on the imagined "expanse" of U.S. landscapes that has come to symbolize U.S. nationalist self-definition since the doctrine of Manifest Destiny, which shaped the nation's imperialist westward expansion through the nineteenth century. With the belief that in the United States freedom is represented by the spaces that Americans can "wander freely," Lee imagines her fundamental difference from the Russians she encounters through her mobility. Moreover, while Lee's earlier description of the Moskva highlights the west to east flow that symbolizes the U.S.S.R. encroaching into the Middle East, the Mississippi's north to south flow alludes to the historical movement to freedom that slaves undertook when escaping from bondage in the U.S. South. Although Lee's choice of a canonical U.S. literary work such as *Huckleberry Finn*, which has been highly criticized for its racist portrayal of Jim, might be interpreted as an indirect commentary on the incomplete project of liberation within the United States, when read from the context of the Soviet Union, as Lee does, this reference to Twain's novel becomes an allegory for the continued upward mobility made possible for people of color within the United States by the civil rights struggle.

Alongside contrasts, such as the one Lee makes between the Moskva and the Mississippi Rivers, that draw on the racialized symbolism of darkness and freedom to oppose the Soviet and U.S. landscapes, *Russian Journal* is at times even more direct in ascribing the United States' racial past to the U.S.S.R.'s present. For instance, the entry entitled "Cleopatra" describes the opening of the movie *Cleopatra*, a U.S. "antique," in Moscow theaters:[59]

Instead of Egypt in circa 40 B.C., it was America in 1962. . . . While the unquestioning arrogance of the assumption that Taylor, with her white Celtic skin intact, could rule over a country of Egyptians showed the innocence of the time, when none of our ideas about race, about sex, about leadership had been shaken, and we still rejoiced in heroes. . . . I thought about the last time I'd seen it, when I'd shared as much as a child can in the boundless material self-confidence of the country—when Russia lay, a clearly articulated evil, on the other side of the world. Now here I am in Russia, and that particular innocence and arrogance have departed from me and from other Americans, probably forever. Strangely enough, it's this lost America that Russians seem most to admire, although they denounce it: the dream landscape made up of our big cars, big wasteful meals, sprawling suburbs, tough military stance.[60]

Lee's post–civil rights, post-Vietnam vantage point did not foresee the near future revival of Cold War rhetoric and the longing that would emerge in the United States itself for "lost America." Viewing *Cleopatra* from the Soviet perspective, Lee reads the movie's representation of the United States (Egypt) in 1962, and especially of sex and race, to be "innocent" and "arrogant." *Russian Journal* thus takes the civil rights movement to be a turning point in U.S. history and a collective, national learning experience that has allowed the nation to move forward. Lee's own crossing of the East–West divide that had once represented "a clearly articulated evil" parallels the U.S. national crossing of the color line through the struggle for civil rights. According to *Russian Journal*, the United States' past, and in particular its racial past, can now only be replayed within the Soviet imagination of a United States that was big, sprawling, and wasteful.

Just as in the United States the south to north movement has historically evoked the movement toward liberation, the end of *Russian Journal* indicates that in the U.S.S.R. the road westward brings with it a sense of freedom. When she describes her departure from Russia, Lee focuses on the moment her train crosses the Brest–Litovsk border with Poland. She feels a "lightening of the mood" and a "sense of celebration."[61] She reports experiencing "a crazy sense of freedom; we felt released from a subtle and deadly confinement, which, we only now realized, had sapped our spirits for ten months."[62] After a short stay in Poland, she "traveled south to the Aegean, to awaken further from Russia in the purest, most logical light in the world."[63] Though Lee would later miss "life in the tower," her movement westward is described in terms of an enlightenment, moving from imprisonment to liberty, from darkness to light. The "logical" light recalls one of her earliest descriptions of Russia's monuments that sought to evoke "raw emotion," in contrast to the "measured rationality" of U.S. ones.[64] If, as Kate Baldwin suggests, earlier instances of African Americans traveling across the East–West divide exposed the connection between the United States' fears of Soviet imperial expansion and domestic racial transgression, in the post–civil rights context of the late 1970s, Lee's *Russian Journal* reveals that the United States' concerns with Soviet expansion in the Middle East, articulated in U.S. foreign policy as a human rights concern, displaced American racial inequalities and imperial ambitions onto the U.S.S.R. Lee's reflections on the "measured rationality" of U.S. liberalism, which had nominally fulfilled the promise of racial equality under the law, no longer imagined the U.S.S.R. as a place from which to launch a critique of U.S. racial politics.

Because Lee's *Russian Journal* did not explicitly depict racism in Russia, her observations about the U.S.S.R. stand in contrast to her later reflections, expressed in her 1990 lecture, about her attraction to Russia as linked to her personal memories of U.S. racial politics during the civil rights era. Reading *Russian Journal* side by side with Lee's lecture, in which she described the book as a relic of the past, also speaks to a particular cultural amnesia about the Cold War, one that naturalizes the dominant U.S. presumption of itself as the foremost democracy by decontextualizing it from the Cold War logics that underwrote such claims. Lee's connection between totalitarianism in the U.S.S.R. and U.S. domestic race relations, while gesturing toward the mutually defining discourses of the Cold War and racial progress, also implies that U.S. racism stands as a relic of the past alongside the nation's Cold War vision of the U.S.S.R.

Transitional Aspirations: Multicultural Futurity and Reconciliation

Whereas Lee's portrait of the U.S.S.R. as an incarnation of the racist past emerged in a late Cold War moment when geopolitical tensions were escalating, the Afro-Russian journalist Yelena Khanga's journey to the United States in the late 1980s and the publication of her memoir *Soul to Soul* in the early 1990s coincided with the excitement surrounding the fall of communism and the disintegration of the U.S.S.R.[65] Reversing Lee's spatial and temporal orientation by writing about the United States from a Soviet perspective, Khanga's travelogue, though focused on recounting her family's history, espoused a future-oriented outlook for the possibilities of multiculturalism as a way to heal past racial incursions and as a model for the Soviet transition to liberal democracy. Khanga captured the interest of the U.S. media after the disintegration of the U.S.S.R. because through her Soviet upbringing and her African American heritage, she embodied the hope that former enemies would come together in a global celebration of democracy.

In 1988, at the height of glasnost during the Gorbachev years, Khanga traveled to the United States on behalf of *Moscow Weekly News* as part of a professional exchange with the American paper the *Christian Science Monitor*. Since this was the first exchange between journalists from a Soviet paper and a U.S. paper, Khanga was carefully selected as one of the participants because she traced her family's lineage to the United States. The granddaughter of American émigrés Oliver Golden, an African American son of a slave, and Bertha Bialek, a Polish Jew, Khanga's professional journey as the first journalist to officially represent the Soviet Union in the United States was intricately linked to her personal journey of discovering the complexities of her own racial and national identity. Her presence as a Soviet journalist in the United States evoked the liberalization of the U.S.S.R. because it stood for the possibility of a free press. In addition, as a black Russian, she represented the multiplicity of voices—including those with historical ties to the United States—coming to the fore with glasnost. Khanga thus became a minor media celebrity during her year at the *Monitor* in Boston.[66] The *Washington Post* article "A Child of Many Cultures" noted that of "the contemporary characters who straddle the mighty distance between Russia and America [and who constitute] a colorful and eclectic group . . . , none of them has a saga more poignant than Yelena Khanga."[67] The piece went on to specify that Khanga's "coffee color" skin and "the cultural heritage that comes along with it" make her the most "poignant" figure for bridging the "mighty distance" between East and West. *Ebony*, a monthly magazine that is aimed at a black readership, headlined its review "How a Black/Jewish/Polish/Russian/African Woman Found Her Roots."[68] Calling Khanga's book a "weave" of "multicultural strands," the article, and especially its title, implied that Khanga's mixed ancestry produced a story that, in and of itself, could recommend the memoir as an exemplary text of post–Cold War diversity. *Essence*, another monthly magazine targeted at black readers, praised the "multicultural saga, extending from American Slavery to glasnost, [as] an insightful and ironic journey not only into racial attitudes, but also into the profound cultural gulf separating Russian and American society."[69] By connecting U.S. progress toward racial "equality" and multiculturalism to Russia's progress toward democracy, the U.S. media implied that Khanga's embodied multiculturalism was the ideal allegory for Russia's post–Cold War potential for liberal tolerance.

Khanga's grandparents, who met through the Communist Party in New York City during the 1920s, set sail for the U.S.S.R. in 1931 along with sixteen black agricultural experts from the United States in search of professional opportunities unavailable to them in the United States due to racism. Their daughter, Lily Golden, Yelena's mother, grew up in Moscow, where she married Abdullah Khanga, who was an exchange student from Zanzibar (later called Tanzania).[70] Khanga's 1988 trip to her grandparents' homeland was momentous, since no one in her family had set foot on U.S. soil since 1931. The process of uncovering her family's roots, her experience of meeting her U.S. relatives for the first time, and U.S. media enthusiasm over her family's

diverse history elucidate the connections between the shifting racial paradigms within the United States during the transitional moment of the late
1980s and early 1990s and the changes in U.S. foreign policy toward the
Soviet-led Eastern Bloc. It is no coincidence that Yelena Khanga became an
embodiment of multiculturalism at this time. Her reunification with her
black and white American families became symbolic of U.S. domestic and
geopolitical reconciliation. Khanga was first "discovered" in the United
States as she was waiting, amid hundreds of reporters, to hear that Gorbachev
and Reagan had signed a tentative strategic arms control agreement. In *Soul
to Soul* she explains that, for the U.S. media, she "was more interesting than
boring old arms control—a young black woman talking casually about 'we
Russinas.' "[71] This young black Russian's rediscovery of her family's American ancestry seemed to parallel the cautious beginnings of conciliation
between the two global superpowers in the arms control agreement.

Khanga's initial trip to the United States as a reporter was soon followed
by a second visit, made possible by a grant from the Rockefeller Foundation,
which funded her to chronicle her family's "roots" in the Mississippi delta
and Chicago. In 1992 Khanga published the memoir based on her research,
Soul to Soul, which was an exploration of her perceptions and experiences
of being black in the Soviet Union and in the United States, set against
the backdrop of her family's history. "Soul to soul," a Russian term used to
describe intimate friendships, is deployed throughout the text as a metaphor not just for Khanga's reunion with the black and white sides of her
family in the United States but also for the potential of a renewed U.S.–
Soviet friendship. The term *soul* itself, as Dale Peterson points out, is evo-
cative of the parallels between Russian and African American cultures'
conceptions of ethnic soul as "essentially multicultural and syncretic."[72]
Khanga's use of "soul" as the framing mechanism for her memoir resonates
with the term's "ethnic" connotation, which is especially evident in the
book's focus on how Khanga found a multicultural connection with African
American and Jewish American cultures in the United States.

On the level of allegory, *Soul to Soul* envisions the transformation of
the post–Cold War global order and U.S.–Russian cooperation through
Khanga's reunification with the Goldens—the black side of her family—and
the Bialeks—the white Jewish side of her family. In the spring of 1988,
Khanga taped an interview with the weekly *ABC News* magazine *20/20,*
after which her African American relatives contacted her. Khanga writes, "I
gradually came to understand what it meant to belong to a large African
American family with a proud history. We were of the same blood; we

shared a past even though we had been separated by time, language, and culture."[73] Overcoming the prejudices and intolerances of the "past," whether in the U.S. civil rights struggle or through "democratization" in the U.S.S.R., laid the foundation for new racial and historical frames. Khanga's familial reconciliation, however, could not be complete without an encounter with the Bialek family. Khanga's great-grandparents had disowned her grandmother, Bertha, for having married a black man. In the memoir, Khanga confesses that she was reluctant to find the Bialeks until Frank Karel of the Rockefeller Foundation urged her to complete the story of her family by meeting her white Jewish relatives. Though Jack, Bertha Bialek's brother, had concealed from the rest of the family that they had black relatives living in Russia, by the time Khanga met the younger generation they seamlessly integrated Yelena's blackness into their conception of the family: "You mean the big secret is that we have a black cousin? So what?"[74] The cousins' insistence that race no longer matters resonates with *Soul to Soul*'s perspective on changes in U.S. race relations on the level of the family; what was understood as miscegenation in the 1930s, when Khanga's grandparents left for the U.S.S.R., became a sign of multicultural unity in one family in the 1990s. A 1992 *Essence* review of *Soul to Soul* completed this narrative by recounting how at a Thanksgiving reunion of the Golden and Bialek families Khanga and her Polish American cousin, Nancy Bialek, performed a rendition of Stevie Wonder's "Ebony and Ivory."[75] The concluding lines of *Soul to Soul* rearticulate the dual processes in the "perfect harmony," as the song goes, of multicultural (domestic) and post–Cold War (geopolitical) healing: "We need a common language through which we can accept differences while embracing common humanity; that was my grandparents' real dream, and I have shared it since the day I first heard Martin Luther King's voice on a scratchy tape in a Moscow elementary school—a black, Russian, American, human dream."[76]

Although *Soul to Soul* invited its U.S. readers to imagine the possibilities of reconciliation between former enemies in the immediate post–Cold War moment, the memoir nevertheless unwittingly perpetuated the Cold War binaries it proposed to tear down. In spite of funding from the Rockefeller Foundation for Khanga to explore her family history on her father's side in Zanzibar, *Soul to Soul*'s limited treatment of her African heritage excludes Africa from the possibility of progress that it imagines for post-Communist nations should they succeed in overcoming their illiberal prejudices in order to pursue the politics of tolerance, diversity, and free-market capitalism. Khanga writes that immediately after her birth, "the cultural rift between

[her] parents grew into a chasm."[77] Yelena's mother never moved to Zanzibar with Abdullah Khanga because "his attitudes towards women were the product of a culture very different from our own. She did not criticize that culture but emphasized that she, brought up with a very different way of thinking about women's possibilities, could not adapt to his attitudes."[78] Even after Khanga herself visited Zanzibar as part of her research, she discovered that the instinctual and intimate connection she had with her American family was completely lacking in Africa. Khanga writes, "I can't claim to have experienced any special revelation about my African 'roots' during this journey. Walking along the streets of Dar, I kept waiting for a click, the sense of recognition and identification I've felt so many times among black Americans."[79]

Khanga's sense of alienation from "Tanzania, a country strongly influenced by Islam," in which she describes the exclusion of women from public participation that is still prevalent, thus imagines Africa as apart from, if not antithetical to, her future-oriented fantasy of reconciliation through tolerance and diversity.[80] *Soul to Soul*'s self-proclaimed feminist critique of Yelena's father, as well as of Africa, suggests an insurmountable cultural difference between Africa and the U.S.S.R. that, even though it is not yet Western, is seen to espouse modern notions of equality shared by Western Europe and the United States. The temporal distancing of Africa from the progress narrative of postsocialist transition is here articulated through the figuring of unreformed, and therefore intolerant, Islamic formations. *Soul to Soul* thus exemplifies multiculturalism's dual movement of incorporating racial difference into a story of progress and transition while displacing fears of illiberalism onto religious difference. In order to include Eastern Europe and the U.S.S.R. in a narrative of historical progress, religious intolerance, here located in Africa, becomes the new landscape through and against which U.S. citizens can understand themselves as a nation that has shed its past of racial intolerance, and citizens of the U.S.S.R. can understand the present-day need to shed their past of totalitarian intolerance. Africa, in other words, functions in the travelogue as the container of past prejudices.

The figuration of Yelena Khanga as a multicultural emblem who could stand as a bridge between former ideological rivals in the East and West is indicative of the shift to the transnational marketability of difference in the realm of the global free-market economy celebrated in the post–Cold War transition. Shortly after the publication of her book, Khanga capitalized on her multicultural value to become an entrepreneur. She invited black professionals to travel to Russia and to teach Russians how to shed the vestiges of the Communist state-run economy. Khanga observed:

> Right now, Russia is one of the biggest markets in the world. Hotels are filled with foreign businessmen who are planting the roots for various spheres of business. But when I mention this to black business people, they say it is too expensive. They are afraid they might be rejected because they are black. Russians want resources and profits. If you can do that, there is no problem.[81]

Khanga's invitation to black businesspeople represents a historical irony in light of the radical Afro-American diaspora's past in the former Soviet Union, of which her grandparents were a part. Oliver Golden and Bertha Bialek left the United States both because they wished to escape racism and because they believed in building an alternative to the capitalist model of national development. In contrast to her grandparents, Khanga herself returned to the U.S.S.R. (as hers is not an immigrant's story of coming to the United States) and urged black businesspeople to travel to capitalist Russia because race no longer mattered—only profit. Kate Baldwin has suggested that in the context of post-Communist Russia, "Khanga's embodiment of [the] unusual routings [of the black diaspora] reads through the screen of earlier black Americans in the U.S.S.R. But her Soviet upbringing in the 1970s and 1980s also shifts the image broadcast to new interpretive frames."[82] The rearticulation of Khanga's complex family history also reflects the new interpretive frames of the post–Cold War moment in the context of the United States, in particular, the racialized currency of multiculturalism within the global free-market economy. In conflating multiculturalism with the ideals of freedom, democracy, and equality, Khanga's vision for black businesspeople reflects how the celebratory rhetoric in the United States during the 1990s failed to substantively address the changing forms of racism and discrimination in the domestic context.

Through their focus on developing Eastern Europe economically, politically, and culturally, these U.S. post–Cold War discourses in fact worked to displace U.S. racial anxieties by positioning the United States as a model for liberal tolerance. They did so by eliding domestic histories of racial inequality and uneven development in favor of marketing multiculturalism and difference to promote the free market as a stand-in for democracy. Indeed, U.S. knowledge of Eastern Europe as a region in transition established a connection between freedom and diversity as minority civil rights are used alongside capitalist development to measure the spread of "freedom" and democracy. According to the "Freedom Rating" published by the Freedom House, a nonpartisan organization that provides a metric for classifying countries as "free," "partly free," or "unfree," there are three clusters of conditions for ranking the formerly Communist "nations in transition" that follow economic variables: (1) "freedom," which encompasses civil liberties and political rights; (2) the competitiveness and institutionalization of political parties and elections, as well as the accountability of politicians to the electorate; and (3) the rule of law.[83] The Freedom House, founded in 1941 to encourage support for U.S. intervention in World War II, originated in the idea that the United States could spread freedom abroad.[84] The Freedom Rating classifications were developed in 1973, after civil rights were enshrined in U.S. law, thus establishing the United States as a model of what "freedom" looks like. In the postsocialist period, the Freedom House expanded its on-the-ground-projects in Eastern Europe. The Freedom Rating took on a new significance, establishing a developmental narrative within which Eastern European nations strive to overcome the legacy of communism in the transitional period—understood here in terms of the lack of civil liberties and rights due to Communist legacies of intolerance— and to achieve legitimate democracy and tolerance exemplified by the U.S.-led West. Political imaginaries like those produced by the Freedom House, and like Khanga's perspective on Soviet transition, imply that capitalist development breeds tolerance, justice for minorities, and modernity. Postsocialist "freedom" in Eastern Europe has thus meant not only participation in the U.S.-dominated free-market economy but an espousal (even if only a nominal one) of multicultural values.

"A Journey through History": Religious Legacies, Ancient Hatreds, and the Balkans

While Khanga's travelogue, as an allegory for the former Eastern Bloc's transitional aspirations, promoted multiculturalism as the racial promise of liberal democracy and civil rights in Eastern Europe, already by the early 1990s the rise in ethnic and religious nationalism in some formerly Communist countries suggested that multicultural reconciliation would not be the fate awaiting the entire postsocialist world. In the Cold War era formulation of historical progress, the fall of the Berlin Wall should have led to the incorporation of the former Eastern Bloc nations into the realm of political and economic freedom. Yet in the former Yugoslavia, which came to epitomize the failures of transition, conflict and civil war only escalated as the decade wore on, moving eastward from Slovenia and Croatia (1990–1992) to Bosnia and Herzegovina (1992–1995) and, eventually, to Serbia and Kosovo. In contrast to the future-oriented fantasy of liberal multicultural-ism, U.S. media and politicians portrayed instances of ethnoreligious vio-lence in the Balkans as a contemporary enactment of primordial hatreds and ancient grievances. "Ethnic conflict," the commonplace descriptor of postsocialist troubles, was construed as the greatest threat to the progres-sive vision of the new world order. Thus the Cold War era's racialized oppo-sition between U.S. freedom and Communist totalitarianism gave way to a new opposition between multicultural tolerance and ethnoreligious hatred. In the temporal refiguring of racial geopolitical imaginaries in the post-socialist era, multiculturalism came to represent the fulfillment of U.S. domestic racial progress, while ethnoreligious nationalism became a sign of the racial time of the other—those landscapes that were not yet, and might never be, ready for freedom.

Perhaps the best-known book that contributed to shaping the U.S. post-socialist racial and temporal imaginary is Robert Kaplan's travelogue *Bal-kan Ghosts: A Journey through History*. *Balkan Ghosts* is widely believed to have influenced first Bill Clinton's policy of inaction during the civil war in Bosnia and Herzegovina and later, in a seeming contradiction, his deci-sion to lead the first purely "humanitarian" war, the 1999 Operation Allied Force in Serbia and Kosovo. The well-known association between Kaplan's travelogue and U.S. foreign policy in the 1990s exemplifies the intertextual circulation of postsocialist knowledge about the world produced in travel-ogues, as well as the interconnectedness of cultural and political discourses about transition. Kaplan's record of his journey in the late 1980s and 1990 across Croatia, Kosovo, Macedonia, Romania, Bulgaria, and Greece nar-rates the Balkans as a region distinct from Europe as a whole. Depicting the Balkans as steeped in a backward religiosity that is incompatible with lib-eral democratic reform, he sums up the territory as "a time-capsule world: a dim stage upon which people raged, spilled blood, experienced visions and ecstasies."[85] Emphasizing that Americans need to rethink regional his-tories and geopolitics in the part of the world that had been known as the Eastern Bloc, he writes, "the Cold War and the false division of Europe were over. A different, more historically grounded division of Europe was about to open up, I knew. Instead of democratic Western Europe and a Commu-nist Eastern Europe, there would now be Europe and the Balkans."[86]

Arguing that the United States and the West must no longer consider Eastern Europe to be outside of Europe proper, Kaplan proposes subsuming the Balkans into what he calls the "New Near East" in order to grasp the social and economic "drifting from the Second to the Third World" that occurred in some, but not other, parts of formerly Communist nations.[87] Separating the Balkans from Europe was essential for dismantling the alternative economic and social vision symbolized by the Cold War designation of the "Second World." In the new global map, nations were either already modern, capitalist, and democratic (First World), or failed and in a state of perpetual crisis (Third World). The 1990s reframing of global crisis, which no longer signaled the threat of Communist infiltration but, rather, the inherent failings evident in both the nature and culture of some "Third World" nations, was central in morally underwriting new modes of U.S. and Western military and economic interventionism.

The spatial and ideological reorganization of postsocialist geopolitics thus produced new fantasies of otherness that would take the place of communism as a foremost sign of Eastern alterity. Comparing Kaplan's work to print and visual media that represent the victims of famine and war, Cynthia Simmons addresses the way in which the otherness of suffering bodies is "intimately tied to issues of political policy and, by way of that, to issues regarding human rights."[88] She argues that works like Kaplan's, which are at best Orientalizing and at worst examples of "Baedeker Barbarism," eliciting and justifying "barbaric apathy" toward the other, have at times of war "affected policies that resulted in human rights disasters."[89] In this connection, Simmons suggests that "the insidiousness" of *Balkan Ghosts* lies not in its Orientalism but, rather, in its "confusion as to its genre, and therefore, its claim to serious discourse on the tragic events in the former Yugoslavia."[90] As a "politicized travelogue," a "genre somewhere between serious journalism and travelogue," Kaplan claims for himself an unwarranted expertise on the region that proved quite dangerous in relation to U.S. policy.[91] Particularly troublesome for Simmons is Kaplan's misrepresentation of religion as the root cause of the wars. She herself emphasizes that, contrary to Kaplan's claims, most former Yugoslavs, including Bosnians, Albanians, and Serbs, were adamantly secular.

While Simmons's analysis astutely foregrounds the importance of religion in the narrative of *Balkan Ghosts*, her emphasis on the book's inaccuracies and her ensuing claim that a more truthful portrait of the Balkans would have led to better U.S. policy in the region miss the broader shift in the U.S. transnational racial imaginary occurring in the early 1990s.

Whether correct or not, Kaplan's vivid depiction of religion as the driving force of Balkan barbarity was one cultural cornerstone of the emergent post-Communist racial fantasy portraying monstrous religiosity as the new great evil threatening global development and the liberal ideal of freedom. An analysis that insists on separating cultural works from policy, such as Simmons's, neglects the interconnectedness of the two in the production of global imaginaries. Ironically, Kaplan himself agrees with Simmons. Reacting to accusations that *Balkan Ghosts* affected Clinton's foreign policy, he stresses that he never imagined his "travel book on a region in its last moments of obscurity might later be read as a policy tract."[92] Opposing what he sees as a predominant tendency in the United States to politicize all works, Kaplan presents his view of the travelogue genre as a narrative record and a portrait of an individual traveler's experience of his or her surroundings and encounters occurring in a particular time and place. One should not, according to Kaplan, read travelogues as " 'progressive' or 'illiberal,' 'deterministic' or 'humanistic,' 'interventionst' or 'noninterventionist.' . . . The real questions should be: do the characters and descriptions come alive."[93] As Kaplan concludes, "realists know this. They don't need to idealize a region, a people, or a history in order to take action, and so they don't need to see a book through a filter of what they want to believe: whether it be a President searching for an excuse to do nothing in 1993, or for inspiration to do something in 1999."[94]

The "confusion" about the political circulation of Kaplan's book (and travel literature more generally) with which Kaplan and his critics are concerned points to the controversial yet productive role of travelogues in bringing to life geopolitical imaginaries in which political acts are narrated as moral or amoral, ethical or unethical, and just or unjust. In spite of the predominant critique of *Balkan Ghosts* as a book that, through its political influence, exacerbated human rights violations, its portrayal of temporal, racial, and religious otherness was in fact constitutive of a postsocialist imaginary that divided the globe between landscapes defined by human rights violations and those defined through minority rights and tolerance. In order for citizens in Europe and in the United States to understand their nations as spaces of rights and as humanitarian actors, there was a need for images of humanitarian crises. In other words, there was a demand for answers to the question Robert Kaplan asked himself while traveling in the Balkans: "What does the earth look like in the places where people commit atrocities?"[95] Throughout the 1990s, U.S. and Western European cultural and political discourses produced ethnoreligious conflict in the Balkans as an exemplary site of atrocity. Through the region's confounding location both within and outside of Europe, the postsocialist human rights catastrophe of ethnic and religious warfare in the Balkans that played out throughout the decade conjured the need for military intervention in the region so as to bring it into the fold of Euro-American modernity. The presumption within the United States that it had, as a liberal multicultural nation, achieved human rights for its diverse citizens, meanwhile, morally authorized U.S. interventionism as humanitarian.

Against spectacularized portraits of ethnic and religious rivalries, in the postsocialist era U.S. Americans distinguished their nation's power from earlier European imperial ambitions by conceiving of their national present not just as humanitarian but as antiracist. The racialization of religious difference, such as in the narrative of Kaplan's *Balkan Ghosts*, signaled the emergence of a new racialized imaginary in the United States that produced "unreformed" religious formations as the ideological other, distinguishing those parts of the former Eastern Bloc that were fit for liberal democracy from those that were not. In *Balkan Ghosts*, Kaplan makes the case that to grasp the significance of the Balkans in the new world order, U.S. and Western readers must come to terms with two regional realities: the first, that nonmodern religious beliefs were foremost in the resurgence of Balkan nationalism; the second, that Balkan people espoused a fundamentally different and opposing view of history from Western citizens. He suggests that whereas in the West, the Protestant Reformation led to the separation of church and state, in the Balkans, unreformed religiosity precluded the development of secular history, democratic institutions, and the principles of tolerance. In this view, communism, rather than revolutionizing religious worldviews and instituting modernity in the East, had simply repressed religious feeling. This is why, as the argument goes, religious clashes erupted so violently in the 1990s.

Kaplan's travelogue proposes to describe the cycles of repression and return in the Balkans, which led to a perspective on history that has little in common with the Western belief in progress. In the book's prologue, he explains that in the Balkans, the Western traveler can grasp how "an entire world can be made out of very little light."[96] *Balkan Ghosts* develops a connection between physical darkness—the book's overarching metaphor for Balkan unenlightenment persisting through the eras of Ottoman imperial rule, Communist rule, and nationalist self-rule—and ethnicized and nationalized religious identification, which makes Balkan worldviews incompatible with democratic values and tolerance. Kaplan begins his journey in a Serbian Orthodox monastery in Peć, Kosovo (then a province in Serbia): "Inside the Church of the Apostles, painted in A.D. 1250, my eyes needed time. The minutes were long and, like the unbroken centuries, full of defeat. I carried neither a flashlight nor a candle. Nothing focuses the will like blindness."[97] Framing his account, Kaplan contrasts his own ability to see in the darkness with the blindness of Balkan natives, whose wills and minds have been stunted by religion and defeat through the "unbroken centuries." Describing the church's painted apostles and saints, who "all appeared through a faith's distorting mirror" as the "haunted and hunger-ravaged faces of a preconscious, Serb past," Kaplan explains that "the distance these monumental forms had to travel while my eyes adjusted to the dark was infinite: through Ottoman centuries, the most evil wars, and communist rule. Here, in this sanctum of dogma, mysticism, and savage beauty, national life was lived. Only from here could it ever emerge."[98] Kaplan is explicit that the Western traveler who truly wants to understand the region must journey through history as well as across space. Only in doing so can the Western observer reorient his entire mind-set: "*Superstition? Idolatry? That would be a Western mind talking.* A mind that, in Joseph Conrad's words, did 'not have a hereditary and personal knowledge of the means by which an historical autocracy represses ideas, guards its power, and defends its existence.'"[99]

In order to associate the Western mind, from the era of high British imperialism in which Joseph Conrad was writing to the present day, with a fundamental belief in the freedom of thought and conscience, Kaplan displaces recent instances of Western barbarity onto the Balkans.[100] In his interpretation of the historical record, "Nazism, . . . can claim Balkan origins. Among the flophouses of Vienna, a breeding ground of ethnic resentments close to the southern Slavic world, Hitler learned how to hate so infectiously."[101] Austria, however, is no longer Balkan. As Kaplan enters Croatia at the Austrian border, he ruminates that "the offspring of the SS" are now safely "tucked away in middle-class box houses." Kaplan proposes that as advanced capitalism and consumerism render anti-Semitism unacceptable and fully displaced from the public sphere in Western Europe, emblematized by the fact that Israel has become "just another winter destination for local sun worshippers," "the Balkans no longer begin at the gates of Vienna, or even at those of Klagenfurt."[102] The new landscape of atrocity begins, instead, with the former Yugoslavia, at whose border men with "grimy fingernails" crowd the train, shouting at each other, "slugging back alcohol," and working "their way quietly through pornographic magazines."[103] Kaplan, himself Jewish, uses ongoing anti-Semitism in the Balkans as an example of racial and religious hatred that transcends differences between the Balkan nations he visits. From the nationalist rehabilitation of the World War II era Croatian fascists in the late 1980s, to the renewed popularity of the Legionnaires of the archangel Michael in Romania, who executed "one of the most brutal pogroms in history," Kaplan recounts the death of communism as having reawakened an unchanged form of fascism in the Balkans.[104] After all, he writes, communism was simply "fascism, without fascism's ability to make the trains run on time."[105] Like Lee, who referenced her experience of racism in the U.S. pre–civil rights era to racialize Communist totalitarianism, and Khanga, who built on her multiracial background to portray multiculturalism as a future-orientated frame for Eastern European transition, Kaplan uses his position as a Jewish American from a nation that values religious freedom to assess contemporary religious animosity and prejudice in the Balkans through the familiar referent of anti-Semitism. At the same time, Kaplan's positionality as a U.S. religious, rather than a racial, minority also demonstrates the shift to the privileging of religion over race as a foremost signifier of conflict and freedom in the post-socialist era.

In addition to associating the Balkans with the European evils of Nazism, in his geopolitical remapping Kaplan points to the Balkans as the historical locus of all the world's evils: "Whatever has happened in Beirut or elsewhere happened here first, long ago, in the Balkans. The Balkans produced the century's first terrorists. . . . Hostage taking and the wholesale slaughter of innocents were common. Even the fanaticism of the Iranian clergy has a Balkan precedent."[106] Kaplan's displacement of U.S. and Western readers' fears of terrorism and irrational death dealing onto the Balkans produces a new racial geography that extends the "Third World" to encompass the Balkans, a part of the former Eastern Bloc that cannot adapt to liberal reform: "The Balkans were the original Third World, long before Western media coined the term . . . in an age when Asia and Africa were still a bit too far afield."[107] Using his experience of writing and reporting from Africa, Kaplan liberally draws comparisons between the Balkan landscape and the "dark continent" to illustrate the region's difference from the rest of Europe. In Transylvania, Kaplan describes how "there was so much dust and garbage in the vicinity that I felt as if I were back in North Africa."[108] In another part of Romania, taking a boat to Sfintu Gheorghe along the Danube, Kaplan admits, "conditions exactly like these had scared me away from taking riverboats up the Nile in the Sudan and down the Zaire (Congo) river in Zaire."[109] Citing the British traveler E. O. Hoppe, he adds that the Danube delta consists of "Conrad-like stretches—the Conrad of *Heart of Darkness*."[110] Indeed, Kaplan elaborates, "The passengers around me intensified my feeling of having passed beyond Europe. . . . Romania was an original mix: a population that looked Italian but wore the expression of Russian peasants; an architectural backdrop that often evoked France and Central Europe; and service and physical conditions that resembled those in Africa."[111]

The new racial geography described by Kaplan, in which the Balkans are portrayed as akin to Africa and not of, or in, Europe, can no longer be apprehended through physical differences. After all, Romanians look Italian; their buildings French. Rather, the new racialized landscape can only be mapped through an exploration of interiorized difference of feeling and mind-set. In Croatia, for instance, Kaplan notes, "since Croats are ethnically indistinguishable from Serbs—they come from the same Slavic race, they speak the same language, their names are usually the same—their identity rests on their Roman Catholicism. Therefore, the Croatian crowd symbol might be the *Church*."[112] In the new geopolitical environment, where the differences that matter are not visible on the surface, Kaplan implies that religious beliefs and institutions are the essential modes of difference that must be excavated and explored. Ultimately, however, *Balkan Ghosts* locates Eastern Orthodox Christianity and Islam, not the Croats' Roman Catholicism, as the root of Balkan backwardness and irrationality—the region's core difference from the West. As he explains:

> Because Catholicism arose in the West, and Orthodoxy in the East, the difference between them is greater than that between, say, Catholicism and Protestantism, or even Catholicism and Judaism (which, on account of the Diaspora, also developed in the West). While Western religions emphasize ideas and deeds, Eastern religions emphasize beauty and magic. . . . Even Catholicism, the most baroque of western religions, is, by the standards of Eastern Orthodoxy, austere and intellectual.[113]

The division between Western and Eastern religions in *Balkan Ghosts* allies Western religions (including Protestantism, Judaism, and Catholicism) with the mind and, less directly, with the political and economic systems of liberal democracy and capitalism that follow rational thought and foster individuals' desire for freedom of "ideas and deeds." For instance, in Transylvania, where Kaplan encounters a large Protestant Saxon minority, he is shocked at how unlike the rest of Romania the people and place are. In the town of Sibiu, he finds that everything is clean, and people are hard at work doing their jobs. "It was like coming up for air. The clay tiles and metal spouts in the bathroom had been polished to a shine. . . . The Romanian waiters, like the Romanian maids who attended my room, worked quietly and efficiently, and didn't whisper in my ear about exchange rates and prostitutes."[114] Unlike Romanian waiters and maids in the rest of the country, who do not adequately perform the tasks for which they are paid, in Sibiu Kaplan discovers Romanians who value work similarly to how it is valued in the West. According to Kaplan, these Romanians adopted their work ethic from the Saxons, who strengthened their German identity after the Protestant Reformation. Though the Saxons migrated to this part of Transylvania in medieval times, Kaplan notes that their post-Reformation conversion to Lutheranism led them to create a town in the middle of Romania where "the hotel, plus many of the shops and eating places, operated at (for Romania) an unusually high standard of efficiency. . . . It had clearly helped the Romanians a great deal."[115] Reiterating a belief in the benefits of a Protestant work ethic, Kaplan implies that unlike Eastern Orthodoxy, Protestant values are conducive to making capitalism and democracy function. He thus concludes that the Balkans must turn westward and accept tutelage in order for real change to occur, change that would involve a conversion of the Orthodox heart and mind. He writes:

> The Saxons, along with the Jews, were the only people in Romania with a tradition of bourgeois values. . . . The era of Soviet domination in the Balkans was about to give way to an era of German domination. German economic imperialism, I realized, offered the most practical and efficient means of bringing free enterprise, democracy, and the other enlightened traditions of the West to Romania.[116]

As Kaplan's hopeful affirmation of German economic imperialism indicates, in *Balkan Ghosts*, religious distinctions are never simply about identity, faith, or practice. They are, instead, conceived of as a mind-set and value system produced through political, economic, and ideological systems. As such, Kaplan's engagement with the religious is simultaneously a commentary on old imperial legacies and new postsocialist geopolitical shifts. In this context, what he calls Eastern religions, described as mystical and tied to the body rather than to the mind, are conceived of as incompatible with how the West might imagine capitalist transformation in the postsocialist world. In spite of the Balkans' Christian majority, Kaplan enfolds the region into the Muslim world because Orthodoxy developed under Ottoman rule. In Jassy, a town in the Romanian province of Moldavia, he describes worshippers in the Metropolitan Cathedral:

> I watched a throng of Romanians wait in line to touch and kiss the skeleton [bones of St. Friday]. What struck me was the fervor and terror of the faces waiting in line. Not merely were the people repeatedly crossing themselves, but they were doing so with their knees on the floor, and some of them were sweating profusely. . . . Only in Shiite holy places in the Middle East had I experienced such a charged and suffocating religious climate, rippling with explosive energy. It frightened me.[117]

The embodied practices of Orthodoxy, which remind Kaplan of Islamic rituals in their "fervor and terror," frighten him because they are unrestrained, "suffocating," and "explosive." Privileging the body and not the mind, Orthodoxy counteracts the Balkans' possible connections with Germany, in which Kaplan finds hope for democratic and economic progress. Meanwhile, Orthodoxy's associations with Islam and the East provide *Balkan Ghosts* with its explanation for why time and history are experienced differently in the Balkans than in the West.

According to Kaplan, five hundred years of Ottoman rule are to blame. He writes that, following the Serbian defeat at Kosovo Polje in 1389, "as the living death of Ottoman Turkish rule began to seep in, with its physical cruelty, economic exploitation, and barren intellectual life, the Serbs perverted the myth of noble sacrifice."[118] In Kaplan's perspective, Orthodox Christianity became "perverted" through its encounter with and subjection to Islam. Serbs "filled their hearts with vengeful sadness and defeat: feelings whose atmospheric effect bore an uncanny resemblance to those that for centuries propelled the Iranian Shiites."[119] For this reason, "like Shiites, unreconstructed Serbs . . . granted no legitimacy to their temporal rulers. . . . They ignored the physical world."[120] In contrast to the Reformation, which led Protestants and, by extension, religious practitioners in the West to live and work on developing the ideals of religious freedom, tolerance, and the betterment of life in this world, Kaplan proposes that Orthodoxy, like certain sects of Islam and the formerly Ottoman world, bypasses the human drive to work for a political and economic system that would allow for individual self-realization and national development. "While the plain of Athens below the Parthenon—not to mention Moldavia and Wallachia—dozed under an Oriental, Ottoman sleep, Transylvania was proclaiming the Enlightenment, with freedom and equality for both Catholics and Protestants."[121] In spite of the fact that the Ottoman Empire is generally known for its tolerance of religious minorities, Kaplan imagines that Ottoman rule has led to historical stagnation and a view of history and temporality that is antithetical to Enlightenment values. Thus he concludes that in the Balkans, "history is not viewed as tracing a chronological progression as it is in the West" but is instead cyclical and productive of mythology.[122] In short, Eastern religiosity, consolidated under Ottoman rule, continues to influence a stagnant conception of temporality antithetical to the forward momentum of democratic transition.

As Kaplan argues in his sequel to *Balkan Ghosts*, Orthodox Christianity and Islam are both "oriental" rather than European religions because they neither engage, nor seek to change, the world as it is.[123] Moreover, he posits that Ottoman and Communist rule both encouraged and exacerbated the religiously motivated tendency of Balkan natives to ignore life in this world. According to Kaplan, the Ottoman Empire had never stimulated modern development, while communism "was simply a destructive force, a second Mongol invasion."[124] *Balkan Ghosts* ultimately racializes religious formations in the Balkans through a narrative that distinguishes Christian development under "Western" and "Eastern" rule. The travelogue suggests that any possibility for historical progress in the postsocialist era depends on the reshaping of stagnant Ottoman/Oriental and Communist mind-sets through Western dominance. Importantly, for Kaplan, imperialism is not in and of itself the key historical problem manipulating Balkan politics. Rather, the central problem in the postsocialist era is the kind of belief and value systems promoted by imperial formations opposed to modernization and human and economic development and progress. Whereas the Ottoman Oriental Empire and the Communist empire promoted defeatism and despotism, precluding the development of infrastructures necessary for the emergence of liberal capitalist nation-states for Kaplan, other imperial formations can not only engender such change but also humanize previously tyrannical and illiberal parts of the world. Indeed, in his chapter on Transylvania, Kaplan celebrates German economic imperialism as the hope for the future. Similarly, in his chapter on Croatia, he recounts how, in spite of the Austrian exploitation of Slavs, "to the modern Croats, the Habsburgs represent the last normal and stable epoch in Central European history prior to the horrific detour through Nazism and Communism."[125] In this sense, in

Balkan Ghosts, secular historical progress depends on the reformation (or Western reorientation) of "unreconstructed" Orthodox Christians and Muslims, a conversion of their inner being and belief to make them suitable for capitalist transition.

Balkan Ghosts thus reframes the idioms of otherness used to justify imperial domination. This is evident in the book's focus on describing interiorized differences of being and feeling (made manifest in this world as religion) rather than racial differences legible on the skin. As such, the travelogue should be read as part of a shifting racial imaginary of the 1990s that facilitated the consolidation of new imperial projects. The Balkan postsocialist landscape, with its complex, overlapping imperial histories and often confusing mix of religious practices, became laden as a site in which U.S. political and cultural discourses narrated ideological and imperial life and death, and the meaning of humanity and inhumanity in the aftermath of communism. The book begins with an epigraph from Rebecca West's famous Yugoslav travelogue, *Black Lamb and Grey Falcon*: "I hate the corpses of empires, they stink as nothing else." Paralleling its opening frame of the Balkans as a twentieth-century landscape of imperial death, *Balkan Ghosts* concludes by comparing the "decline of the Ottoman Empire and the decline of the Soviet Empire."[126] Implying that the decade of the 1990s represents a similar moment to the 1910s, in which the rotting remains of an empire continue to shape regional politics, Kaplan writes that the ethnic conflicts that proliferated in the Balkans were "inflamed by the living death of Communism."[127] With certain regions emerging as places where life was not life but living death, and in which inhumanity was as much a part of the landscape as the architecture, it seemed clear that the United States' task was no longer just to defend freedom against communism but to defend humanity and life itself through a mode of imperialism very much alive in the present day.

A New Imperial Fantasy

Whereas Cold War geopolitics coincided with massive decolonizing movements in the Third World, the postsocialist era can be thought of, as Shumei Shih has suggested, as ushering in a post-postcolonial moment.[128] In light of emergent temporal and racial fantasies morally underwriting the need for Western intervention, it is crucial to contextualize the post-1990 proliferation of U.S. and Western European political and cultural discourses celebrating certain forms of imperialism alongside the demise of communism. In popular accounts of geopolitical transformation like *Balkan Ghosts*, past empires, such as the Ottoman Empire and Western European colonial empires, are portrayed as ideologically out of time with the present moment. When the Ottoman Empire does enter the U.S. imaginary of the European continent, it is remembered as having fallen apart with the advent of modern nationalism and capitalist expansion. The Western European colonial empires, meanwhile, though viewed as modernizing projects, are nonetheless criticized for their racist policies, which are incompatible with the ideals of freedom, equality, and tolerance made manifest in the transnationalization of U.S. multicultural racial logics. Through popular critiques of dead empires and bygone eras, economic imperialism and humanitarian imperialism are experiencing an afterlife in the postsocialist moment as they become linked to progress, a capitalist work ethic, and enlightenment ideals. Since the demise of the last "empire" that was out of sync with the capitalist conception of individual freedom and the "free world," the Communist empire, imperialism no longer in and of itself has a negative connotation. Instead, economic and humanitarian forms of imperialism are seen as the only possible way to incorporate certain regions, like the Balkans, into the secular historical time of capitalist and democratic progress.

Robert Kaplan's trajectory as a journalist and popular travel writer exemplifies the shift in the temporal frame through which global "trouble spots" enter the U.S. national imaginary as a foremost power in the world and, consequently, how this shift affects public perceptions of imperial ideologies. During the last years of the Cold War, in the 1980s, Kaplan portrayed the Second and Third Worlds' potential for historical progress quite differently than in *Balkan Ghosts* and his subsequent writings. He argued in both his 1988 book on the famine in Ethiopia and his 1990 book on the Soviet–Afghan War that communism, a morally and economically bankrupt political and ideological system, was to blame for the humanitarian and refugee disasters.[129] Following the demise of communism, however, Kaplan began to write travel and journalistic accounts of Africa, the Middle East, and the Balkans that no longer blamed a form of government. Rather, in texts like *Balkan Ghosts* and his infamous dystopic piece on Africa, "The Coming Anarchy," Kaplan suggests that contemporary global conflicts, wars, and famine are rooted in nature, ancient and unchanging civilizational clashes, and religious systems antithetical to modernity and democracy.[130] Framing conflict and suffering as ahistorical, forever rooted in those regions that have, due to "unreconstructed" religion or untamed nature, never entered modernity, the post–Cold War temporalizing of the globe fundamentally changed the view of historical progress dominating U.S. interventionism since the Second World War. Whereas during the Communist era, regions such as the Balkans, Africa, and the Middle East were portrayed as having the potential to enter the temporality of progress as part of the "free world" once communism was defeated, the postsocialist era produced a fissure in interventionist progress narratives by depicting these regions as forever outside of modern time. This has, ironically, strengthened the feeling that the United States has arrived as a nation that now represents the timeless and universal values of human rights and humanitarianism— values applicable across time and space, even in those nether regions of the world where history is cyclical.

Although Kaplan has ardently denied supporting or believing in the successes of Western humanitarian interventionism in global trouble spots, he, just like liberal thinkers supporting humanitarian intervention, has explicitly endorsed U.S. imperialism, particularly in the post-9/11 era.[131] The understanding that contemporary U.S. imperialism no longer represents the "white man's burden" but, rather, a universal human burden has in large part supported liberal and "realist" conservative imperial apologists.[132] As public intellectual Michael Ignatieff argues, "America's empire is not like empires of times past . . . [but] an empire lite, a global hegemony whose grace notes are free markets, human rights and democracy."[133] Three developments, exemplified in the travelogues I have analyzed in this chapter, have been crucial to giving old empires their "afterlife" as the new enlightened, antiracist, human rights empire built by the United States in the postsocialist era. The first, the consolidation of multiculturalism in the late years of the Cold War, was essential to the fantasy of the United States as an antiracist nation where people of different colors and creeds have the same access to rights and equality. The second, the shift in the racialization of otherness, ranging from the racialization of unreconstructed religious formations to the racialization of nature and the environment in the case of Africa, enabled novel depictions of difference that did not, at least on the surface, repeat the scientific racism of the eighteenth and nineteenth centuries. Finally, these emergent modes of racialized difference depend on the fantasy of distinct yet coexisting temporalities, which divide the globe between nations such as the United States and those of Western Europe that have reached the end of history, and nations mired in ancient traditions, if not nature, that have remained sites of atrocity. In the chapters that follow, I trace these three developments through distinct instances of U.S. warfare and military intervention in the late Cold War years and the postsocialist era. The seeming contradiction of promoting universal humanitarianism and rights through war needed a new landscape of otherness—a landscape that works such as Lee's, Khanga's, and Kaplan's helped produce in the popular U.S. imaginary.

2 THE VIETNAM WAR AND THE ETHICS OF FAILURE

Heart of Darkness *and the Emergence of Humanitarian Feeling at the Limits of Imperial Critique*

THE 2008 DOCUMENTARY *An Unlikely Weapon: The Eddie Adams Story* engages the life and work of the photojournalist made famous by his photograph capturing a Vietcong insurgent's moment of execution at the hands of the Saigon police chief.[1] Foregrounding Eddie Adams's artistic genius not just in the field of war but across a range of human experiences, the photographer is nonetheless figured as representative of how the human search for perfection inevitably fails. The documentary opens with Adams's musing that the desire for greatness is both universal and unattainable. While his colleagues and contemporaries attest to the unparalleled impact and importance of his work, Adams is plagued with doubt. For instance, speaking about the execution photo that won the 1969 Pulitzer Prize, *ABC News* anchor Peter Jennings posits that as a single visual statement, that image brought home the "evil" and "cruelty" of the war for U.S. citizens in the most intimate of ways, changing public opinion and the course of that war, as well as the course of national history. Adams, meanwhile, dismisses the image as a terrible photo, poorly composed and taken in bad lighting. Ultimately, Adams's self-critique is upheld as the driving force that allows him to strive to improve the world through his images. Indeed, later in the film, when Adams speaks about the Vietnamese refugees, the "boat people," whom he photographed, inspiring Congress to allow them to enter the United States, he declares it is the only truly good thing that he has done.

Adams's life story, narrated as a search for progress through self-reflection, an experience of the horrors of war and a journey toward humanitarian action, and an exploration of new narratives about humanity, life, and death in the realm of the visual, in many ways parallels the recuperation of the Vietnam War in U.S. politics and culture that has taken place over the last three decades. Because the Vietnam War (1954–1975) is remembered as a "war of images," photojournalism and televised images of war are viewed as the impetus behind the development of domestic opposition to the war, leading to subsequent shifts in U.S. modes of militarism.[2] The commonplace national narrative of the Vietnam War as one that the U.S. military lost but that the camera, an unlikely weapon that effected moral outrage in the U.S. citizenry, won, inscribes the failures of the Vietnam War as the condition of possibility for the emergence of the U.S. nation as humanitarian. The Vietnam War is often historically situated as the event that exploded the nation's early Cold War innocence, boldness, and belief that its wars enabled the spread of global freedom. Yet far from ending future instances of U.S. military intervention, the failures of the Vietnam War produced an inwardly directed national critique that enabled a refiguring of U.S. national greatness by consolidating a distinct nationalist vision from that of the early Cold War years.

In a sense, the post-Vietnam era ushered in postsocialist fantasies about the globe, as the early Cold War understandings of the world shattered. Images, as condensed articulations of U.S. brutality in Vietnam, developed America's humanitarian gaze as one that could perceive a moral victory even in the face of military atrocity. During and after the Vietnam War, documentaries and photographs depicting the horrors of war allowed U.S. audiences to experience outrage at having caused the suffering of Vietnamese women, children, and civilians, affirming the ability of U.S. citizens to distinguish right from wrong. Most important in this regard was the myth that the Vietnam War was completely transparent, open, and available to the U.S. media.[3] The idea that Americans were able to see for themselves the horrors of their own nation's military actions and to take a moral stance against those actions suggested that U.S. democracy was still vibrant.

This chapter contends with the association between visual fantasies of atrocity and redemption, national self-reflection, and the emergence of humanitarian feeling in the post-Vietnam era. Arguing that cultural criticisms of imperial brutality and excess are not apart from but rather constitutive of future imperial projects, I contextualize the Vietnam War as a decisive event in the history of U.S. postsocialist empire building. Although the Vietnam War is generally addressed as the moment when U.S. Cold War imperialism came under attack by its own citizenry, I contend that the critique of U.S. militarism in this instance was necessary for the consolidation of postsocialist imperial and humanitarian fantasies of the 1990s and beyond. Whereas the first chapter explored the racial temporalities of postsocialist transition, this chapter turns to the crisis of previous temporal and narrative frames through which the U.S. nation apprehended its global role. Photojournalistic images of the Vietnam War that froze human suffering, such as the iconic Eddie Adams photo, seem to forever return the nation to the moment of moral disintegration. Yet the pain of the other depicted in prominent photographs—supposedly transparent reflections of the horrific truths of war—became linked to the possibility of national transfiguration and resurrection rather than deterioration. Wartime atrocity, captured in images that perpetually arrested the moment of death or injury, was written out of the secular, progress-oriented time of the nation, working instead as part of a symbolic past. Vietnam War photography can thus be thought of as instituting a sacred temporality, which Dana Luciano has described as an affective and regenerative mode that, through grief, transcends secular, linear, and forward-moving temporalities.[4] In the context of the Vietnam War, photojournalism provided the compensatory images for the horrors of the highly mechanized war, allowing U.S. citizens to affirm their enduring humanity by feeling grief on behalf of the war's victims. The halted temporality thus reworked the opposition to the war as hallowed history, enabling the spiritual reemergence of a democratic nation.

While wartime photographs formally encapsulated the puncturing of the nation's early Cold War progress narratives, other cultural forms, particularly documentaries, films, and even literary works, self-reflexively struggled with the possibility of making new narrative frames through which to make meaning of the images of national evil and moral failure that saturated post-Vietnam culture. The crisis of post-Vietnam era nationhood was made manifest as a crisis in representational frames. At this moment, U.S. culture turned to an earlier moment of imperial crisis—that of nineteenth-century European imperial atrocity. As one of the most well-known portrayals of how ostensibly noble ideas can lead to savage acts, Joseph Conrad's 1899 novella, *Heart of Darkness*, was commonly referenced and refigured as anchoring national reflexivity. According to Edward Said, *Heart of Darkness* is as much a reflection on the narrative practice of empire as it is an exposition of moral crisis. As such, the novel has circulated in cultural works that self-consciously foreground the creative processes through which the crumbling of past worldviews and the emergence of new ones takes shape. Said proposes that "by accentuating the discrepancy between the 'idea' of empire and the remarkably disorienting reality of Africa, [the novel] unsettles the reader's sense not only of the very idea of empire, but of something more basic, reality itself. . . . With Conrad, then, we are in a world being made and unmade more or less all the time."[5] In this sense, *Heart of Darkness*, as a book not just about imperial atrocity and failure but also about the fading of certain lifeworlds and the emergence of new ones, enabled post-Vietnam U.S. fantasies about building new, more ethical worlds out of ones that had crumbled.[6] In other words, the post-Vietnam ethical dilemma of how to portray the nation's encounter with its own heart of darkness, which played out largely in the realm of visual culture, can be read as an attempt to grapple with questions about how a nation maintains or loses its faith in its own ideals when it encounters their destructive and deadly force.

Of course, even as geopolitical formations shifted and conceptions of humanitarian intervention and moral action evolved with the unfolding of the Cold War, ongoing cultural and political allusions to *Heart of Darkness* as a frame for imperial critique bear the legacy of European imperialism. The racial contradictions in Conrad's novel structured the post-Vietnam U.S. imaginary of what it means to be human and to recognize the humanity of another, to feel "moral shock" at the violence and brutality brought about by supposedly altruistic ideas. Conrad's imperial critique racialized and objectified the other's pain as a locus around which the European subject could prove his or her humanity. Like Conrad's novel, which flattens the African space as the backdrop in which Europeans have the opportunity to prove their humanity, visual images of "Vietnam" facilitated the reemergence of U.S. politics as ethical in the aftermath of a wartime loss. Indeed, the post-Vietnam insistence on exposing the horrors of war reworked Conrad's racial imaginary by affirming the United States as a space of human and democratic potential through and against depictions of the Vietnamese victims of U.S. violence.

Highlighting the imbrication of humanitarian-based criticisms of empire with the work of empire, as well as the ironies of establishing humanitarian ideals and ideas about democracy through war, this chapter traces the racial and imperial foundations that enabled the association between morality and violence in the United States at the Cold War's end. I begin with a brief overview of the early Cold War ideals that were disrupted with the Vietnam War, focusing on John F. Kennedy's conception of the "New Frontier" as a site of darkness that the United States could enlighten through liberal democratic and capitalist ideals. To understand the cultural apprehension of the Vietnam War as the event with which the darkness turned inward as the nation came face-to-face with its own brutality, I turn to the text of *Heart of Darkness* itself, highlighting how the European imperial conception of humanity depended on the racialization of humanitarian affect. Building on the analyses of these two earlier geopolitical imaginaries of the early Cold War and the European imperial eras, the remainder of the chapter contends with post-Vietnam cultural works that self-reflexively dealt with the disintegration of earlier notions of human–historical progress. Making reference to Conrad's novel as a postwar ethical frame, avowedly antiwar documentaries and photojournalism associated with the critique of American brutality paradoxically reproduced older racialized frames of human redemption. Throughout, I show how U.S. humanitarian affect, haunted by the Vietnam War, is necessarily simultaneously about racial and imperial aspiration and failure. Founded in the legacy of the Vietnam War, U.S. humanitarian ethics and culture are thus bound to reproduce the cycles of imperial war and violence.

The New Frontier and Its Disintegration

In *Heart of Darkness*, Joseph Conrad famously articulated that what redeems the violence accompanying the conquest of the earth "is the idea only. An idea at the back of it; not a sentimental pretense but an idea; and an unselfish belief in the idea—something you can set up, and bow down before, and offer a sacrifice to."[7] Throughout the early years of the Cold War, U.S. "ideas" about democracy and freedom were positioned against the global spread of Communist oppression, inscribing the nation's interventionism in the nonaligned world with benevolent intentions. As the gruesome materialization of these ideas, the Vietnam War, which wore on for two decades, caused nearly sixty thousand U.S. military deaths and over one million Vietnamese deaths. Leading to massive antiwar demonstrations and widespread opposition to the war at home, Vietnam represented a breaking point in U.S. citizens' belief that war was a means by which to win hearts and minds. In other words, Vietnam is that failed "idea" behind the U.S. ideological conquest of the free world.

The early Cold War "idea" of what the United States was fighting for abroad was most clearly articulated by, and is perhaps best represented in, John F. Kennedy, whose presidency is remembered as a moment of national promise and arrival on the global stage, the golden days of "Camelot." Certainly, with Kennedy's presidency, the U.S. military presence in Vietnam escalated, setting the stage for the war's future devastation of the Vietnamese nation and its people. Yet Kennedy is not remembered for the war but, rather, for embodying the post–World War II U.S. promise that was later ruined. When accepting the nomination from the Democratic Party for the presidency in 1960, Kennedy outlined his vision for the nation's role on the global stage. The first principle he affirmed for himself and the United States was that of the Rights of Man—"the civil and economic rights essential to the human dignity of all men."[8] In a purposeful distancing of U.S. interventionism from European imperial worldviews, Kennedy cited the hope of furthering civil rights and capitalist opportunity at home and abroad. The global workings of the U.S. military were thus enfolded into the rhetoric of liberal rights rather than viewed as part of the nation's imperialistic accumulation of land or wealth in the Third World. Elaborating on this unique U.S. Cold War mission, Kennedy asserted:

> We are not here to curse the darkness, but to light the candle that can guide us through that darkness to a safe and sane future. . . . For the world is changing. The old era is ending. The old ways will not do. Abroad, the balance of power is shifting. . . . One-third of the world, it has been said, may be free—but one-third is the victim of cruel repression—and the other one-third is rocked by the pangs of poverty, hunger, and envy. More energy is released by the awakening of these new nations than by the fission of the atom itself.[9]

Kennedy attributes darkness to European imperial rule that preceded U.S. geopolitical ascendance. In contrast the United States leads by enlightened example, uniting in freedom the three worlds suffering from distinct forms of oppression. Conceiving of European imperialism as a past form of darkness, from which the Third World is "awakening" after World War II, Kennedy further underscores that contemporary darkness is located in communism's imperial ambitions. He thus calls for an end to "Communist influence [that] has penetrated further into Asia."[10]

In spite of Kennedy's rejection of Old World philosophies through his portrayal of U.S. geopolitical ascendance as constitutive of a nonimperial future based on racial equality and rights, he makes recourse to European conceptions of historical progress to make his point. As Dipesh Chakrabarty has argued, "Imaginations of socially just futures for humans usually take the idea of single, homogeneous, and secular historical time for granted. Modern politics is often justified as a story of human sovereignty acted out in the context of a ceaseless unfolding of unitary historical time."[11] Kennedy conceives of a third of the world, in which the battle between U.S. light and Communist darkness is being fought, as a blank space whose entry into history is yet to be written. With two competing geopolitical conceptions of historical unfolding—the Communist and the U.S. democratic—Kennedy frames the American-led future as the one that is redemptive. This is made explicit in his notion of the new frontier as the theme of his presidential campaign. The frontier has underwritten U.S. narratives about the nation's uniqueness ever since colonial times. In the supposedly empty expanses of the New World, U.S. democracy was mythologized as developing and distinguishing itself from the spatial confines of the Old World that settlers had left behind. By the late nineteenth century, when the United States extended from the Atlantic to the Pacific coast, it seemed that, as Frederick Jackson Turner famously argued in 1893, the frontier was closed. However, American national imaginaries have mobilized new frontiers beyond the continental United States as metaphors for the spatial and historical momentum associated with the renewal of U.S. democratic promise. Rejecting the idea that an American frontier no longer exists, Kennedy argued that "the New Frontier is here, whether we seek it or not. Beyond that frontier are the uncharted areas of science and space, unsolved problems of peace and war, unconquered pockets of ignorance and prejudice, unanswered questions of poverty and surplus."[12] Similar to the imperial excitement that Marlow, Conrad's protagonist, feels as a child looking at the vast blank spaces on the European imperial map, Kennedy sees the blankness of the Cold War map in which history has yet to be written as an ideological blankness—one in which the United States can inscribe its values of racial equality, human rights, scientific progress, and peace. Standing "on this frontier," Kennedy proclaims, "we must prove all over again whether this nation . . . with its freedom of choice, its breadth of opportunity, its range of alternatives—can compete with the single-minded advance of the Communist system."[13]

Writing about Kennedy's New Frontier, Richard Slotkin argues that this midcentury framing of the war on poverty and the war on racism was paradoxically built on the racial violence of the old frontier, in which Native Americans symbolized spiritual darkness that had to be defeated.[14] According to Slotkin, throughout U.S. history, the frontier and the idea of America's Manifest Destiny represented the possibility of spiritual regeneration through violence over and against the figure of the Indian.[15] In a chapter evocatively entitled "A Home in the Heart of Darkness," Slotkin elaborates on the racialization of the Puritans' spiritual quest for their souls in the wilderness. Reading Indian war narratives, Slotkin argues that the Puritans saw Native Americans as the darkened and inverted mirror image of themselves in the New World. Portraying racial divisions as absolute, Puritans established an analogy between Indian warfare and the struggle between good and evil in man's soul.[16] Indian darkness was thus framed as a spiritual darkness that had to be suppressed in order to affirm the moral character of the Puritan settlers in the New World.[17] For Slotkin, even as the Christian eschatological structure of the original frontier myth was subsumed by a more secular narrative of progress and expansion in subsequent eras, the moral justification for racial violence against Native American peoples continued to underlie new borders between good and evil in new frontiers, through which U.S. democratic values were to be defined and enforced through violence.

Although the Cold War was built on the racializing discourses of the frontier, it is worthwhile to emphasize that in the post–World War II era, the memory of the racism that was a part of the "old" frontier signified past times of trouble that the United States had transcended with the advent of civil rights. Certainly, as Slotkin points out, war continued to be the primary mechanism through which the United States spread its values in the second half of the twentieth century. However, the wars of the Cold War's New Frontier were depicted as saving the lives of racial others from the threat of communism rather than as exterminating them. War was thus reframed as a moral burden that the United States had to assume to promote peace and bring the Third World into the fold of secular history and progress.[18] Against this dominant conception of U.S. democracy fighting for the "rights of man," during the turbulent decade of the 1960s social justice movements agitated for racial and gender revolutions and an end to U.S. imperialism. By 1964, George Ball, the under secretary of state in the Kennedy and Johnson administrations, expressed concern that escalating the Vietnam War would give the impression that the United States was fighting a white man's war.[19] In spite of this, the war continued to escalate during the Johnson administration, and by 1967 the United States experienced, in Slotkin's words, a "disorientation within the frame of history" as Americans had understood it in the early Cold War years. White liberals reacted with surprise when the urban riots erupted so soon after the major legislative victories represented by the Civil Rights Act of 1964 and the Voting Rights Act of 1965. Simultaneous with the disruption of the idea that the United States was making racial progress at home was the growing disbelief that the United States was gaining ideological ground against communism abroad. By the time the photos of the My Lai massacre were released in 1969, it became clear that U.S. actions were not saving the Vietnamese people from the horrors of communism; rather, they brought horror to Vietnam.[20] The heart of America's darkness that unfolded in the Vietnamese jungle revealed that the United States was not that different from its European predecessors and their forms of racial imperialism. Along these lines, William Spanos argues that the Vietnam War represented the "self-destruction" of America's exceptionalist discourses, as the genocidal violence of U.S. militarism exposed the lie behind hegemonic discourses of America's "planetary promise" to fulfill the moral obligations and ideals that had been betrayed by the Old World.[21]

It appeared that in what John F. Kennedy called the "New Frontier" of the post–World War II era, the United States had come face-to-face with the violence inherent in its supposed geopolitical acts of benevolence. In order to conceive of Vietnam as an ongoing site of regeneration for U.S. democracy, the nation had to integrate the experience of its own savagery—not to overcome the savagery of the other. In this sense, Vietnam, as the New Frontier, became the site of U.S. imperial disintegration. The frame of *Heart of Darkness*, which, as James Clifford argues, presents a "record of white men at the frontier, at points of danger and disintegration," thus became a somewhat uneasy complement through which to subsume the Vietnam experience into the foundational myth of America's "regeneration through violence" in the frontier.[22] Because Vietnam represented a moral regression toward savagery, *Heart of Darkness* provided a thematic reference through which to understand the irrationality and horrors of Vietnam. Unlike the frontier mythology that depicts, in Turner's terms, the "meeting point between savagery and civilization" as the historical engine for U.S. democratic development, *Heart of Darkness* is about European imperial and temporal regression—as much about the horrific encounter with the savagery inherent in civilizational ideas as about the savagery of the racialized other. As a narrative frame for the Vietnam War, not only does Conrad's novel appear to align U.S. Cold War politics with the brutal racism of Old World imperialism, but it also calls into question national mythologies about the global promises of democratic progress. Yet it is *Heart of Darkness*'s textual ambiguity regarding the precise content of imperial horror and its embedded truths about human nature, humanitarian action, and the possibility of transcendence that animated postwar cultural fictions about the sacredness of the Vietnam experience and the survival of U.S. ideals.

Heart of Darkness and the Racialization of Humanitarian Feeling

Joseph Conrad's *Heart of Darkness* was originally written between 1898 and 1899, when it was serialized in *Blackwood's Magazine*. The novel is concerned with the meaning of moral darkness at the point at which the civilizational ideas behind European imperialism and the brutal realities of imperial rule collide. At the time of its publication, it was credited with influencing British policy and public opinion regarding the atrocities being perpetuated in the Belgian Congo. It thus became a point of orientation for future attempts to formulate enduring cultural statements opposing violence, war, and imperialism. *Heart of Darkness* includes a powerful insistence that Europeans need to recognize a common and universal humanity against which the excesses of imperial subjugation must be condemned. At the same time, the ambiguity of Conrad's text, particularly its racialized objectification of Africa as the backdrop for Europe's self-critique and its upholding of Europe as a space that produces humanitarian feeling, has continued to structure and delimit contemporary Euro-American debates about the morality of military intervention. Because the novel has become a cultural shorthand for denouncing wartime excesses, reexamining *Heart of Darkness* in relation to how atrocity came to be understood and condemned in post-Vietnam U.S. culture brings to light the imperial origins of humanitarian outrage and moral shock in the contemporary context.

As a call for recognizing the humanity of the other in a space of colonial subjugation, *Heart of Darkness* exemplifies how the emergence of humanitarian discourses, which affirmed Europe as the space of ethical feeling, was enabled by imperial geopolitics. Published after Conrad's journey to the Belgian Congo in 1890, the book has often been read as a fictionalization of Belgian brutality that he witnessed during his travels. In 1876, King Leopold II of Belgium convened a geographical meeting in Brussels, forming the International Association for the Exploration and Civilization of Africa. Between 1878 and 1884, a variety of committees and groups, ostensibly formed to advance scientific and civilizational missions in the Congo, solidified Belgium's supremacy over the rubber and ivory trade in the region. At the 1884 Conference of Berlin, Leopold was awarded the Belgian Free State. By the early 1900s, the Congo Free State came under criticism in Europe for a variety of reasons, including Leopold's claims to "vacant land," which compelled native people to contribute their labor and produce, the inhumane treatment and brutal methods of killing and punishing native populations, and the limitation and disregard of free-trade provisions provided by the Berlin Act.[23]

Heart of Darkness relays the horrors that took place in the Congo for a British audience. The novel begins with an unnamed narrator's introduction of a story told to him by Marlow, an English sailor and captain, while the two are on a boat anchored on the river Thames. Marlow's tale is about his past assignment with a Belgian company in Africa, where he was sent to retrieve a company agent, Kurtz. Kurtz was "an exceptional man, of the greatest importance to the Company," but he had, as the company manager put it to Marlow, fallen "ill" in the deepest reaches of the Continent.[24] Throughout his journey, Marlow eagerly awaits meeting the great man, but when he finds him, he discovers the extent of the brutality involved in Kurtz's "methods" of obtaining ivory and spreading civilization. Kurtz's moral degeneration is encapsulated in Marlow's description of rebel heads displayed on stakes facing Kurtz's compound, natives worshipping Kurtz as a god, and Kurtz's infamous last words, "the horror, the horror."

Alan Simmons reads "the horror" in Conrad's short novel as part of the broader discussions about the atrocities of the Congo in Britain. He focuses on the relationship between Conrad and Roger Casement, the British consul to the Congo who authored the 1904 "The Congo Report," which caused an outcry in Great Britain regarding Belgian conduct in Africa. Simmons suggests that Casement's report and *Heart of Darkness* are twin depictions of imperial brutality: one, a report intended for the British Parliament, which in 1903 passed a resolution to investigate the abuses of the Congo Free State; the other, a fictional account intended for an audience of the broader British public. Posing the question "What is the language of atrocity?" he concludes that

> when communicating atrocities, a discourse is required that is capable of conveying the "unspeakable" truth without sounding exaggerated or preposterous. . . . The contribution of "Heart of Darkness" to the reform movement may lie, ultimately, in helping to create the context and the conditions for believing the tales of atrocity coming out of the Congo precisely because the scale of the "horror" to which it alludes cannot be adequately conveyed through facts anyway.[25]

For Simmons, the importance of *Heart of Darkness* is its status as an ethical fictional accounting of an otherwise unimaginable atrocity.

Keeping in mind the contributing role of *Heart of Darkness* in influencing British foreign policy at the time of the book's publication, it is important to note that Conrad was writing about atrocities that were committed by a competing imperial power in their colonies. His representation of another nation's savagery conceives of their colonized victim as an object through which the English subject emerged as capable of self-critique, reform, and development. Conrad's association with the reform movement and his judgment against imperial brutality are haunted by the limits of liberal humanitarian discourses about the Congo Free State in the sense that these discourses instrumentalized the African victim to articulate the European subject's capacity for humanitarian sentiment and failed to disrupt the foundational belief in the goodness of properly implemented imperial projects. As Adam Hochschild has argued,

> *Heart of Darkness* is one of the most scathing indictments of imperialism in all literature, but its author, curiously, thought himself an ardent imperialist where England was concerned. . . . Conrad's stand-in, Marlow, muses on how "the conquest of the earth, which mostly means taking it away from those who have a different complexion or slightly flatter noses than ourselves, is not a pretty thing when you look into it too much." Yet in almost the same breath, Marlow talks about how the British territories colored red on a world map were "good to see at any time because one knows that some real work is done there." . . . Conrad felt that "liberty . . . can only be found under the English flag all over the world."[26]

Conrad's indictment of certain forms of imperialism as inhumane seems to have been paradoxically enabled by his belief in the goodness and morality of the British imperial project, thought to free human subjects and facilitate the humanization of the African other. This foundational imperial formulation of humanitarian feeling continues to structure contemporary humanitarianism, which in the postsocialist era perpetuates modes of imperialism deemed to be ethical while justifying the demise of other forms of governance and worldviews.

Constitutive of humanitarianism's selective and limited opposition to imperial rule is that European conceptions of universal humanity, like Conrad's, were built on the same racial distinctions as the imperial projects they sought to critique. Indeed, European liberal humanitarianism is perpetually haunted by the very "horror" that it proposes to redress. This was one of Chinua Achebe's points in the famous essay "An Image of Africa."[27] Though best known for accusing Conrad of racism, Achebe's critique draws attention to the foundational limits of the liberal notion of common humanity that depends on the reestablishment and stabilization of racial categories. Achebe writes, "The kind of liberalism espoused here by Marlow/Conrad touched all the best minds of the age in England, Europe, and America. It took different forms in the minds of different people but almost always managed to sidestep the ultimate question of equality between white people and black people."[28] For Achebe, it is not imperialism that represents the "horror" in *Heart of Darkness* but the "lurking hint of kinship, of common ancestry," between Europe and Africa.[29] The European ability to recognize a common humanity actually reinscribes Africa and Africans as objects by conceiving of "Africa as setting and backdrop which eliminates the African as human factor. Africa as a metaphysical battlefield devoid of all recognizable humanity."[30] In liberal imperial discourses about dehumanizing conditions in Africa, Europe was able to affirm its humanity through feeling for the African other, who continued to be produced as a racial object of that feeling. Thus though scholars have noted that the enduring legacy of *Heart of Darkness* is the text's critique of atrocity and human rights abuses, as Achebe insists, these representations are made possible only through the production of Africa as "a carrier onto whom the master unloads his physical and moral deformities so that he may go forward, erect and immaculate."[31] In other words, liberal reformers, like the ardent imperialists they critiqued, constructed a flattened African space as the setting in which the Western subject could either prove and maintain, or lose, his or her humanity.

Although much has been made of whether *Heart of Darkness* is a racist portrayal of Africans, the more interesting question might be how Conrad's novel participates, as a racializing narrative frame, in producing liberal critiques of imperialism and calls for moral action through its temporalizing imaginary of human universality. *Heart of Darkness* dramatizes the evolution of European humanity in the African "setting and backdrop." In a 1903 letter to Casement, Conrad wrote, "It is an extraordinary thing that the conscience of Europe which seventy years ago has put down the slave trade on humanitarian grounds tolerates the Congo State today. It is as if the moral clock has been put back many hours."[32] As a metaphor, the "moral clock" suggests that the proof of the imperial subject's humanity is made manifest in one's actions toward and encounter with the African other, who is an emblem of otherness frozen in historical time against which European moral progress can be ascertained. The idea of common humanity that structures *Heart of Darkness*'s condemnation of brutality and atrocity against one's fellow man is built on a racialized temporal imaginary—a looking back in time that is necessary to understand Africans as human. Marlow's journey through the African continent is described as "travelling back to the earliest beginnings of the world."[33] The deeper one travels into the continent, the further back in time one moves. In Conrad's critique, Europe's moral regression, manifest in its atrocities against colonized natives, is racially metaphorized through Africa as a stand-in for European prehistory. Because of the temporalizing relationship that underlies Europe's discovery of a common humanity across continents and races, the moment of recognition that Africans and Europeans share a common humanity is horrifying since it has the power to destabilize dominant historical narratives of civilization and progress. As Marlow muses,

> Well, you know that was the worst of it—this suspicion of their not being inhuman. . . . What thrilled you was just the thought of their humanity—like yours—the thought of your remote kinship with this wild and passionate uproar. Ugly. Yes, it was ugly enough, but if you were man enough you would admit to yourself that there was in you just the faintest trace of a response to the terrible frankness of that noise, a dim suspicion of there being a meaning in it which you—you so remote from the night of first ages—could comprehend.[34]

Europeans' hidden and buried primitive interiority, "the wild and passionate" uproar that is an aspect of the European self, is here equated with Africans' racialized exteriority, a primitiveness visible on the surface of the skin. This racialized perception of the other, frozen in time, would continue to shadow future liberal formulations of moral responses to violence that made recourse to Conrad's narrative frame.

The commingling of repulsion and thrill that Marlow ascribes to recognizing common humanity across continents and racial temporalities parallels the novel's understanding of imperialism as having the simultaneous potential to destroy and to spark enlightenment. Paradoxically, even as *Heart of Darkness* opposes imperial excesses on the grounds that it turns back the "moral clock" of European civilization, the novel's opening indicates that imperialism, when properly implemented, can end the brutality of human prehistory, bringing enlightenment in its wake. On the river Thames, Marlow declares, "And this also . . . has been one of the dark places of the earth."[35] He goes on, "I was thinking of very old times, when the Romans first came here, nineteen hundred years ago. . . . We live in the flicker. . . . But darkness was here yesterday. Imagine the feelings of a [Roman] commander. . . . Imagine him here—the very end of the world."[36] In this historicization, the Roman Empire sparked Great Britain's emergence from darkness and its entry into the time of historical progress. Yet considering that in Conrad's novel Africa's darkness is literal, inscribed on the bodies of its inhabitants rather than symbolizing a pre–enlightenment era as it does in Europe, it remains unclear whether European imperialism is conceived of as capable of bringing enlightenment to Africa, or whether Africa can only ever lead to European racialized regression.

Ultimately, the novel resolves the racial contradiction inherent in the attempt to distinguish good and evil modes of imperialism through the racialization of humanitarian feeling. Before being subsumed by the darkness by "going native," Kurtz represented the "idea" behind European imperialism in Africa—the "mission" that would justify, in moral terms, Europe's accumulation of African natural resources and exploitation of native labor. In spite of the fact that Kurtz represents the loss of the European soul and civilized self in the imperial struggle between progress and savagery, it is through Kurtz that *Heart of Darkness* maintains the importance of a belief in something. Toward the end of the novel, Marlow affirms that Kurtz is a "remarkable man" because

> he had something to say. . . . He had summed it up—he had judged. "The horror!" He was a remarkable man. After all, this was the expression of some sort of belief; it had candour, it had conviction, it had a vibrating note of revolt in its whisper, it had the appalling face of a glimpsed truth—the strange commingling of desire and hate. . . . It was a moral victory paid for by innumerable defeats, by abominable terrors, by abominable sanctions. But it was a victory.[37]

For Marlow, judging a failed mission and recognizing the horror of imperial brutality when it is unleashed in its encounter with the wilderness represent a moral stance that redeems a failed idea. "The horror" might be read as the appeal of British reform groups that denounced atrocities in the Congo Free State in spite of their own participation in maintaining British imperialism. In this historical context, humanitarianism can be viewed as the moral by-product of imperial excess, the idea that redeems the European soul. Yet if the belief in a common humanity stands in opposition to imperial racial violence brought upon the colonized natives by European savagery, in Conrad's vision it is paradoxically Europe's encounter with those others that led to the unleashing of savagery to begin with. Since the African can never be the selfsame as the European, humanitarian feeling inevitably fails to recognize the full humanity of the racial other, leaving the European with only feelings of moral victory. The separation of moral victories from death dealing and violence reemerged powerfully in post-Vietnam humanitarian critiques in the United States.

The Ethics of Representation in Post-Vietnam Culture

As a work that has been hailed as an ethical representation in the face of imperial excess and atrocity, the afterlife of *Heart of Darkness* in post-Vietnam U.S. culture calls for an analysis of how the emergence of humanitarian feeling in the shadow of wartime horror necessitated the making of new fictions that would frame an emergent humanitarian ethos. Like Conrad's novel, which grapples with the disintegration of certain imperial ideas about morality and civilizational progress, post-Vietnam cultural texts have participated in questioning and constructing a novel ethics of representation in the face of national fragmentation. Two contemporary works that both reference and reflect on the circulation of *Heart of Darkness* in post-Vietnam U.S. visual culture, attending to the relationship between cartographies of "darkness" and the making and unmaking of imperial lifeworlds, are *Hearts of Darkness: A Filmmaker's Apocalypse*, a 1991 documentary about the making of Francis Ford Coppola's *Apocalypse Now* (1979), and Jessica Hagedorn's 2003 novel, *Dream Jungle*. Each references Conrad's novel as the touchstone of post-Vietnam U.S. historical fictions that have contended with national failure and redemption. The 1991 documentary and Hagedorn's novel are both metacommentaries on the process of making national fictions whose role was to apprehend the tension between order and chaos in the post-Vietnam global landscape. However, where *Hearts of Darkness* is concerned solely with how American subjects become ethical simply by struggling to portray their nation's imperial irrationality and violent failure, *Dream Jungle* foregrounds the interrelatedness of imperial histories and the objectification of colonial space as always already enabling acts of nation making and ethical self-fashioning in the metropole.

Hearts of Darkness uses footage shot by Francis Ford Coppola's wife, Eleanor Coppola, during the filming of *Apocalypse Now* in the Philippines. Because of the war's vast unpopularity on the home front, films about Vietnam were rare in the United States until the success of *Apocalypse Now*, which garnered the prestigious Palme d'Or Award at the Cannes Film Festival.[38] Part of the film's success was due to the fact that, departing from previous conventions of stylistic realism in the war-film genre, Coppola structured his approach to war through surrealism as a way of getting at the irrationality and futility of U.S. violence in Vietnam. To do so, he used Conrad's *Heart of Darkness* as the inspiration. According to Margot Norris, *Apocalypse Now*'s dialogue with Conrad's novel resulted in a political critique of the Cold War "hearts and minds" rhetoric, exposing the darkness and colonial inflections inherent in U.S. claims of spreading democracy and defending the free world from Communist infiltration.[39] For Norris, Coppola's transposition of U.S. domestic histories of colonial genocide onto the space of Vietnam echoes Conrad's attention to narrative transmissibility in its structure of double storytelling. *Apocalypse Now,* she concludes, is thus able to perform an ethical commentary on colonialism itself as "a movable horror prone to displacement and repetition."[40] Yet like Conrad's own condemnation of the moral failings of colonial violence and excess, which was limited by existing imperial worldviews, Coppola's use of *Heart of Darkness* as the structure for an ethical critique of the Vietnam War relied on previous and ongoing imperial racializing and exploitative economies. The film could not have been made without the structural legacies of U.S. imperialism in the Asia Pacific. As Amy Kaplan writes, *Hearts of Darkness* simply relocates Conrad's Africa to Vietnam and the Philippines.[41] Kaplan suggests that although Coppola's aim was not to deny empire but to expose U.S. brutality in Vietnam through an antiwar stance and to connect U.S. imperialism to European imperialism through Conrad's novel, the documentary "refuses recognition of the film's complicity with the imperial context that enables its production."[42] For instance, six hundred native workers were paid only one dollar each day. Meanwhile, Coppola paid exorbitant sums to rent bodyguards and helicopters from Ferdinand Marcos's repressive dictatorship, with which the United States maintained close ties in the 1970s. Noting the filmmaker's frustration when these helicopters were continually called off the set to repress local political insurrections, Kaplan argues that

> the blatant evidence of the surrounding reality of imperialism generates excitement in the voice-over about being in the "thick of the jungle," about being so close to the battlefield. They find in the Philippines a way of retrieving nostalgically the intensity of the battlefield experience they may have rejected on political grounds. By turning the Philippines [and, by extension, Vietnam] into a timeless "jungle," like the African "jungle," . . . the Coppolas deny the imperial history which brings them to the Philippines.[43]

Hearts of Darkness demonstrates the extent to which the instrumentalization of colonial spaces to dramatize imperial self-reflection reaffirms the United States as the foremost domain of human transcendence. Contending that his film will save lives, Coppola implied that the contemporary moral struggle occurs in the realm of representation. Though, as Norris proposes, *Apocalypse Now* might succeed in critiquing early Cold War rhetoric, Coppola's grandiose vision for his film inadvertently parallels the Cold War idea that Americans can go abroad (as he went to the Philippines) to save lives and capture hearts and minds. Ultimately, *Hearts of Darkness* reduces the struggle over life and death in the making of *Apocalypse Now* to the figure of Francis Coppola as a filmmaker.[44] In spite of the millions of dollars he spent to borrow Marcos's helicopters, the documentary positions Coppola as an ethical artist and underdog trying to undermine big Hollywood and the sorts of stories they deem marketable. In her footage of the production process, Eleanor Coppola frames the making of the Vietnam epic as a metaphor for her husband's journey into himself. She notes that though it was difficult for her to watch him confront his innermost fears, such as the fear of the future, of death, and of going insane, one must do a little of each to come out on the other side. Many of Francis Coppola's fears stem from his feelings of becoming the Kurtz of Conrad's novel, as the Philippine jungle and its natural and political caprices threaten his sanity. Fearing that he has lost his integrity, Francis Coppola's chief concern is that *Apocalypse Now* would be a $20 million disaster—a pompous, bad movie about a very important subject. He seems to ask: Is this film simply another American disaster that started with good intentions? In recorded conversations with his wife, Francis Coppola laments that he constantly dreams about how to achieve his vision for an appropriate ending, but that he cannot translate his dreams into a script. Like American politicians' nightmare of being unable to find a peace with honor in Vietnam, the finales Francis formulates are, he worries, weak because they lack answers to the moral questions his film asks. Yet, as his wife predicts, the great director's descent into the darkness ends with the film's success in Cannes and with American audiences—the only ending that matters in the documentary.[45]

Through the figure of Francis Ford Coppola, *Hearts of Darkness* suggests that descent into one's own place of darkness is the condition of possibility for ethical representation and, consequently, ethical action. In the parallels it draws between Francis Coppola falling to pieces during the making of *Apocalypse Now* and the U.S. national experience of fragmentation during the Vietnam War, the documentary indicates that America's moral victory rests in coming face-to-face with its time of darkness in Vietnam. In this formulation, films and photography, as documents of the war, become the tools for reanimating democracy. At the end of the film, Francis expresses his "great hope" for the democratization of representation but stays within the confines of the United States. He muses that with the growing availability of 8 mm video recorders, those who have thus far been unable to make movies will begin to do so. "Suddenly, one day, some little fat girl in Ohio is going to be the new Mozart, and . . . make a beautiful film with her father's camera recorder."[46] In his vision, a girl inherits a camera from her father, indicating gender equality as the "great hope" for the future. It is a hope that

Figure 1. *Hearts of Darkness* documents Francis Ford Coppola's personal descent into darkness during the filming of *Apocalypse Now*.

upholds a liberal progress narrative. Reaffirming America's creative capacity, the documentary reinstates the nation's potential for democratic development in spite of the moral failures exhibited in Vietnam.

Hagedorn's *Dream Jungle* sketches an alternate history of the making of *Apocalypse Now* and the politics of culture in the Philippines. Hagedorn reframes Conrad's conception of empire as a system of representation by foregrounding the way in which both *Heart of Darkness* and Coppola's film produced the colonial space as a backdrop, frozen in time, against which to dramatize the possibility for an ethical critique of the American self. *Dream Jungle* weaves two parallel and seemingly unrelated stories from the 1970s: the "discovery" of the Tabao, a Paleolithic tribe of cave dwellers whose members have ostensibly had no contact with the modern world, and the arrival of an American film crew shooting a Vietnam War epic called *Napalm Sunset* in the Philippines.[47] The Tabao story line focuses on Zamora Lopez de Legazpi Jr., a millionaire man of leisure residing in a prominent Manila mansion, who wishes to bring to the world's attention the tribe's existence. Eventually, suspicion mounts that his project is an elaborate hoax meant to procure rain forest lands for the Marcos regime. The novel makes clear that whether or not the Tabao are authentically prehistoric or paid actors, they are a necessary national fiction. As an untouched indigenous people, they embody a prehistory that highlights the lengths traveled by the Philippine nation, spurred by Spanish and American imperialisms, to enter global modernity. Hagedorn emphasizes that as an "ethnological find of the century" and, simultaneously, as one of the century's most elaborate hoaxes, fictions about one's own prehistory, written through the racialized other, are essential for conceiving national transcendence.[48] *Dream Jungle* marks these fictions as acts of godly creation. In one instance, Zamora invites Ken Forbes, a photojournalist working in Saigon, to come to the Philippines to document the existence of the Tabao. Forbes describes his first impressions of the Tabao in the mountains: "They were naked except for loincloths fashioned out of leaves and strips of what looked like bark. They carried no weapons or tools. As soon as they set eyes on me, they threw themselves on the ground and began to wail. I aimed my Nikon at them . . . I clicked away at the marvelous, prostrate people. Click, click."[49] In this scene of "discovery and conquest," as Hagedon titles the first part of the novel, conquest happens through representational technologies—the camera is a weapon. For Forbes, the move from documenting the Vietnam War to documenting a prehistoric tribe is seamless. As prehistory, embodied by the naked Tabao, bows down before modernity, symbolized by the Nikon, the association between the godlike act of creation through representation ("In the beginning there was the word, and the word was God") and the process of being folded into humanity is solidified. In this scene of first encounter, in which capturing the other through representational technologies is a scene of violence and conquest, Hagedorn thus presents a conflicting perspective on the possibility of ethically representing the other to that of the Coppolas. For her, the act of documentation is also always an act of violation—of violently creating and inserting an "other" into one's own historical and national narrative about humanitarianism and national transcendence.

Dream Jungle uses the Tabao story line and the story of Tony Pierce and his crew to portray parallel modes of what Hagedorn has called "cultural mythmaking."[50] In the sense that the camera is already understood to be a weapon, the presence of an entire film crew might be read as a full assault on the Philippine landscape. Like Zamora, who is referred to as "Father" by the Tabao, and whose espousal of their cause gives him an almost godlike stature among the tribe, Tony Pierce's wife, Janet, who is there to film the process of making *Napalm Sunset*, secretly refers to her husband as "Tony God." Paz Marlowe, a Filipina American journalist, describes Tony "God" Pierce's film project as having the simultaneous authority to create and destroy. The crew was "always blowing things up. Building elaborate sets only to blow them all up. Paz had observed two days straight of a simulated Vietcong hamlet's being bombed, coconut trees on the shoreline of Lake Ramayyah ablaze with fire and smoke. . . . Sometimes the children were tapped for the spontaneous scenes Pierce was fond of creating. They played fallen, bloody corpses or extras in crowd scenes with humor and enthusiasm."[51] Through its portrayal of Tony God's reduction of the Philippines to nothing more than a set or a backdrop for his creation of a post-Vietnam American epic, *Dream Jungle* implies that this approach to representation necessarily produces the local inhabitants as "bloody corpses" or "extras" in their own homeland. Later in the novel, during an interview Paz obtains with Pierce, he elaborates on his inspiration for making the film. "The beauty of a location like this is that it offers you everything you need. Beach, ocean, jungle, lake, mountains, waterfalls, cheap labor."[52] Interrupting Pierce's rumination on the Philippines as putting all of its natural resources, including its people, on offer, Paz comments, "And of course there's Mayor Fritz, your protector, your fixer, your landlord, your biggest fan." Pierce ignores her contemporary political commentary, responding instead by quoting *Heart of Darkness*: "The earth seemed unearthly," he tells her. "We could not understand because we were too far and could not remember because we were travelling the night of the first ages, of those ages that are gone, leaving hardly a sign—and no memories."

Bypassing contemporary geopolitics, Pierce romanticizes his desire for the natural resources on offer in the Philippines through *Heart of Darkness*'s journey into prehistory. Fantasizing about the blank spaces of the earth that the American filmmaker can mold through an act of creation necessitates fictions of prehistory, like Conrad's. After all, a land that has yet to enter history enables history to be written by its conquistadors. Linking back to *Dream Jungle*'s story line about the Tabao as a necessary fiction in Philippine national modernity, Pierce's fantasy makes clear how the tribe activates older imperial yearnings for blank spaces and prehistoric people, the yet to be discovered, which enables the fiction of the Euro-American man as creator. These are imperial fictions that, like Conrad's, reproduce the very racial structures they critique. Immediately after quoting Conrad, Pierce moves into a discussion of how he discovered one of the young black actors for his Vietnam epic. "Isaiah. I discovered him. . . . Playing the guitar. . . . His guitar was out of tune, and his little amp kept feeding back. It was awful."[53] Isaiah, a subject who is "discoverable," is himself not capable of acts of creation, as he cannot produce good music with his broken amp and out-of-tune guitar. But Pierce likes this. He continues, "I'd been auditioning lots of black actors for the role of Monk. They could do Shake-speare, all that shit. But they were all too old. Too *trained*. I needed a kid. A raw, vulnerable type."[54] The black actor, like the Philippine prehistoric landscape, must be raw, open to Tony God's molding and shaping, and someone through whom he can see his own creativity.

Exposing embedded imperial desires and narratives in post-Vietnam fictions of America's failure, loss, and moral fragmentation, *Dream Jungle* suggests that the United States reactivated its self-conception as a morally transcendent nation after Vietnam through the divine politics of ethical representation. Hagedorn's connection between godlikeness and the pro-cess of producing necessary national fictions is particularly insightful as a way through which to understand how and why the history of the Vietnam War came to be represented as hallowed, or sacred, after the conclusion of the war. If, as Hagedorn suggests, representation has the power to make certain lifeworlds legible by instrumentalizing, objectifying, and covering over other lifeworlds, then it becomes possible to begin to analyze how U.S. "ideas" were given life anew in post-Vietnam fictions.

Frames of Humanity and Atrocity

The connection that Hagedorn makes in *Dream Jungle* between representa-tional technologies, war and violence, and temporalizing national fictions helps to elucidate how U.S. cultural representations of the Vietnam War enabled images of wartime brutality to ironically activate the ability of U.S. citizens to "feel" human once again. In post-Vietnam U.S. culture, there is a well-developed national mythology that reporting during the Vietnam War—in particular, photojournalism—was an uncensored representation of U.S. ruthlessness that ruptured dominant early Cold War discourses about U.S. exceptionalism. The idea that during the Vietnam War the free-dom of the U.S. press led to an ethical critique of the U.S. nation has, con-tradictorily, worked to reaffirm the idea of the United States as an exceptional nation that could heal from its irrational descent into savagery in Vietnam. Keeping in mind that there is an inherent violence involved in acts of docu-mentation, it is important to consider the relationship between depictions of Vietnam itself and the broader project of American self-critique.[55] Vietnam-era photojournalism and the enduring and iconic images it has produced, particularly those that portray the suffering of the Vietnamese people, have come to embody the nation's capacity for democratic regen-eration. As Sara Ahmed has argued in a different context, the appropriation of the other's pain into our sadness retains the other as the object of our feeling.[56] She suggests that our shame at causing the other pain as part of past wrongdoing is often put into the service of national reconciliation projects. The process of recognizing past failures thus becomes the ground for renewed patriotic love.[57] When we feel shame for not living up to an ideal, as the United States felt when early Cold War ideals were ruptured in Vietnam, rather than signaling the inadequacy of those ideals, that shame can work to reaffirm the idea to which the nation has not lived up.[58]

After the Vietnam War, coming face-to-face with the horrors brought about by the failure of national ideals was seen as important in recuperating the exceptional status of the United States. Whereas the nation lost its sense of moral superiority through the brutality of its military campaign during the war in Vietnam, the images produced during that war became a parallel and oppositional site through which the war was refought and U.S. democracy was reaffirmed. More than any other visual medium, the photographs of the Vietnam War are remembered as having exposed U.S. military atrocities igniting the antiwar movement at home. Yet even as the camera was a tool for documenting U.S. state violence, as *Dream Jungle* suggests, it is also a weapon of conquest.[59] In the case of the Vietnam War, it became a weapon that won the war that America's military technology could not. In light of the notion that Vietnam-era photojournalism was a democratic medium that exposed the war's horrors, signaling American potential for feeling outrage on behalf of the other, it is worth remembering that what and who will fall into the realm of humanity at any given moment in time can reveal particular values, morphologies, and power relations that are differentially inhabited.[60] As Judith Butler argues, when our humanity is defined by feeling moral horror, we tend to disregard the ways in which social interpretations already determine the subjects for whom we feel and those whose lives and deaths do not touch us.[61] What might it mean, then, to rethink Vietnam War–era photojournalism not as simply revealing the horrific acts committed by the United States but also as affirming American humanitarianism?

Peter Davis attempted to address this problem in the 1974 documentary *Hearts and Minds*, which self-reflexively demonstrates the capacity of the camera to be a weapon that is as powerful as the military technologies that devastated the Vietnamese landscape. To critique U.S. violence, the documentary develops a dialogic structure that juxtaposes scenes of America's technologized vision of the war in Vietnam and interviews with U.S. policy makers with the suffering and devastation of the Vietnamese people who were bombed on a daily basis, their families callously killed. Following an interview with U.S. pilots, who expressed pride in how they were able to use American advanced weapons systems, the documentary cuts to scenes of Vietnamese peasants walking next to horse-drawn buggies carrying water from a well. The contrast between the high-tech war waged by the Americans and the simplicity of Vietnamese "village people" was a common antiwar representational strategy.[62] In *Hearts and Minds*, the critique of Western modernity is more formally complex, as Davis makes recourse to the temporal mode of photography as the freezing of a moment in time to puncture early Cold War triumphalist ideologies and to capture the grief of the other. In an attempt to apprehend the anguish of people who lost their homes and whose lives were destroyed by the spectacular demonstration of American war technology, the film uses a close-up shot of a Vietnamese man crying, saying, "I'm so unhappy." There is a lengthy, uncomfortable silence that the long take refuses to break. Like a photograph, it fills the frame with misery and sorrow caused by U.S. violence. As David Grosser points out, in this moment that forces the audience to confront Vietnamese emotions, "time seems to stand still, and no other image comes to the rescue."[63] Unlike a photograph, however, in Davis's documentary the subjects who suffer speak back to the camera. Two Vietnamese men later in the documentary comment on the filming: "Look, they are focusing on us now. First they bomb as much as they please, then they film." Davis's documentary indicates the complicity of the project of documenting the sorrow of the other with the violence inherent in war. At the same time, the nonsubtle antiwar message conveyed through Davis's purposeful editing and dialogic structure maintains a belief in the ethical possibilities for non-nationalist forms of representation.[64]

One reason photography is widely regarded as the predominant Vietnamera mode of critique that caused a rupture in U.S. Cold War ideologies is the medium's distinct temporality, which stops time. The photojournalism of the Vietnam War captured moments of death and suffering to which U.S. militarism subjected the Vietnamese people. These images thus exposed the brutal miscarriage, if not downright duplicity, of early Cold War ideologies and the New Frontier rhetoric about bringing the Vietnamese a better future and a life safe from Communist oppression. Through their temporal mode, the Vietnam-era photographs appeared to seize and lay bare the breaking point of U.S. narratives about racial and democratic progress. What Roland Barthes called the "punctum" in a photograph, that which exceeds the photograph's connotation and denotation, was, in Vietnam War photography, the rupture in the idea that the United States was promoting a better life in the Third World. Whereas films narrativize an experience, photographs, as Barthes argued, arrest the coming of the future.[65] For Barthes, because of its unique temporality, "the photograph produces death while trying to preserve life."[66] Although he was writing about the effects of an image that has been captured and that endures even as it conjures up the inevitable death of the subject, in a different context, Vietnam War photographs exhibit a similar contradiction, though in a more literal sense. On the one hand, many of the most powerful Vietnam-era photographs captured the moment of death.[67] On the other hand, in their circulation, the viewer of the image was made to understand his or her own life through the other's death.

Not only does the frozen moment of the other's injury or death highlight our aliveness, but in feeling moral outrage and shock at the pain of others we establish our own humanity. This is, of course, a racialized structure of seeing and feeling. Within the iconic Vietnam War–era photographs, "the race of their subjects is what allows the violence of these images to be shown."[68] In this sense, the humanitarian gaze constructed through these images is itself racializing. In *Regarding the Pain of Others*, Susan Sontag traces the history of photographic depictions of anguish as providing an invitation to look and serving as a tool for developing a moral feeling in the viewer that is a response to the horror portrayed in an image. Sontag argues that the shame and shock that follow from looking at photographs of suffering and violence lead to a sense that unless action is taken we are nothing more than voyeurs.[69] Photos that are seen as raw, taken in the moment, and not set up thus carry a special "moral authority" that, when seen as part of a national or cultural image archive, creates a "modern ethical feeling" formed in relation to the pain of the other.[70] Importantly, Sontag points out that in the post–World War II era, the ubiquity of photos that represent suffering and death in the Third World produces a space in which tragedy seems inevitable, as the other is reduced to someone to be seen, not someone who returns the gaze.[71]

Like Conrad's Marlow, who comes to a novel understanding of humanity and a critique of imperial violence through his conception of Africans as frozen in a time outside the realm of historical progress, Vietnam War photography created a "modern ethical feeling" in U.S. citizens by freezing Vietnam as a locus of misery in the national imaginary. Later, these same photographs became evidence of U.S. democracy. They are remembered as having sparked mass demonstrations that led to the government's eventual response to its citizens' objections to the war. The narrativizing of Vietnam

War photography as rekindling America's democratic potential is the prominent framework of several recent coffee-table books commemorating the famous photojournalists of the era. For instance, the front cover of *Eddie Adams: Vietnam* reproduces the famous image taken by the photographer of the Vietnamese National Police Force chief, general Nguyen Ngoc Loan, executing a guerilla insurgent in 1968.[72] At the time, the photo circulated widely in the U.S. press and on television. Antiwar demonstrators cited the photo as an example of the brutal practices of America's South Vietnamese allies. Vivian Sobchack writes about the Saigon execution photo as eliciting a "humane gaze": "the bodily paralysis and inertia it represents" can acknowledge "the inadequacy of action to respond to 'something intolerable and unbearable.'"[73] At the same time, as I am suggesting, the very paralysis produced by the photo in relation to Vietnam that leads to a "humane gaze" opens up a future frame for humanitarian action. In a series of introductions by well-known Vietnam War–era journalists, the book's cover photo is discussed as exemplifying the ethical dilemmas and universalizing potential of Adams's photography, as well as the unique place of the Vietnam War in the development of America's moral futurity. The Pulitzer Prize–winning journalist David Halberstam begins by ruminating, "How ironic that Eddie's most famous photo was also his cruelest. How strange that a man whose extraordinary body of work celebrates the richness and complexity of the human family is best remembered for an image he captured detailing the ultimate act of inhumanity."[74] For Halberstam, however, it is precisely the ability to distinguish between "the most violent impulses and the most generous ones" that allows us to retain our humanity. He suggests that capturing cruelty as a way of distinguishing it from goodness empowers a great combat photographer like Adams to show "the singular humanity that runs through his photos." Halberstam proposes that through Adams's work, the history of the Vietnam War is overturned, becoming a mark not of our violent inhumanity but of our enduring humanity, a time when "we did what we were supposed to do, and then, on occasion, we reached out and did even more."[75]

While it seems incongruous with the predominant conception of Vietnam as an epistemic break in American exceptionalist rhetoric to analyze the war as essential to the evolution of humanitarian feeling in America, recent remembrances of Vietnam War–era journalistic documentation do just that by framing Vietnam as a space that was made completely transparent by the actions of the press. Well-known reporter Peter Arnett recalls in his reflection on Adams's work, "The Vietnam War was the last great war for the American Press."[76] For Arnett, Vietnam laid the ground for ethical action because it was accessible to journalists. "In Vietnam the world was open to any of us. We could get on a medevac helicopter and go into the center of action." Like the longing for the once blank spaces on the earth, that kind of transparency is, for Arnett, no longer possible with today's media and military relationship in the Middle East. It is only the full accessibility offered by Vietnam that allowed Adams to capture in that famous image "a moment of truth about the war. The picture was a tangible reality that came to characterize the whole conflict." Television journalist Bob Schieffer confirms this understanding: "There was virtually no censorship, and it is one of the only wars America has fought where there was no censorship."[77] With the journalist and photographer becoming the heroes of the Vietnam War, actions taken by Americans during the war can be remembered nostalgically as being part of an ethical structure of feeling in the United States that is divorced from military actions. As television news correspondent Morley Safer puts it, "Correspondents saw more war than many in the military, more than most generals."[78] Eddie Adams's picture thus saw what the military could not. It captured "everything that was wrong with that war. The brutality of it, the pointlessness of it; who were the good guys and who were the bad guys of it."[79]

Although it is important to remember that culture was the site through which political lies and the brutality of U.S. militarism in Vietnam were exposed, it is equally important to foreground the ways in which antiwar images and texts have been subsumed into an understanding of U.S. democracy as robust. The framing of photojournalism in particular has been used to conceive of the possibility of morality in a post-Vietnam world. For example, in their discussion of iconic images, Robert Hariman and John Lucaites argue that certain photographs become sacred images for a secular society.[80] Because they view photojournalism as a "characteristically democratic art," they argue that the iconic photo "reproduces idealism essential for democratic continuity" and serves as a conversation piece for the "vernacular public sphere."[81] The preponderance of iconic Vietnam War images, including the Eddie Adams photo and Huynh Cong Ut's *Accidental Napalm*, highlighted America's moral fragmentation through the capture of its immoral actions abroad. As Hariman and Lucaites suggest in their reading of *Accidental Napalm*, the traumatic moment of moral failure, encapsulated in the image of a naked young girl running, her skin burning from a Napalm attack, is stopped in time.[82] Yet Americans' ability to recognize the nation's moral failing in the suffering of the naked girl symbolizes the overcoming of the moral and social breakdown of the United States in Vietnam, what Halberstam's introduction to the Eddie Adams book characterizes as the human ability to transcend the breakdown by recognizing right from wrong. As contemporary discourses about photojournalism and the Vietnam War demonstrate, what makes the iconic Vietnam era photos "sacred" in U.S. history is that they ultimately reaffirm the relevance, vibrancy, and moral superiority of U.S. democracy in spite of periodic lapses. In the dominant reading of Vietnam War images, the national outrage at the moral failings of the United States, exposed through transparent journalistic practices, became the foremost symbol of the nation's ability to recognize and overcome the horrors it had wreaked upon Vietnam and to emerge an ethical and humanitarian actor on the global stage yet again.

From Vietnam to Afghanistan

In a collection of essays on the aftermath of the Vietnam War in U.S. culture, Noam Chomsky proposed that the dual tendency of focusing on human rights and deflecting U.S. self-critique as an empire upon the Soviet Union was part of the political process of recovering from the Vietnam War. He begins his analysis by citing the perspective of Zbigniew Brzezinski, President Jimmy Carter's national security adviser, regarding the 1979 Soviet invasion of Afghanistan: "Soviet policy in Afghanistan is the fourth greatest exercise in social holocaust of our contemporary age: it ranks only after Stalin's multimillion massacres; after Hitler's genocide of the European Jews and partially of the Slavs; and after Pol Pot's decimation of his own people; it is, moreover, happening right now."[83] Brzezinski blames U.S. liberals for critiquing only "unfashionable" imperialisms, namely, that of the United States, and turning a blind eye to the humanitarian horrors of the more dangerous contemporary empire, the U.S.S.R. Chomsky argues that for Carter and his administration to conceive of themselves as the "patron saint[s] of human rights," who had the moral authority to condemn human rights abuses committed by others, required not the forgetting of Vietnam but, rather, the reframing of what happened in Vietnam.[84] Whereas the Soviets' overwhelming military power in Afghanistan could be conceived of as genocidal and therefore a human rights issue on which the United States should take a stance, Vietnam was reimagined as a war of equals. The equality between the Americans and the Vietnamese became legible through "loss," where "losses" rather than military power supposedly leveled any discrepancies in technology or manpower. Importantly, the emphasis on the U.S.S.R.'s human rights abuses in Afghanistan throughout the 1980s, addressed in the next chapter, indicates that Ronald Reagan's policy of remilitarization did not necessarily represent a complete departure from Carter's interest in human rights as a post-Vietnam War way of conceptualizing the United States' role in the world. Rather, Reagan-era descriptors of U.S. geopolitical and moral duties built on the lessons of Vietnam, citing human rights abuses as the reason for military aid.

Whereas the images of Vietnamese suffering became the condition of possibility for reviving U.S. humanity in the post-Vietnam War context, in the 1980s Afghanistan became the site through which the morality of U.S. militarism was reaffirmed and past U.S. military methods were condemned. The way in which this critique was staged in political and media discourses reframed the relationship between an idea, imperialism, and violence in *Heart of Darkness.* In Afghanistan, the United States was able to salvage early Cold War discourses about freedom and democracy by condemning the "methods" it had used to fight the Vietnam War without questioning the ideas that led to the war in the first place. Reagan's foreign policy refused large-scale military actions, supporting instead guerilla fighters who were opposed to the Soviet Union. It is possible to read discourses about the Reagan Doctrine, which posited that the United States should provide covert aid to anti-Communist guerillas, as well as the doctrine itself, as emergent frames for U.S. militarism reproducing the moment in Conrad's *Heart of Darkness* when the company removes Kurtz while continuing to justify its objectives through a critique of Kurtz's "methods." In the novel, the company manager claims:

> We have done all we could for him—haven't we. But there is no disguising the fact, Mr. Kurtz has done more harm than good to the Company. He did not see the time was not ripe for vigorous action. . . . I don't deny there is a remarkable quantity of ivory—mostly fossil. We must save it, at all events—but look how precarious the position is—and why? Because the method is unsound.[85]

By maintaining the need for accumulating ivory, the manager describes the damage done by Kurtz to the company as a methodological error rather than an error of principles. With the advent of the Reagan era, new forms of U.S. militarism limited the critique of what occurred in Vietnam to that war's methods, reaffirming the ideals underlying the war and leading to a revival of early Cold War rhetoric.

∃ RESTORING NATIONAL FAITH

The Soviet–Afghan War in U.S. Media and Politics

IN SPITE OF being one of the decisive events that precipitated the demise of the Soviet Union and the Communist world, the Soviet–Afghan War (1979–1989) has been largely forgotten in the United States, having been overshadowed by America's own imperial occupation of Afghanistan over the last decade. *Charlie Wilson's War* (2007) is a rare mainstream film that reflects back on U.S. aid to the mujahideen in the 1980s.[1] Released in a year that was "the deadliest for U.S. and NATO-led forces in Afghanistan since the Taliban regime fell in late 2001," its focus is on U.S. senator Charlie Wilson, a politician advocating on behalf of the Afghan guerillas opposing the Soviet-supported regime.[2] A rogue playboy who adopts the Afghan cause, Wilson forms unlikely alliances to raise millions of dollars for smuggling weapons to the "freedom fighters," as the mujahideen were known in the United States. The dramatic opening scene depicts a silhouette of an Afghan man praying under a crescent moon. As he starts to rise, his RPG, a portable antitank grenade launcher associated with the mujahideen, comes into view. Standing up, the silhouette turns toward the audience and fires his weapon directly at the camera and thus the viewers. Wresting the familiar visual figuration of the RPG-toting guerilla fighter of the Soviet–Afghan War from the past into the present, the scene reiterates a post-9/11 understanding that the weapons and training provided to the mujahideen by the United States are now being turned against "us." This establishing sequence, which is both Orientalizing and unnerving, has been read as representing a "return of the repressed."[3] More than just a forgotten past that haunts the United States today, however, this faceless shadow, whose history the film then unfolds, poses the question, like Joseph Conrad's *Heart of Darkness*, about the possibilities and limits for representing the failure of an imperial project and "idea." *Charlie Wilson's War* recalls U.S. humanitarian

Figure 2. Mujahideen silhouette turning the gun on the United States, *Charlie Wilson's War* (2007).

aid to the Afghan people in the 1980s, conjuring up a previous relationship to the region not associated with the contemporary disappointments of U.S. military occupation. The memory of the United States helping two million Afghan refugees displaced by Soviet aggression both redeems the current U.S. position in the region and suggests that it could have been otherwise. As Charlie Wilson puts it at the end of the film, "We fucked up the end game."

The contradiction between the messianic overtones of President Ronald Reagan's foreign policy promising a postsocialist future and the place of Islam and Muslims in that future came to a violent head after 9/11. Currently, the memory of U.S. military and humanitarian aid to the mujahideen has become an alibi for the perpetual military occupation of Afghanistan. The implication that humanitarian investments unaccompanied by U.S. military oversight fail to properly "discipline" Islam frames the necessity for U.S. imperialism in the Middle East. Indeed, the association between humanitarianism and direct U.S. military intervention in the 1990s facilitated this reformulation. Reexamining 1980s political and media depictions of the U.S. alliance with the mujahideen in light of present-day imperial formations reveals the extent to which discourses about humanitarian intervention inevitably produced the racial and religious victim of atrocities and persecution as aspiring to be like "us," but not yet our equal and therefore in need of our perpetual supervision. Throughout the Reagan presidency, the Afghan freedom fighters were enfolded into a U.S. narrative of secular progress, which would bring about a free world, as well as into a messianic narrative of deliverance from Communist oppression. They were central to the production of Reagan-era fantasies of a postsocialist futurity. Yet because of the objectification of the mujahideen for the purposes of a U.S. global vision, after the fall of the Berlin Wall they themselves came to embody the totalitarian and oppressive evil once associated with Communist ideology.

It is argued in this chapter that U.S. political and media depictions of the Soviet–Afghan War were constitutive of an emergent articulation of humanitarian militarism that reflected a religious reordering of the U.S. worldview about freedom and democracy in the 1980s. The shift from early Cold War nationalist conceptions about the United States' need to save the racial other from communism in Vietnam to calls for saving religious minorities from Soviet imperialism represents a late Cold War development in humanitarian fantasies of redemption. These would continue to be consolidated in the postsocialist era, first in the Balkans and later in the post-9/11 U.S. wars in Afghanistan and Iraq. The Soviet–Afghan War was crucial to early formulations about the role of religion in humanitarian intervention, because although it was one of several sites in the Global South in which the Reagan Doctrine of covert support for guerilla warfare played out, it was the only nation where the piousness of the guerillas seemed to align itself with the Reagan-era emphasis on renewed faith in the U.S. nation. It was also the only nation where the Soviet Union was directly involved in fighting a war. The mujahideen, who were portrayed as America's Muslim brothers-in-faith, struggling against the atheistic Communists, were framed within the Christian eschatology underlying U.S. frontier mythology about the struggle between good and evil as the engine for democratic regeneration.[4] In this sense, when the media's prior focus on the Vietnam War shifted to the Soviet–Afghan War, the religious undertones of the frontier mythology became explicit as the mechanism for the renewal of U.S. democratic potential. The contradictory embracement of Islam within the Protestant–Christian tenor of the Reagan regime's geopolitics, of course, came to a crisis in the post-9/11 era, as the former victims of Soviet oppression themselves became the oppressors in the U.S. worldview.

In contrast to the overtness of the U.S. postsocialist imperialism of the 1990s, the topic of chapter 4, the association between religious freedom and humanitarianism established during the Soviet–Afghan War in U.S. politics and media utilized the frame of imperial projection that functioned alongside the mode of imperial critique developed vis-à-vis the Vietnam War.

How a superpower like the United States could recoup after the Vietnam War was in part explained through portrayals of how the Soviet Union met its demise in Afghanistan. Although Afghanistan came to be known as Moscow's Vietnam, U.S. citizens were asked to distinguish U.S. violence in Vietnam from Soviet imperial violence in Afghanistan. That the United States survived its tour in Vietnam, a postcolony associated with the decline of French imperialism, while Afghanistan became the Soviet Union's "graveyard" as it had been to the British, appeared to reaffirm U.S. moral uniqueness as a nation that embraces and comes to the aid of racial and religious minorities persecuted by imperial and totalitarian domination.[5] The chapter begins by addressing the unprecedented collusion between notions of morality, religiosity, and humanitarianism underlying the Reagan Doctrine as a post-Vietnam mode of militarism. Whereas the Vietnam War became a locus of humanitarian feeling for the United States, the Soviet–Afghan War became a site in which military aid, if not direct intervention, materialized the nation's potential for humanitarian action. The discussion next turns to the ongoing importance of visual transparency in U.S. notions of humanitarianism. As discussed in chapter 2, the idea that the U.S. media could freely transmit images of the Vietnam War, allowing U.S. citizens to feel moral shock at the violence perpetuated by their own nation, resignified the failures of that war as crucial to the development and renewal of American democracy through notions of ethical representation. Meanwhile, the fact that Afghanistan was closed to foreign journalists throughout the 1980s turned Afghanistan into a symbol of darkness and unfreedom brought on by Soviet totalitarian oppression. As the moral decay associated with U.S. violence in Vietnam was displaced onto the Soviet Union, the remilitarization of U.S. culture and covert support for guerilla warfare were justified by the nation's having already affirmed its humanity. Afghanistan thus became a contemporary space of darkness in which inhuman Soviet acts and the mujahideen's enduring faith in God demanded that Americans rekindle their own faith in the U.S. ideals of freedom and democracy. Finally, the chapter addresses the U.S. media's own engagement with the mujahideen, focusing on U.S. journalists' attempts to make Afghanistan transparent for American audiences. Tracing the shift in journalistic portraits of Muslim piousness in the region from the era of the Soviet–Afghan War to the contemporary moment, I conclude by considering the extent to which the buried memory of the Soviet–Afghan War reaffirms U.S. morality in the Middle East in the present.

Reagan's Moral Revolution and the "Soldiers of God"

During Ronald Reagan's presidency, Afghanistan, which was known as the Soviet Union's Vietnam, reanimated early Cold War discourses through an emergent emphasis on the need for the United States to defend religious freedom from the spread of Communist imperialism. Afghanistan was significant not simply because it represented a parallel space of loss for the Soviet Union as did Vietnam for the United States in previous decades. Rather, Afghanistan was conceived as a site of religious persecution and violence through which the United States could once again act as a benevolent nation protecting the freedom of conscience from Soviet-imposed monoculturalism and atheism. An opportunity to help the Afghans defend themselves against the Soviet Union reaffirmed U.S. morality in the frame of liberal democratic progress. Through covert U.S. action and media coverage of the Soviet–Afghan War, the failure of Vietnam became the ground for a rekindled patriotism and militarism, as the United States was able to prove that this time it was on the side of a weaker Third World people. With U.S. support for the "freedom fighters," the United States was no longer a superpower being defeated by Vietcong guerillas adamantly committed to their cause but was instead working alongside guerillas who would never give up in the face of the Soviet invasion. In Afghanistan, the mirror turned away from the United States itself and started reflecting the horrors of Soviet actions as Americans had the opportunity to witness the evils of another superpower invading a poorer and less technologically advanced non-European nation.

The consolidation of the Reagan Doctrine in the 1980s as the predominant mode of U.S. military intervention concealed "the colonial origins of the Vietnam War and [obfuscated] two critical historic associations: Vietnamese communism with anticolonial nationalism and the United States with foreign domination."[6] As Reagan himself asserted in a 1986 discussion of U.S. foreign policy, since the 1970s the United States has been an "ardent champion of decolonization."[7] Distancing the United States from colonial contexts was necessary to revitalize early Cold War worldviews that conceived of a free world in need of defense from Communist aggression. In the 1980s, the Soviet–Afghan War offered concrete proof that Communist forces were indeed expansionist occupiers of small Third World nations, a worldview that had come into question in Vietnam. Like a number of late 1970s leftist coups in Africa, Latin America, and Asia, in 1978 a leftist regime came into power in Afghanistan. To support this regime when it came under attack by Muslim clerics, in December 1979 Soviet troops entered Afghanistan to install Babrak Karmal as its president. According to the Soviets, they were not an invading force but, rather, "advisers" in what they presented as an Afghan civil war. The U.S.-supported guerilla fighters continually frustrated Soviet efforts, leading to numerous comparisons between Afghanistan and Vietnam. By 1988, when the last of the Soviet troops left Afghanistan, the United States had renewed confidence in the humanitarian ethos of its military interventions, while the U.S.S.R. would cease to exist in two years' time.

Throughout the Soviet–Afghan War, the U.S.S.R. was depicted as an old-fashioned empire, out of step with the democratizing march of history toward a postsocialist future. In a televised interview about why the U.S.S.R. invaded Afghanistan and what its aspirations were in the Middle East, Helmut Sonnenfeldt of the Brookings Institution argued that the Soviets "want to have positions that resemble the positions of the great colonial and imperial powers of the past."[8] In contrast, according to Francis Fukuyama, U.S. methods were modern. He contended that while the Soviet Union was fraying at the edges because of oppositional indigenous guerilla movements in Angola, Ethiopia, Nicaragua, and Afghanistan, where the Soviet Union had installed Marxist–Leninist regimes, the United States, which was on the side of these guerillas, had become a "worldwide subversive power."[9] Samuel Huntington did not even make recourse to comparisons with previous empires to proclaim the backwardness of the Soviet project. He argued that, historically speaking, the main Soviet export has been revolutionary idealism. However, he continued, no one considers the Soviets to be on the cutting edge of revolution any more.[10] For Huntington, all the Soviets had left to export were guns. Lacking ideals, lacking God, and even lacking revolution, by the 1980s the U.S.S.R. became emptied of all meaning in U.S. discourses, save as an outdated imperial and military force with which the United States had to reckon.

Meanwhile, Reagan's rhetoric appropriated the concept of "revolution" to represent the shift in U.S. policy and ethical investments. For Reagan, the changes that took place under his watch and the transformation in U.S. methods for achieving moral and political ends in the geopolitical sphere represented nothing short of a "revolution" in international relations.[11] Reclaiming global "revolution" for the United States, Reagan sought to coopt and displace leftist politics and aspirations for economic, social, and racial justice that could profoundly remake the capitalist world order. Instead, the Reagan Doctrine of covert aid, the military engine of America's geopolitical "revolution," emerged out of the belief that the Soviet military should be depleted through having to fight indigenous guerilla groups the same way that the United States was depleted in Vietnam. In Reagan's view, the Vietnam War left the United States weak and divided, which allowed for Soviet imperialistic expansionism in the 1970s.[12] However, in spite of conceiving of Afghanistan as the Soviet Union's Vietnam militarily, Reagan and the U.S. media did not actually equate America's devastation of Vietnam to Soviet aggression in Afghanistan. Rather, Vietnam was used as a flattened reference conjuring up moral horror at the actions of an imperial power, now disassociated from the United States' past. In what seemed to be a reversal from the Soviet and U.S. positions in Vietnam, where the Vietcong subverted U.S. military goals, in the 1980s the United States could again be seen as being "on the side of progressive change."[13] The political portrayal of a contemporary Vietnam War being waged by the Soviet Union in Afghanistan reframed that fraught history of the Vietnam War as part of the evolution of U.S. morality. With accounts of the United States offering its support to guerilla fighters as opposed to a puppet regime, in the 1980s Afghanistan became a concretized negative reflection of U.S. actions in Vietnam. As Central Intelligence Agency (CIA) director William Casey noted, "Usually it looks like the big bad Americans are beating up the natives. Afghanistan is just the reverse. The Russians are beating up on the little guys."[14]

As political commentators of the time noted, from its inception, the formulation of the Reagan Doctrine entailed an "unusual fusion of power, politics, and morality" unseen in recent American politics.[15] While some observers criticized Reagan's policies as being too open-ended, contending that the understanding of "democracy" and "freedom" differs for each group receiving U.S. support, and that their understanding might not overlap with that of the United States, others, like Charles Krauthammer of the *New Republic*, praised the "universalism and moralism" of aiding, in principle, all opponents of communism.[16] Indeed, throughout the 1980s, the United States was aiding groups as diverse as the Contras in Nicaragua, anti-Marxist guerillas in Angola, and the mujahideen in Afghanistan. For Reagan, however, the diversity of these aspirations for freedom against communism proved the universal morality of the United States as a nation to which these groups could look for aid, and the universal immorality of the Soviet Union to which the world stood opposed. Toward the end of his presidency, Reagan reflected that though "the structure and purpose of American foreign policy decayed in the 1970s," that is, after Vietnam, in the 1980s the United States could no longer continue to accept that only half the world would be free.[17] Speaking of his achievements, Reagan underscored that "we refused to believe that it was somehow an act of belligerence to proclaim publicly the crucial moral distinction between democracy and totalitarianism."[18] The implication of Reagan's words is that, following Vietnam, even articulating a belief in the morality of U.S. ideologies was considered an act of belligerence. Throughout his term, Reagan thus sought to reclaim interventionism on behalf of U.S. ideals as divinely ordained.

With Afghanistan taking Vietnam's place as a contemporary Cold War site of imperial horror, religious language predominated U.S. political discourses about contemporary geopolitics. This was enabled through a rhetorical framing of Afghans' faith in God as symbolic of the United States' need to revive its faith in its national ideals so that it could successfully stand opposed to communism once again. In the early days of the Soviet invasion, Jimmy Carter explained to American audiences that the "massive" Soviet force of fifty thousand heavily armed troops represented a "powerful atheistic government" that wished to deliberately "subjugate an independent Islamic people."[19] The emphasis on Afghan piousness represented a new direction in the late 1970s and 1980s reworkings of the domino theory. In the same postinvasion press conference, Carter instructed the camera to zoom in on a map of the Middle East, telling U.S. citizens that it was once again necessary for the United States to protect the freedom and independence of one nation, Afghanistan, for the sake of all other nations in the region. "Freedom" and independence, in this context, conflated religious freedom with opposition to the forces of Communistic atheism. Reagan similarly associated U.S. global progress with the nation's embracement of racial and religious yearnings for freedom. In a conception of the U.S. global mission as sacred, he proclaimed that "the American spirit . . . knows no ethnic, religious, social, political, regional or economic boundaries; the spirit that burned with zeal in the hearts of millions of immigrants from every corner of the earth who came here in search of freedom."[20] In this formulation, America's "spirit" depends on the ethnic and regional diversity of its people and their beliefs, establishing as divinely ordained the nation's role in the world. Reagan continued:

Can we doubt that only a Divine Providence placed this land, an island of freedom, here as a refuge for all those people in the world who yearn to breathe free? Jews and Christians enduring persecution behind the Iron Curtain; the boat people of Southeast Asia, Cuba and of Haiti; the victims of drought and famine in Africa, the freedom fighters in Afghanistan, and our own countrymen held in savage captivity. . . . Can we begin our crusade in a moment of silent prayer?

Reagan's "crusade" both references the religious impetus of the medieval Christian crusaders and reinvents the meaning of "crusade" in a secular frame of diversity. Subsuming the Afghan story into the U.S. story of religious redemption, in this formulation, like the New World Puritans and immigrants to the North American continent before them, Afghans desire religious freedom, but in their own land. In this sense, Afghanistan embodies the transnationalization of the American dream on a global scale. Refusing to be persecuted like Christians and Jews behind the Iron Curtain, the Afghan "freedom fighters" struggle and persevere in the name of their religion—Islam. As journalist Nick Doney put it, Afghan "tribesmen" may not know the meaning of communism, but they know that the Communists are atheists, and this is cause enough for a holy war—jihad.[21]

Through the emphasis on Afghan religious conviction, Reagan viewed U.S. military aid to the freedom fighters as being both "material" and "moral."[22] Beginning with his 1980 campaign for the presidency, Reagan argued that the divine status of the U.S. nation predetermined its duty to support a people of faith. In the historical context of the 1980s, the religiosity of the mujahideen, who refused to give up their beliefs even in the face of the Soviets' superior military strength, seemed to parallel the United States' refusal to give up faith in America's geopolitical duty to intervene on behalf of freedom even after the setbacks of Vietnam. Thus in spite of the Christian messianic tenor of Reagan's crusade rhetoric, there appeared to be an affinity between the United States and Muslim Afghan opposition to the Soviet-supported Afghan Army and the Red Army. Even though the Iranian hostage crisis that occurred simultaneously with the Soviet Union's invasion of Afghanistan prevented a blanket acceptance of all devout Muslims, the distinction between the "militant terrorists," as Carter called the Iranians, and the "freedom fighters," as the Afghan rebels came to be known, had to do with which superpower was being opposed. As Walter Cronkite put it in a 1980 CBS special report, both events led to a "national awakening," because the United States once again had enemies that one could "see" and, therefore, "fight."[23] According to the report, for most Americans the more satisfying villain was in the Kremlin rather than in Iran. As godless, Soviet actions readily lent themselves to being portrayed as inhuman in their cruelty, and the U.S.S.R. could be seen as lacking America's divine destiny. Speaking to Afghan refugees in Pakistani camps, Zbigniew Brzezinski affirmed his belief in the ultimate defeat of the Communists when they face an opponent who holds a deep belief in God. Pointing across the border to Afghanistan, he proclaimed, "God is on your side."[24]

News reports represented religious conviction as the one weapon that the Soviets could not overcome, either ideologically or militarily. In descriptions of Afghan rebels as freedom fighters, 1980s political and media rhetoric linked their fight with other global struggles for "freedom," such as those in Nicaragua and Angola. However, in portrayals of the mujahideen's war as a jihad, or a holy war, the fighters' religious devotion was seen as a unique arsenal possessed by the Afghans that enabled and motivated them to endure in their struggle against Communists as the "infidel invader."[25] One news story focusing on the Soviet Central Asian province of Tashkent, which is predominantly Muslim, explained that Communist ideology could not overcome Islamic piousness.[26] According to the report, the "communist education system, which savagely mocks all religion, seems to have had little effect after years of indoctrinating Muslim children." This information, presented as a narrative voice-over framing images of men in mosques bowing toward Mecca, makes the point visually and verbally that Communist ideology is powerless in this part of the world. Other reports framed faith less in opposition to ideology and more in opposition to weapons and military might. Dan Rather, one of the first U.S. journalists to produce an extensive report on Afghanistan following the Soviet invasion, concluded his 1980 *60 Minutes* segment by predicting that this is "a war [the mujahideen] will have to win on faith. Islam is their strongest weapon now."[27] Another news segment concluded that the mujahideen, with "combined bravery and faith [and] with a few bullets," could "frustrate the Soviet army."[28] To explain the persistence of the mujahideen in the face of immense injuries and deaths, the media used the frame of religious conviction to explain how the freedom fighters, because of their interior strength, exceed their physical body on this earth. In scenes from a Red Cross orthopedic center, where wounded fighters came for rehabilitation, one report affirmed that these images of broken bodies did not in any way represent the breaking of the mujahideen spirit.[29]

The Afghans' enduring faith in Islam eventually came to be imagined as the force that defeated previous empires, of which the Soviet Union was only the most recent. A 1984 episode of *Frontline*, "Red Star over Khyber," begins by metaphorizing Afghanistan as a place of death for dreams of imperial expansion.[30] Situating the Red Army's aspirations in a long series of failed invasions, including Alexander the Great's and Genghis Khan's attempts to conquer the Central Asian nation, the program predicts that victory is not possible. After chronicling the Red Army's frustrations, the segment concludes with a reading of Rudyard Kipling's ode to Afghanistan: "When you're wounded and left on Afghanistan's plains / And the women come to cut up your remains / just roll to your rifle and blow out your brains / and go to your God like a soldier." The Kipling poem links the Soviet Union to previous empires that met their demise in Afghanistan. The words of the poem function as an obituary for the Soviet Union, and as they are recited, black-and-white images of Russian soldiers killed in action pass across the screen, a slide show of death. Cutting to shots of Red Army issue boots and fur hats, signifying the passing of many a Russian soldier who once wore these clothes, the program proclaims, "And for their God, Allah, the mujahideen fight on." In closing, *Frontline* tells its audience that the Afghans have only two things—their land and their God—and once their land is taken away through hostile invasion, they are left only with faith and holy war. The episode's ending thus posits that the faith of the Afghan people endures, defeating superpowers of the past and the present.

Reporting Atrocities from the "Hidden War"

While U.S. aid to the mujahideen aligned Reagan-era policies with the side of God, the enduring "faith" of the mujahideen also allegorized the importance of maintaining faith in moral ideals that oppose communism—including those that the United States seemed to have lost in Vietnam, such as promoting human rights instead of perpetuating atrocities. The emphasis on faith as the foundation for a universal moral stance that could cover a variety of Third World aspirations for "freedom" against communism thus resurrected early Cold War discourses, but with a twist. Specifically, the United States sought to prove that post-Vietnam military actions were not just undertaken in the name of "freedom" and "democracy" but that any U.S. militarism was also now moral because it was humanitarian. Deflecting the memory of its own imperial darkness in Vietnam onto the Soviet Union, the United States had a chance to articulate the way in which its methods of waging war had been transformed. Whereas the Vietnam War was reimagined to be outside of the nation's secular time of progress, symbolizing a national descent into darkness and a testing ground for U.S. ideals, Soviet violence in Afghanistan was portrayed in concrete and horrific terms as moral darkness that must be opposed, through humanitarian action, in the present.

Unlike the early Cold War years, when the conflict between the United States and the U.S.S.R. was seen as an ideological conflict, in the post-Vietnam era the United States positioned itself as a champion of universal human rights against Soviet-instigated humanitarian disasters. In vivid descriptions of Soviet savagery, commentators connected Communist imperialism with human rights abuses. For instance, Rosanne Klass, then director of the Afghan Information Center for Freedom House, argued that Soviet policy in Afghanistan was a "calculated policy of terrorization" and a series of "systematic campaigns of butchery."[31] In an account of moral shock that rivals Marlow's encounter in *Heart of Darkness* with the trophy heads in Kurtz's compound, Klass explains in horrific detail how the Russians cut off Afghan rebels' heads, putting men's heads on women's bodies and women's heads on men's bodies. She asserts that the Soviets purposely leave "the mutilated dead as a warning and an omen to survivors." Other commentators also used graphic depictions, relating how Soviet soldiers plucked out men's beards and fingernails and urinated into the mouths of prisoners.[32] When the U.S. Helsinki Human Rights Committee went to Afghanistan, it concluded that "just about every conceivable human-rights violation is occurring in Afghanistan, and on an enormous scale."[33] The most commonly cited violations included accounts of Soviets killing entire villages filled with women and children, which resonated with, but also displaced, the moral horror of the My Lai massacre.[34] The Soviet invasion of Afghanistan was framed as the ultimate morally horrifying act not just because of the scale of the human rights abuses they were committing in Afghanistan but because, unlike U.S. citizens, they were incapable of recognizing the humanity of the other.

One way in which Soviet citizens were rendered as quite literally incapable of seeing atrocities was through the emphasis on Afghanistan being closed off to journalists. The "hidden war," as it came to be known, framed Afghanistan's inaccessibility as exacerbating the human rights abuses happening there, and as a central aspect of the Soviet campaign of terror.[35] At the time, Jean-François Revel argued that Communists shape their image in the world by barring journalists, and even doctors, from entering Afghanistan: "Soviets have kept the Afghan horror story from being told by the mass media."[36] In this assessment, the "horror" of Afghanistan is the result of not just Soviet military violence but also of representational violence that constitutes the nation as a literal space of darkness into which the world cannot peer. Proposing a correlation between reporting, documentation, and morality, Revel suggests that to see would be to awaken moral responsibility in the West. Rosanne Klass had a slightly different take on the lack of reporting from Afghanistan. She accused journalists themselves of refusing to report what they could not see and verify for themselves, comparing the situation to the Holocaust, when the U.S. press at first refused to believe reports of Nazi death camps.[37] Though Klass critiques the idea that horrors must be verifiable in a way that privileges the need for visual documentation, she nonetheless, like Revel, conceives of a closed-off Afghanistan as a human rights abuse.

Unlike the popular idea that Vietnam was a transparent television war, or a war in which journalists had full access to take photographs of shocking violence that elicited moral outrage from the U.S. public, during the Soviet–Afghan War the Soviet population was imagined as incapable of an ethical response to atrocity because it was in the dark about what was happening in Afghanistan. In this sense, U.S. militarism was aligned with truth and morality, while Soviet atrocities were seen as enabled by the media blackout. For instance, U.S. news coverage of the 1980 Moscow Olympic games, which the United States boycotted because of the Afghan War, contended that the Russian people did not even know why there was a boycott. Discussing the Soviet media's complicity, U.S. reporters accused their counterparts of "snappy editing" and extensive use of zoom lenses to quickly redirect the public's attention from any signs of protest, such as teams that chose to march behind the Olympic flag rather than their national flags.[38] It is rare for a news report, such as this one, to draw attention to the fact of editing in journalism. In this case, editing became a tool of deceit that the Soviet media used to dupe their public. Implicitly, the U.S. media showed themselves as conveying the truth in a complete and unbiased manner to their U.S. public.

In accounts of the Soviet media, U.S. news sources portrayed the Soviet Union as a regime that offered no space for debate, critique, or an antiwar movement that could morally redeem the horrors of its imperial misadventure in Afghanistan. For instance, some news stories that addressed Muslim populations within the borders of the Soviet Union underlined that the nonexistent coverage of Afghanistan led to an erasure of religious and ethnic opposition to communism through concealment. The segment on Tashkent claimed that there is "no mention of fighting in Afghanistan in ethnic language newspapers that most people buy and read."[39] That there were no scenes of mass protest and violence like in U.S. cities and universities during the Vietnam era—and that Soviet Central Asian Muslims went peacefully about their everyday business rather than supporting their fellow Muslims—was explained in terms of the Soviet populace being kept in the dark. By 1985, when Soviet television began to broadcast news of the war, U.S. reports of their coverage continued to stress censorship. One 1985 ABC segment showed black-and-white footage of Red Army soldiers during World War II to emphasize the misplaced patriotism and analogies that Soviet news sources were using to describe this war that for years the U.S.S.R. pretended did not exist.[40] According to the report, their government told Soviet "boys" that they were fighting to raise the Afghan standard of living.

U.S. politicians seized on the association between Soviet inhumanity and Afghanistan's media blackout to distance U.S. militarism from that of the U.S.S.R. Aligning transparency with U.S. democracy, Ronald Reagan contended that the Soviets "have a different standard of morality than we do. We tell the truth."[41] Similarly, Utah senator Orrin Hatch argued that even though its unpopularity among the soldiers and citizens led to the analogy of Afghanistan as Moscow's Vietnam, the analogy ended there— first, because the U.S.S.R. did not pay attention to public opinion, and second, because the Afghan War was "largely hidden from the eyes of the world." Hatch's statement provides an apt example of two of the ways in which Vietnam was reinscribed as sacred in U.S. culture—that it was a war in which American popular opinion mattered, therefore affirming U.S. democracy, and that it was journalistic access that enabled and fueled the democratic debate. For him, both were missing from the Soviet Union's actions in Afghanistan, giving that war no redeeming qualities. Hatch warns that because of the media blackout, the "Afghan horror story has not penetrated our consciousness." As a 1980s study put it, "Vietnam . . . was a high-tech television war, [while] Afghanistan is one of those old fashioned encounters that takes place in the dark."[42] Unlike Vietnam, this war was not fought in the living rooms of citizens but was "out of sight, out of mind."

The "hidden" nature of the Soviet War in Afghanistan was ultimately conceived of as a key mechanism for Soviet imperialism and religious persecution. Erik Durschmied, an independent journalist for CBS, who, having received special permission to film in Kabul for five weeks, produced the special three-part story, "Under the Soviet Gun," made the point that when the borders of Afghanistan were "sealed off" following the Soviet invasion, the story was "killed."[43] The report implies that "killing" stories conceals killing people and immoral (imperialistic rather than humanitarian) motivations for waging war. According to Durschmied, Kabul is a "forbidden city," and his account emphasizes censorship as the enabling condition of

Soviet colonialism. First he recounts how he was only allowed to film Afghan civilians going about their daily lives, and that he was not allowed to film any Russian soldiers. However, the report explains that the Soviet military was present everywhere in spite of the Afghan civilians' contempt for the "shuravi"—a derogatory name for the Russians. Visually, the story is edited to emphasize the Soviet military's attempts to become invisible. For instance, footage of a Russian soldier gradually fades to static on the screen. The word "CENSORED" is stamped in red letters across the television snow. Similarly, Durschmied discusses how even images of distant helicopters were censored. What this censorship conceals is, according to the report, old-fashioned racial imperialism. The story explains how Russian civilians have moved to Afghanistan to live in special apartment complexes, bringing over their children and families. Durschmied also exposes how only the Russians are using a university ostensibly built for the Afghans. Cutting to images of young children reciting Communist slogans, he asserts that even attempts at increasing literacy are little more than propaganda tools. Durschmied's conclusion is that Afghanistan has "in effect become a province of the Soviet Union," and that the Soviets' goal is to make Afghanistan a "carbon copy" of the U.S.S.R., a conclusion that is affirmed as the show ends by zooming in on a Russian soldier's belt buckle that has on it the insignia of a hammer and sickle.[44]

Becoming Afghan

The closing off of Afghanistan to foreign journalists led to a unique genre of reporting in the 1980s, one in which the reporters attempted to dress and look like Afghans in order to cross the border and deliver news that in their view the U.S. public needed to hear. Having already established its ability to feel for the victim of imperial violence during the Vietnam War, in Afghanistan, the United States represented itself as selfsame to that victim through portraits of American journalists becoming one with the mujahideen. Endeavoring to blend with the "natives," white U.S. reporters distanced themselves from an association with foreign intervention and aligned themselves with the resistance to Soviet expansionist aggression. Moreover, by making themselves look like the mujahideen, the reporters' disguise visually emphasized the absence of American bodies in this war. Yet because Afghanistan symbolized a new kind of geographic darkness formed through a media blackout, a crucial way for the United States to assert its duty and morality in that space was through penetrating it with journalistic exposure. The U.S.

journalist, recognizable as a figure of democratic and moral outrage in Vietnam, became once again the cartographer of imperial immorality for U.S. audiences.

Dan Rather's 1980 *60 Minutes* report set the tone for what would become a common mode of reporting resistance to Soviet rule. In an introduction to the segment, Rather explained that little or nothing comes out of Afghanistan as news, and therefore, one must go and see for oneself. By way of rationalizing the disguise that viewers were about to see, he noted that in Afghanistan, an "American would stand out like a beacon." The story then begins with Rather positioned at the Afghanistan–Pakistan border, dressed in a recognizably Afghan *pakol* (hat) and *chapan* (coat), his face darkened and tanned. Though he would humorously be referred to as "Gunga Dan" in popular culture commentaries, such as the *Doonesbury* comic strip, the camouflaged Western journalist became a staple figure in reports on Afghanistan following Rather's *60 Minutes* story. The undercover reporter was the human complement to the Reagan Doctrine of covert aid. Like U.S.-built weapons that flowed into Afghanistan, which were made to appear as if they were of Soviet origin and confiscated by the Afghan fighters in battle, the reporters' Afghan costumes emphasized the need for concealment and American ingenuity.

Figure 3. Dan Rather dressed as a mujahideen, reporting "Inside Afghanistan" for *60 Minutes*.

Because Rather's report was taped and broadcast at the very beginning of the Soviet invasion, before the entrenchment of the new U.S. military policy favoring covert aid, the notion that the U.S. role in Afghanistan was that of an anti-imperialist force collaborating with the persecuted resistance was made explicit through allusions to Vietnam. Early on in the episode, Rather, still dressed as a mujahideen, questions one witness about whether or not the gas he saw used was napalm. With napalm's characterization as the most inhumane of the weapons deployed by the United States in Vietnam, the reference establishes that the Russians' mode of fighting is at least as merciless and vicious as the United States'. Later in the episode, the comparison to Vietnam becomes more explicit. In another interview, a mujahideen tells Rather that Afghans feel like "America is asleep." Rather tells the translator, "I'm sure he knows that in Vietnam America got its fingers burnt, and we got our whole hands burnt when we tried to help in this kind of situation." Interestingly, unlike in his question about napalm, in this more overt association of Afghanistan and Vietnam Rather does not equate U.S. militarism with that of the Soviet Union but posits that the Soviets were the aggressors in Vietnam as well.

With the Reagan Doctrine, the worry expressed by George Ball that in Vietnam it looked as if the United States was fighting a white man's war was no longer an issue. Here were Afghan freedom fighters telling Americans what they want and need—weapons that would serve a humanitarian function, protecting a religiously persecuted people from Communist domination. In this respect, the masquerading American reporters underscore the absence of American bodies even as their presence serves the moral function of verifying Soviet atrocities. When Rather tells the mujahideen he interviewed in "Inside Afghanistan" that "no American mother wants to send her son" to fight in a foreign land again, he is informed that the Afghans need weapons, not soldiers, which suggests that the United States can again be militarily active on a global scale, this time supporting indigenous guerrilla groups battling their own wars "with [U.S.] gold but with their blood."[45] Without U.S. aid, these anti-Communist freedom fighters are, as Rather proclaims, "eighteenth-century [men] fighting a twentieth-century war." Asking the mujahideen to put their weapons on display, Rather is dismayed to find that the only automatic weapon they possess dates back to World War I. It is, as Rather puts it, a "real antique." Because of the inadequate weapons, the numbers of refugees continue to increase, as do Soviet atrocities. In his investigation of one camp, Rather finds it entirely peopled with women and children whose husbands were killed in Kurawa, "a name that may one day be as familiar as My Lai." To prevent more such all-too-familiar atrocities, he intimates, the United States need only make a material investment rather than an investment of American lives.

Interestingly, the nonrelevance of "white" bodies in this war was underscored not just through the absenting of American bodies on Afghan soil through the journalists' costumes but also in a thematic and visual way intimated by depictions of Soviet forces as bodily absent. Rendered inhuman by their conflation with high-tech military machines, the Russians were portrayed as godless because, being mechanized rather than made of flesh and blood, they could not feel for the loss of the Afghan people they killed. To solidify the image of the U.S.S.R. as a technologized atheistic empire, many reports showed the Afghans to be a mountain-dwelling, medieval, and tribal people facing a faceless military machine. In an Emmy Award–winning documentary, Hilda Bryant and Richard Pauli conjure up Afghanistan's war-torn landscape as the "mud holes of an ancient people pulverized by heavy Russian artillery."[46] The ancient Afghan peoples' premodernity, in this account, lends them a certain nobility belonging to "brave peasant men who believe they are fighting for Allah." Throughout their report, Bryant and Pauli juxtapose close-up images of Afghans praying and fighting with outdated handheld weapons with scenes of Russian tanks and helicopters but not of Russian soldiers themselves. A common visual technique in most 1980s news stories, this contrast simultaneously signaled the tremendous discrepancy in the quantity, newness, and power of available weapons, thus indicating the vital need for U.S. military aid, and the immorality of a "mechanized, Soviet-trained Army" mercilessly attacking practically unarmed peasant "soldiers of God."[47] Often, news reports introduced stories about wounded civilians and Afghan refugees by establishing shots of Soviet tanks, helicopters, or land mines, made to appear disconnected from the human atrocities that they themselves had orchestrated. According to an *ABC News* report, Russian weapons left only "ghost villages" in their wake.[48] Thus even though accounts of Soviet savagery were meant to shore up support for U.S. military aid, U.S. weapons sent to Afghanistan were given a human face and ascribed a moral function through their association with the rebels' suffering that they were meant to alleviate.

Like Dan Rather before them, Hilda Bryant and Richard Pauli used their disguise as Afghans as a central framing device for their account of faith and inhumanity in the Afghan War. Aligning themselves with the victims of religious persecution, they conceived of their documentary as a record of "smuggling" themselves in, like contraband, with the help of "friendly Afghan guerillas." In addition to shopping for clothing in a bazaar, Pauli went so far as to use black dye on his blond beard. For Bryant, it was more difficult because, as she describes, she was a woman in an all-male Muslim culture. She therefore wore the full chador and was driven in the back of an ambulance as a sister of mercy. Unlike in contemporary reports, in which such an account of the place of women in Afghan society would serve as a marker of antidemocratic Islamic tendencies, in the context of this report it is simply a descriptor of a culture predetermined as "traditional" by the figuration of the primitive and noble rebels, who must be defended against Communist invaders. Since the reporters "became" Afghan through dress and hair dye and, in Rather's case, a tan, these reports imply that Americans, who hail from a racially and religiously diverse nation, can adopt, adapt, and blend into a variety of cultures with ease. Audiences are left to infer that in Afghanistan the United States is not looking to impose its ways but to listen, learn, and help. Through these reporters who "became" Afghan to bring news to the home front, the United States thus incorporated the Afghan fight for freedom into its national narrative of racial and religious progress.

Humanitarian Resonances

Through the spectacle of American reporters looking like Afghan freedom fighters, the human rights abuses committed by the Red Army could be interpreted as abuses committed against U.S. citizens themselves. If Americans were instructed to feel moral unity with the Afghan people, then the humanitarian catastrophe befalling them was befalling the United States as well. Alongside the stories of the mujahideen fighting against incredible odds, with inadequate weapons and endless religious motivation to continue their struggle, images of refugees from camps in Pakistan served as proof of the horrors committed by the Soviets. It is from the refugee camps that the only image of the Soviet–Afghan War to endure in the U.S. consciousness was taken—the famous 1985 picture from the cover of *National Geographic* magazine of a refugee girl who came to be known simply as the "Afghan girl." Steve McCurry, the photographer made famous by the portrait, recounted years later that what drew him to her in the makeshift refugee camp schoolroom was the "haunted look" in her eyes.[49] For McCurry, the photograph's success lies in the girl's iconic green eyes, not because of their unusual color but because "her look summed up the horror because her village had been bombed and her relatives had been killed." Like Conrad's Marlow, who finds redemption and truth in Kurtz's summation of "the horror," for McCurry, the Afghan girl's eyes reveal a horrific truth about Soviet inhumanity that even the media blackout cannot conceal. Unlike Afghanistan itself, which is closed off to the West, her face and gaze invite the U.S. viewer to look back and to see the atrocities she has witnessed.

Since 9/11, many feminist scholars have returned to the image of the Afghan girl and its circulation in U.S. culture. In this context, it is important to ask what is lost if the afterlife of that image is not contextualized through the decade-long history of U.S. support for the mujahideen as a humanitarian cause in the 1980s. According to Rae Lynn Schwartz-DuPre, the salient signifiers of the girl's image—her veil, age, eyes, anonymity, refugee status, and femininity—produced in its U.S. audience the feeling of being ambassadors of compassion and freedom, who were capable of liberating the girl from Communist oppression.[50] By 1985, when this issue of *National Geographic* hit newsstands, Afghanistan was the single-largest covert operation undertaken by the CIA anywhere in the world. In this connection, the girl's youth and femininity symbolized an unaccompanied Afghanistan under Soviet attack.[51] While Schwartz-DuPre rightly points to the function of the Afghan girl's image as an elicitation of humanitarian feeling in U.S. audiences, her reading of the girl's veil and eyes interprets the 1985 photograph through a contemporary post-9/11 lens. She contends that the girl's green European eyes function as a punctum, confronting the audience with the pain that is contained within them. Implicit in this line of argument is the idea that the familiar, yet foreign, eyes, as signifiers for the girl's potential whiteness, elicit a stronger humanitarian feeling in the audience.[52] Keeping in mind, however, the way in which reporters like Rather, Bryant, and Pauli darkened themselves to become like the mujahideen, what becomes more remarkable is that the Afghan girl's eyes, through their racial ambiguity, signal a common, multiracial, and multi-religious humanity shared between the United States and Afghanistan. The color of Rather's skin, Pauli's beard, and the anonymous Afghan girl's eyes are all irrelevant to their mutual yearning for freedom. Collective moral outrage in the face of inhuman Soviet aggression levels religious, and racial, differences.

In a similar recourse to post-9/11 interpretive frames, Schwartz-DuPre contends that the girl's veil, which slightly frames her face in the photo, symbolizes her inferiority to U.S. viewers and therefore functions like her age and femininity.[53] She goes on to suggest that in 1985 unveiling girls and defeating communism went hand in hand in the U.S. geopolitical imaginary. Recalling, however, the ongoing praise of the mujahideens' faith as a sign of their bravery and longing for freedom, this reading would seem out of line with the 1980s media and political discourses. Rather, the veil framing the girl's face might more accurately be read as making her legible as the intended victim of Soviet aggression. The veil has a slight burn on it, and it is ragged, but the girl clings to it as the Afghan people cling to their faith. Because Schwartz-DuPre views the sign of the veil and the reduction of the girl to her European eyes in the *National Geographic* photo through a contemporary lens, when she compares the image of the Afghan girl to *Heart of Darkness* she does so to make the point that the anonymous girl stands for her entire land, and therefore conjures up timeless places in need of civilizing.[54] Although the girl's femininity certainly associates her with all of Afghanistan, the more apt comparison to *Heart of Darkness* might be her appeal to Western audiences to recognize their common humanity and see the horrors of the Soviet invaders that she has witnessed with her eyes.

Almost immediately after the events of 9/11 in 2001, the U.S. public, with news of the Taliban and Afghanistan once again in the public view, recalled the only image they could remember from the 1980s—McCurry's photo, the *Afghan Girl*. With the psyche of the Taliban and the Afghan nation seeming all of a sudden impenetrable to U.S. understanding, there was a longing to recall those eyes that had revealed the truth of the horrors of a different time. In 2002, the National Geographic Channel aired an episode of *Explorer* in which McCurry travels to Pakistan, where the refugee camps had been, to search for the Afghan girl whose name he had never known.[55] Unlike the 1985 *Afghan Girl* photo and 1980s news reports from Afghanistan, which emphasized that the nation's impenetrability was imposed by the Soviets and that the native Afghan people wanted the United States to look upon them and help them, the 2002 search for the Afghan girl accentuates the fact that in the ensuing years, Afghanistan has become closed off to Americans. Narrated by Sigourney Weaver, the *Explorer* episode begins by categorizing the story of the Afghan girl as a mystery that began seventeen years ago involving one of the most "arresting" portraits of our time to which no name can be attached. As the documentary cuts to images of a veiled woman, fully covered, walking with a young child, the narrator asks if it is too late for McCurry to find the face that has haunted him for years. The veil, resignified for the post-9/11 moment, now implies impenetrability.[56] If the girl's face, once open for us to gaze upon, is now covered, she is simply, as

Figure 4. 2002 cover of *National Geographic.* A veiled Sharbat Gula holds the cover of the famous 1985 issue featuring her portrait.

Weaver narrates, "one woman, possibly covered by a burqa, lost among millions." Because of the veil, this has become "one of the most challenging missing persons cases of our time." Whereas in the 1980s the Afghan girl's anonymity could stand for a whole nation in need of U.S. aid, *National Geographic's* "Search for the Afghan Girl" demonstrates that in the post-9/11 context, Muslim women's anonymity can only stand for the subordination of women under Islam. In this case, our new humanitarian duty is to find the Afghan girl and give her a name, and, if she is veiled, to give her a face. That is, the post-9/11 duty is to make her an individual and, therefore, to make her fit for the coming of U.S. liberal democracy.

The documentary's pretense of being a mystery, or a missing person's case, structures the expedition as a search for a lost truth, perhaps a truth in which the United States' role in the world as helping the underdog seemed clearer. When McCurry arrives in Peshawar, Pakistan, he declares that the Afghan refugees there are the victims of a twenty-three-year-old war. Such a claim erases the impact of post-9/11 U.S. intervention. In fact, the documentary makes no mention that in 2002, when it was first aired, the United States expanded its war efforts in Afghanistan, testing out new superbombs on Afghan soil.[57] The show's simultaneous erasure of U.S. weapons technologies and its emphasis on technologies of truth imply that a stable moral ground can be regained in Afghanistan. Throughout, McCurry has the help of an FBI missing persons investigator and the bureau's iris scanning technology. Therefore, if someone comes forward claiming to be the woman from his photograph, the *National Geographic* team will be able to confirm her statements through the identification technologies. Certainly the "technological dazzle" of the story, combined with its human interest element, fits the civilization–premodernity dichotomy discussed by Schwartz-DuPre in the context of the 1985 image.[58] More interesting, however, is what is presented as the real "miracle" of the story—that once Sharbat Gula, which we discover is the Afghan girl's name, has been found, she lifts her veil and "for the second time" reveals her face to McCurry and his American audience, allowing herself to be photographed. In interviews, McCurry expressed his frustration "that the woman, who is a conservative Pashtun, sought her husband's permission to lift the veil of her burqa."[59] McCurry's frustration, however, is well worth the hope that audiences can hear in the first words spoken by Sharbat, "I'd like America to help rebuild Afghanistan." The lost truth that seemed to be hidden behind the veil had not in fact changed since 1985. In searching for the Afghan girl, the *Explorer* episode was also searching for an ethical representation in the new U.S. war in Afghanistan. The memory of the Afghan girl from the 1980s, when U.S. aid was sought after by the Afghan people, and her words in the present moment both affirmed that the United States was still acting out of human feeling and for moral good in the Middle East.

Keeping the Faith

By 2007, when *Charlie Wilson's War* was released, it had become clear that American-instituted "freedom" and "democracy" were failing to win hearts and minds in Afghanistan as they had in Vietnam. That film thus tells a story of a moment in time when those same ideals of freedom and democracy resonated with the Afghans—the story of the Reagan Doctrine and humanitarian aid, now displaced by the U.S. imperial occupation of Afghanistan. The rogue Charlie Wilson, who works alone, stands for a different approach to the problems in the Middle East than the large-scale military operations that have been the hallmark of post-9/11 U.S. policy, and failure, in the region. The film introduces Wilson at a medal ceremony, where he is being honored by the CIA for playing a central role in bringing down the Communist empire. In the flashback that ensues, Wilson is in a Las Vegas hotel Jacuzzi, drinking with scantily clothed women. In the middle of partying, he finds himself distracted by a TV in the background that is tuned into Dan Rather's *60 Minutes* story, "Inside Afghanistan." Wilson poses the question, more to himself than his hot tub companions, "What is Dan Rather wearing?" Although the question is humorous, as has been argued in this chapter the question of what the reporters were wearing is an important one that relates to method—how not to be, as William Casey put it, the "big bad Americans beating up the natives." As the film continues, it becomes evident that this is not a story about the return of the repressed but a story about what could have been if the United States had stayed the course of 1980s-era policies. With numerous scenes of the refugee camps on which the film dwells, it is clear that this triumphalist story puts a humanitarian face on U.S. foreign aid. This is the kind of policy that is represented in the film as having put an end to Communist atrocities. Toward the end of the film, Dan Rather appears on-screen again, this time announcing, in 1988, that Afghanistan is the first country in history to defeat the "mighty Soviet Union," and that the era of Soviet military intervention is over. The film makes clear that the ultimate mistake of the United States was stopping its humanitarian aid. As Wilson laments, millions were spent on weapons, but after the withdrawal of the Soviets, he could not even get $1 million to build schools in Afghanistan: "We always go in with our ideals and change the world, and then we leave. We always leave."

Like the Reagan Doctrine itself, *Charlie Wilson's War* does not ask audiences to question U.S. ideals, just to question the moments when the United States abandons those ideals. For Afghanistan not to become the "graveyard" of the United States, as it had of the Soviet Union, the film appears to propose, paradoxically, maintaining faith in our humanitarian impulse, even as the gun is being turned on us. In contrast, Phillip Noyce's post-9/11 adaptation of Graham Greene's Cold War–era novel, *The Quiet American* (2002), revisits Saigon in the tumultuous decade of the 1950s to question the association between humanitarianism, military moralism, and war waging that was consolidated in the United States after the Vietnam War. The film frames the decline of French imperialism in Indochina and the simultaneous rise of U.S. military opposition to the spread of communism in Vietnam through a murder mystery. The structuring conflict between an idealistic young American, Alden Pyle, and an aging British reporter, Thomas Fowler, which develops through their desire for the same Vietnamese woman, Phuong, symbolizes the distinct imperial fantasies of the old and new worlds. Through its portrayal of the ultimate emptiness of both imperial projects and sets of promises, the film critiques the mobilization of humanitarian ideals to justify geopolitical domination. There can be little doubt that the 2002 adaptation of *The Quiet American*, produced long after the official reasons provided by the U.S. government for its military presence in Vietnam were discredited, uses Pyle's death as a metaphor for the death of early Cold War U.S. ideals in Vietnam. As it turns out, Pyle is not the humanitarian worker he has pretended to be but a covert agent who engages in acts of terror on behalf of abstract ideals, ordering the detonation of explosives in a busy city center brimming with civilians. Considering that the Vietnam War became a major military failure for the United States, Fowler's refusal to fight for an idea resonates as much with the imperial regret that the U.S. nation has been forced to account for the hollowness of its rhetoric of bringing democracy to Vietnam as it does with the decline of British imperialism represented in Greene's 1952 novel.

It might seem surprising that a critique of U.S. militarism in Vietnam, produced three decades after the war's conclusion, should have become as contentious as it did. Yet in the wake of the United States' own experience of an act of "terror" on its soil, and its retaliation against the "terrorists" in Afghanistan following the events of 9/11, *The Quiet American*'s condemnation of previous instances of U.S. military actions as terroristic was deemed too "politically sensitive" for it to be released as scheduled in September 2001.[60] Justifying the nearly yearlong deferral of the film's opening, Harvey Weinstein of Miramax noted, "You can't release this film now; it's unpatriotic. America has to be cohesive and to band together. We were worried that nobody had the stomach for a movie about bad Americans anymore."[61] The controversy surrounding the release of this particular depiction of the Vietnam War in the immediate aftermath of 9/11, when the United States was once again deploying the language of freedom and democracy to justify its war waging, this time in Afghanistan, invites questions about the role of culture as a locus for democratic critique in the United States. Unlike *Charlie*

Wilson's War, The Quiet American represents the ideals of humanitarianism and democracy themselves as hollow, or, if they have meaning, it is only a destructive and violent one. Though it might appear that the story of what the United States did in Afghanistan in the 1980s would be a more difficult one to justify in the post-9/11 context than a story about Vietnam, interestingly, it was *The Quiet American* that was the more controversial of the two films. Certainly this has to do with its release so soon after the events of 9/11. However, it also surely has to do with how histories of U.S. intervention in different parts of the globe are tied to the life and death of U.S. "ideas" and ideals. *The Quiet American*'s critical association between humanitarianism, democracy, and the origins of post–World War II U.S. imperial militarism seemed an unappealing remembrance of U.S. loss and devastation in Vietnam at a time when those same terms were being deployed yet again as the morally justificatory ideals underwriting U.S. warfare in Afghanistan and, subsequently, in Iraq. Even in most post-Vietnam era antiwar representations, the idea of humanitarian feeling for the other was kept alive as part of maintaining faith in the vitality and regenerative capacity of U.S. democracy. The final question *The Quiet American* leaves open is, in many ways, more disturbing than the silhouette of the mujahideen's gun turned on the United States in *Charlie Wilson's War*: What might it mean to seriously contend with humanitarianism itself as a hollow ideal?

4 DRACULA AS ETHNIC CONFLICT

The Technologies of Humanitarian Militarism in

Serbia and Kosovo

THE AMERICAN BLOCKBUSTER *Van Helsing* (2004), a recent adaptation of Bram Stoker's novel *Dracula* (1897), introduces Dracula's by-now-infamous homeland, Transylvania, with a surprising twist. In a black-and-white homage to Universal Studios' monster pictures of the 1930s and 1940s, the film opens with a mob of angry peasants preparing to storm not Dracula's castle but, unpredictably, Frankenstein's castle at the very moment the doctor brings his creature to life.[1] By relocating the birth of Frankenstein's creature to the Romanian province, *Van Helsing* imagines Transylvania as a location that produces multiple monsters. Following the rogue adventurer Van Helsing from Transylvania to Budapest on his mission to find and kill Count Dracula, the film references not just Stoker's novel but a variety of Western European Gothic novels from the nineteenth century, including *Dr. Jekyll and Mr. Hyde* (1886) and *Frankenstein* (1818). Reanimating these stories, *Van Helsing* displaces the cultural memory of Western European monsters and the imperial and racial histories that generated them onto the Eastern European landscape.

Because *Van Helsing* is a movie not just about monsters but about monstrous geographies, the vampire hunter's ability to navigate and command the outermost reaches of European space is key to vanquishing the ancient evil embodied by the count. At the climactic moment when Van Helsing and his companions think they have located Dracula's lair, they find themselves standing in front of a massive wall-mounted map of Transylvania. They realize that the map is actually a door that will lead them to the count. Van Helsing demonstrates his ability to penetrate the secrets embedded in the map and attaches the missing piece that had been safely stored in the Vatican for centuries. In an apt representation of Euro-American and Christian mastery over the region, he shouts the order: "In the name of God, open this door." The topographic depiction of Transylvania's mountains and rivers melts away to reveal a large mirror, leaving Van Helsing and his associates looking back at their own reflection. Recalling that Dracula has no reflection, Van Helsing quickly understands that they can walk through the mirror to enter Dracula's otherworldly realm. In this sense, Dracula's geographic location becomes a negative reflection against which the vampire hunters understand their humanity and moral supremacy, enacted "in the name of God." Through this visual affirmation, the film justifies Dracula's death as necessary for the preservation of humankind.

Much like the post-9/11 vampire hunters in *Van Helsing*, at the start of the 1999 U.S.-led North Atlantic Treaty Organization (NATO) bombing of Serbia and Kosovo, President Bill Clinton found himself deciphering and interpreting a map of the Balkans in order to explain to U.S. citizens the monstrosity of ethnic conflict and religious violence in the post-Communist world. In a televised address justifying the military intervention as "humanitarian," Clinton instructed the camera to zoom in on a map of the former Yugoslavia. Interpreting the on-screen map, he told viewers that

> Kosovo is a small place, but it sits on a major fault line between Europe, Asia and the Middle East, at the meeting place of Islam and both the western and orthodox branches of Christianity. . . . All the ingredients for a major war are there: Ancient grievances, struggling democracies, and at the center of it all, a dictator in Serbia who has done nothing since the cold war ended but start new wars and pour gasoline on the flames of ethnic and religious division.[2]

According to Clinton, postsocialist ethnic and religious division in the Balkans was geographically determined and spatially fixed, erupting, as Samuel Huntington famously elaborated in "The Clash of Civilizations?," at the great "fault-line" between Christianity and Islam.[3] Clinton's use of cartographic and geological metaphors to depict the Balkans as an ahistorical space of racial, religious, and civilizational clashes relied on and reproduced Gothic imagery about the Balkans, which contrasted the post-Enlightenment West with the dangerous, primordial violence of "the East."

These two events—one cinematic, one military—deployed maps not just as tools for orientation but also as representational technologies that rationalized Euro-American leadership and violence in moral terms. Bringing to light new and enduring forms of evil that must be vanquished to spread freedom in what George H. W. Bush called the "new world order" in 1991, *Van Helsing* and Clinton each mobilized and refigured Gothic literary tropes based in Western European imperial and racial ideologies about monstrosity and premodernity. As Foucault notes, nineteenth-century Gothic imagery depicted the opacity of unenlightened locations as "unlit chambers where arbitrary political acts, monarchical caprice, religious superstitions, tyrannical and priestly plots, epidemics and illusions of ignorance were fomented."[4] In the postsocialist era, the new interpretive frames through which *Van Helsing* and Clinton apprehended Balkan maps can be understood as part of an emergent moral geography, which reconceived the role of U.S. military and technological supremacy as a humanizing force that defeats the evil political, racial, and religious formations that endure in some parts of the world.[5]

At the outset of the NATO attacks against Serbia and Kosovo, Clinton told U.S. citizens that "this is not a war in the traditional sense."[6] Though he was referring to the Serbian assault on and displacement of ethnic Albanians in Kosovo, his statement also encompassed the imperative for NATO's military intervention by depicting the air strikes as a humanitarian act in the service of multicultural morality. In Clinton's rhetoric, Operation Allied Force was the only contemporary war to be fought solely on the basis of universal human ideals and not in the name of national interests. Applying a Western "allied force" against Serbia and Kosovo was crucial to legitimizing the post–Cold War doctrine of humanitarian intervention that had unofficial precedents in U.S. military operations in Iraq, Somalia, Haiti, Bosnia, and Rwanda. Of these, the United States' passivity in the Bosnian civil war (1992–1995) and its inaction in Rwanda (1994) were cited as the primary reasons to intervene "in time" in Kosovo. In particular, the United States' bombing of Bosnian Serbs in 1995, which led to the Dayton Peace Accords, seemed to prove that without U.S. military might the United Nations was incompetent to stop humanitarian disasters.

As the decade of violent civil wars in the former Yugoslavia drew to a close, Western politicians and the media alike saw Kosovo as a particularly appropriate geographic and symbolic location in which to legitimize Western interventionism as humanitarian. Through NATO's military actions, the multinational and multicultural coalition was held up as the only force able to use advanced technologies—racial, cultural, and military—to vanquish ancient Balkan tendencies toward ethnic cleansing. The U.S.-led Western Alliance was able to understand itself as modern, enlightened, racially tolerant, and humanitarian by saving the ethnic Kosovar Albanians from the barbaric actions of the bloodthirsty Serbs. As Branka Arsić suggests, in the Western imaginary, the Balkans is "the name for a construct projected into the externality of our internality"; in other words, the

Balkans are imagined to be both within and outside of Europe and function to keep the West "constantly on the move" and "permanently cautious" of internal danger.[7] Keeping a vigilant eye on the Balkans does not just mean that the West periodically saves the Balkans from the region's never-ending cycles of violence, but that the "Balkans" must be continually reinvented in the Euro-American imaginary in order to redefine the meaning of the "West." In contemporary media, political and legal discourses that maintained and legitimized NATO's military intervention in Serbia and Kosovo, the Balkans were construed as Europe's wild and monstrous geographic limit, whose stability was central to a postsocialist world and a united Europe's security and well-being. By envisaging the ambiguously European Balkans as the point of origin of all twentieth-century European violence, including terrorism and Nazism, and by reducing the Balkans to a space of ethnic conflict and ethnic cleansing, U.S. political and media discourses distanced the civilized West from its own racial thinking and racist violence that have been constitutive of Euro-American modernity. In other words, within the West, racism was produced as a monstrous formation of the past, currently playing itself out in the Balkans. During the 1990s, therefore, racial and ethnic differences in the contemporary United States and Europe were represented as productive of progress and civilization in contrast to the Balkans, where such differences were equated with hatred rooted in blood, violence, and primordial evil that would not die.

Political and media discourses have largely relied on Gothic tropes to portray "ethnic hatreds" in the region as unreformed racism that has no place in Euro-American modernity. In his article "Vampires Like Us," Tomislav Longinović suggests that "as a creature of history, the unfortunate count [Dracula] is formed by the colonial gaze of the West, which senses its own bloodthirsty past."[8] In this sense, "the gothic imaginary functions as a time-delayed reflection of past traumas of European collectivities, and this image is then projected onto 'the serbs' through the narratives of global news networks as they recount their Balkan histories in real time."[9] Longinović concludes that the emergence of "the serbs" is a sign of the new "racism without race," a racism that is "couched in the progressive language of human rights" but one that nevertheless perpetuates the enemy within an "Other" Europe.[10] More than just a sign of a new raceless Euro-American "racism," Operation Allied Force signaled the culmination of a transnational refiguring of U.S. racial logics.

Throughout the 1990s, U.S. politicians and the media promoted a post–Cold War vision of cultural diversity, complementing and amending prior notions of racial diversity and operating in tandem with the discourses of humanitarianism and human rights to underwrite U.S. global interventionism as a moral force that spreads freedom and democracy. As Tim Allen argues, the popularity of "ethnicity" as a concept that could explain the motivating factors of the 1990s conflicts in the non-Western world followed the trends of official multiculturalism in the West, which promoted the idea of cultural difference based in geographic descent while eschewing the concept "race," which implied biological hierarchy.[11] At this time, the focus on ethnic conflict as a foremost sign of non-Western violence exemplified the transposition of anxieties about unresolved racial tensions at home that continued to visibly erupt, as they did during the Los Angeles riots in 1992. The idea that Serbs continued to associate race with bloodlines in this sense perpetuated the conception of rogue nations as "vampire nations," whose provincial racial thinking must be vanquished through the coalitional and transnational forces of progress.[12] As I argued in chapter 1, the racialization of religion in the Balkans facilitated such a reworking of normative and perverse modes of inhabiting difference nationally and globally. While the language of religion, ethnicity, and culture clash used to explain conflict in the Balkans certainly borrowed the terms of American multiculturalism, there was nevertheless an important difference in their connotation. The "cauldron image" of "bubbling . . . ethnonationalist sentiments that were sure to boil over unless suppressed by strong states" contrasted with the image of the American melting pot.[13] Thus at the same time narratives about ancient hatreds and wild landscapes naturalized and essentialized ethnoreligious difference in representations of non-Western conflicts, in the context of U.S. multiculturalism, "ethnic" diversity and "racial" diversity were seen as signs of cultural progress and civilization.

Making manifest the force of multicultural, humanitarian action through the technologically advanced death-dealing weapons of war in global "trouble spots," the 1999 bombing represented the zenith of U.S. militarism's paradoxical association between universal human values and advanced technology as the coconstitutive moralizing discourses of postsocialist imperialism. New media and military technologies enabled dominant U.S. discourses to mask the contradictions between humanization and killing. Even as multicultural humanitarianism takes shape through a series of expulsions and incorporations of threatening difference, the fantasy of otherness, in ever-changing forms, is necessary for a continued articulation of its historical and moral authority as a global project. This chapter's analysis of Operation Allied Force therefore addresses technology in two ways:

first, as the advanced military and media technologies that produced and justified the concept of militarized humanitarianism, and second, as the Gothic narrative technologies that produced a novel understanding of Euro-American humanity as nonracist against Balkan racial and religious monstrosity. The first section provides an overview of the political rhetorics through which Operation Allied Force, the culmination of postsocialist imperial action, was framed as a just war, transnationalizing the U.S. multicultural progress narrative. The second section analyzes the Gothic frame through which the technologies of humanitarian imperialism were construed as weapons against atrocity. Next I turn to the extensive use of the Holocaust analogy that made the racialization of religious conflict prominent in the imaginary of a new kind of antiracist humanitarian imperialism in the postsocialist era. The concluding sections lay out how Gothic technologies of documentation and the law, the signs of European modernity in fantasies of racial vampirism and its vanquishing, were referenced and reframed in contemporary depictions of the Balkans to justify U.S. imperial sovereignty during Operation Allied Force. I argue that the casting of U.S. media coverage as a technology for documenting distant human rights violations, by building on the Holocaust analogy, was crucial in transforming the relationship between U.S. warfare in the postsocialist era and the realm of international law.

Framing a Just War

The shift in U.S. racial logics that took shape in the 1990s through the production of Balkan otherness is exemplified in Clinton's address to the nation on his last night as president. Asking U.S. citizens to remember the successes of NATO's air strikes against Serbia and Kosovo, he declared, "We achieve our aims by defending our values and leading the forces of freedom and peace. . . . We must remember that America cannot lead the world unless here at home we weave the threads of our coat of many colors into the fabric of one America."[14] Not only did the president's reminiscences about the U.S. leadership of Operation Allied Force interpret U.S. national interests to stand for universal values such as peace, but his thoughts on Kosovo reaffirmed that over a decade after the fall of the Berlin Wall, the United States still held its rightful position as leader of the free world. Using a common metaphor for multiculturalism—the image of the interwoven threads in a coat of many colors—Clinton's justification of U.S. global interventionism defined and upheld a contrast between U.S. domestic race relations and ethnic conflict abroad. In this way, U.S. multiculturalism rewrote U.S. militarism as a benevolent force that spreads diversity and tolerance around the globe. Affirming the United States as a space of racial harmony that had earned the right to lead the free world by overcoming its own racist foundations through capitalist development meant locating the Balkans as a locus of conflict that represented the antithesis of contemporary U.S. multicultural ideals. The rise of multiculturalism as the predominant mode through which to envision a pluralist democracy during the 1980s and 1990s in the United States differed from the earlier European concept of the ethnic nation-state. In the aftermath of the Civil Rights Act of 1964, when discrimination along racial lines was rendered illegal, the myth of racial progress emphasized the nation's evolution beyond its illiberal racist past. The development of the United States' self-understanding as a multicultural democracy in the 1990s depended on contrasting its "diversity" as a symbol of democracy, modernity, and freedom with the so-called primordial ethnic conflicts in the Balkans, which conjured up premodern, tribal, and violent formations based in "blood and belonging."[15] In this context, the monstrosity of ethnic conflict that reminded the United States of its own past of genocide, slavery, and nativist violence was subsumed by the deployment of the "civilizing technologies" of the U.S.-led Western "humanitarian" imperialism to stop the bloodshed in the Balkans.

The violent disintegration of the former Yugoslavia can be attributed to a number of political and economic factors, none of which had to do with ahistorical ancient hatreds. The most important dynamic leading to the rise of nationalism in the Balkans was the end of Yugoslavia's privileged non-Allied position in Cold War Europe, since foreign loans on which the country depended were no longer available. It is no coincidence that the election of Slobodan Milošević in the late 1980s coincided with the elections of nationalist leaders Milan Kucan in Slovenia and Franjo Tudjman in Croatia. As Jasminka Udovicki and Ivan Torov have shown,

> in nationalism conservative forces found an instrument against fundamental social, political, and economic change that threatened their social privileges. . . . The propaganda Milošević, and later on Tudjman, set in motion appealed to the quite tangible legitimate grievances of the common person: the falling standard of living and the political void. The appeals evolved around the same core: the claim that current economic ills in each of the republics stemmed from the long practice of economic exploitation and political subordination of that republic by all others. . . . In both cases *nationalism*

served objectives that had little to do with ethnicity or grassroots ethnic senti-
ment, were politically motivated, and were orchestrated from above.[16]

Although nationalism was not an isolated phenomenon in Serbia during the 1990s but an ideology that also held appeal for the other Yugoslav republics, during the violent disintegration of the Socialist Federal Republic of Yugoslavia, Western attempts to comprehend the wars of secession focused all of the blame on the figure of Milošević as the rogue nationalist Serbian dictator. According to Susan Woodward, although Yugoslavia lost its significance to the major powers after the Cold War, the ideology of Cold War anticommunism continued to influence the United States' reaction to the disintegration of Yugoslavia: "Anyone who opposed the Communist Party and Communist leaders was, by definition, supported."[17] She argues that the nationalist leaders of Slovenia and Croatia were able to win over Western public opinion by presenting themselves as democratic in contrast to "Communist dictators in Belgrade" and by downplaying instances of their own governments' political oppression. Moreover, after the Cold War, the United States supported regimes that were willing to provide new markets for the West as opposed to ones that were resistant, such as the Milošević regime in Serbia.

Slobodan Milošević, known in the West as the "butcher of the Balkans" and as the primary architect of Yugoslavia's wars of secession, rose to power in Serbia during the late 1980s on the basis of his regressive ethnonationalist policy toward Kosovo. After the death of longtime Yugoslav president Tito in 1980, ethnic Albanians in Kosovo, who constituted 80 percent of the population in that autonomous province of Serbia, began to demand greater self-governance.[18] At the same time, the Serbian minority in Kosovo believed that they were gradually losing their civil rights and suffering harassment at the hands of Albanian secessionists. On April 24, 1987, Milošević, then the head of the Serbian Communist Party, was sent by Serbian president Ivan Stambolić to listen to the Kosovar Serbs' grievances. In a now-famous speech on Kosovo Polje, Milošević told the Kosovar Serbs who claimed to have suffered attacks at the hands of ethnic Albanians, "No one should dare to beat you!" This was a statement that immediately assured him widespread support amid a growing number of Serb nationalists in Serbia proper as well as in Kosovo.

In 1989, when Milošević assumed the Serbian presidency, he immediately revoked Kosovo's autonomous status. Throughout the 1990s, Kosovo's instability was manifest in occasional eruptions of violence between ethnic

Albanian guerillas and Serbian authorities. The violence escalated in the late 1990s, and an estimated two hundred thousand ethnic Albanians were displaced from their homes. During 1998, the Contact Group nations designated by the United Nations to promote peace in the region organized a series of meetings between the Serbian government and ethnic Albanian leadership, and the United Nations Security Council demanded that Serbian hostilities cease. At this time, NATO members backed their threats against the Serbian government by mobilizing forces in the region. The Rambouillet peace negotiations, held in February 1999, represented the culmination of Western diplomatic efforts. Though the Albanian leadership agreed to both plans, Milošević refused to sign the treaty, which would have granted NATO forces full access to Serbia as a whole, not just the Kosovo province. For the Milošević government, the peace plan raised serious concerns about the nation's sovereignty. Less than a month later, on March 24, NATO's aerial bombing campaign began.

NATO was acting without the support of the United Nations and against NATO's own founding charter. Russia and China, both members of the United Nations Security Council, had indicated their opposition to the air strikes. Nonetheless, U.S. political rhetoric stressed that its alliance with NATO countries represented a new global future. Clinton explained to U.S. citizens that while the initial formation of NATO following World War II "made possible the victory of freedom all across the continent . . . Bosnia taught us a lesson. In this volatile region, violence we fail to oppose will lead to greater violence we will have to oppose later."[19] Positing that the problems of the postsocialist era demanded a different solution from those of the Cold War, he noted, "At the end of the 20th century, we face a great battle between the forces of integration and the forces of disintegration, the forces of globalism versus the forces of tribalism, of oppression against empowerment."[20] Although Clinton emphasized that the United States could not intervene in every tragic instance of ethnic conflict, military action in the Balkans was essential because the meaning of fundamental Euro-American principles, such as freedom and tolerance, hung in the balance.

In U.S. political rhetoric, the geographic location of the Balkans on the European continent made it a privileged geopolitical site to be saved at all costs. Even though Clinton framed recent events on the peninsula through the analogy of a violent civilizational fault line, he also emphasized that securing democracy and harmony in the region was important to a unified and peaceful Europe. In his presidential address on the eve of the NATO attacks, he explained that "defusing a powder keg in the heart of Europe" was essential, because "if America is going to be prosperous and secure we need a Europe that is prosperous, secure, undivided and free."[21] The Balkans' symbolic position as neither fully European nor fully other enabled the universalizing rhetoric that legitimized NATO's Operation Allied Force as a just and necessary war for postsocialist restructuring. Meanwhile, because U.S. imperial ambitions within Europe itself seem unthinkable, the nation's economic interests in the region were subsumed within the rhetoric of values. The U.S. administration repeatedly contended that NATO air strikes were not an act of war against the Serbian people nor even, ultimately, against Milošević. Instead, it was a grander war of ideals—tolerance, liberalism, and freedom against intolerance, totalitarianism, and religiously motivated ethnic warfare. Portrayed as a war that was not to be fought in the name of national boundaries or territory, U.S. national interests and European security were deemed to be selfless actions that "[advanced] the cause of peace" across the globe to protect "defenseless people."[22]

Of course, the aerial campaign allowed the United States to reassert its economic and military leadership in Europe as a whole. NATO's origins in Europe's post–World War II devastation and U.S. economic gains from rebuilding the region through the Marshall Plan underwrote U.S. dominance in the alliance. For Clinton, the postsocialist era provided a similar opportunity for the United States, only this time economic prosperity was more clearly connected to diversity and tolerance. In his words, "the United States must do for southeastern Europe what we did for Western Europe after World War II and for Central Europe after the cold war. Freedom, respect for minority rights, and prosperity are powerful forces for progress."[23] Even as the post–Cold War enlarged NATO was refigured as a nonmilitaristic, universal, moral, and just alliance—a symbol for a Europe standing united against a single rogue dictatorship—the U.S. position as leader of that alliance during Operation Allied Force was based in the military superiority of the United States over the other NATO nations. As Michael Ignatieff put it, "Only the United States can muster the military might necessary to deter potential attackers and rescue victims."[24] Ignatieff's statement makes it clear that in the contemporary U.S.-led global order, as in the earlier era of European imperialism, the "forces of progress" are determined and executed only by those nations that possess advanced military technologies.

Several months after NATO declared victory over Milošević, and Serbian troops withdrew from Kosovo, Clinton traveled to Kosovo for the first time. According to one news report, "for Mr. Clinton, the brief visit was the first to a tiny patch of Europe he had studied so closely on maps, on satellite images, and at countless briefings during the NATO air war."[25] The president's now "humanized" vision of Kosovo legitimized the U.S.-led military occupation of the province. Building on the understanding that during the air strikes the United States was the only nation with the military and technological capability to win the war, after the war Clinton asserted that the United States was also the only nation that could exemplify multiethnic peace on a global scale. Addressing the U.S. peacekeeping troops, he urged them to "be a model to the people in Kosovo to show how different ethnic groups could coexist peacefully."[26] Singling out ethnoreligious hatred and violence as one of the world's greatest problems, Clinton referenced U.S. leadership in Operation Allied Force to redefine the role of U.S. military interventions worldwide as being about racial and religious tolerance. Just as in the domestic context U.S. multiculturalism depended on erasing the sedimented histories of racial violence, slavery, and inequality, in Kosovo the U.S. vision of spreading multiculturalism covered over the violence of the fifteen hundred civilians killed as "collateral damage." Adapting the rhetoric of multiculturalism to justify U.S. military aggression and occupation as humanitarian, Clinton concluded that "because of our resolve the 20th century is ending . . . with a hopeful affirmation of human dignity and human rights in the 21st century."[27]

Dracula's Imperial Technologies

As an emergent global morality embodied by the coalition between New Europe and the United States took shape against the atrocities of individual rogue nations, it became clear that transnational ideas about humanity and inhumanity would continue to be consolidated through warfare in the postsocialist era. Thus even as the vampire (and vampire nations) ruptured the ideal of a post–Cold War united humanity, claims to universal human values depended on reviving the vampire figure.[28] As numerous *Dracula* scholars have pointed out, the adaptability of the Dracula narrative is a testament to modernity's unfinished project, which has kept the West ever vigilant of "others" who might reemerge from the dead to strike at civilized lifeworlds.[29] While Stoker's novel can be read as contributing to British imperial discourses that justified British colonialism and exploitation in Asia and Africa as a manifestation of civilizing progress, *Dracula* also portrayed the ambiguity inherent in modernizing imperatives, which could risk reproducing monstrosity. Put otherwise, rather than simply reaffirming a hard boundary between European modernity and its others, the imperial Gothic frame and its political afterlife exemplify how knowledge and technology are constituted through the very horrors they seek to subjugate.

In an astute critique of the merging of Gothic frames and military and media technologies in Operation Allied Force, the Yugoslav Canadian artist and activist Tamara Vukov, known as "Pomgrenade," created a web project entitled *Balkan Mediations*.[30] The three parts of the site, "Proximal Distances," "Ghostly Presences," and "Disjuncture," comment on how the North American God's-eye view of the war as an act of "moralistic humanism against monstrous others" depended on the media staging of the Balkans as a distant set of digitalized targets. *Balkan Mediations* constructs a visual collage that assembles clips from NATO press briefings, televised scenes of the aerial bombardment, excerpts from print media analyzing the war, academic and theoretical critiques of American militarism, filmic constructs of Balkan otherness, and personal e-mails from the artist's family and friends living in the former Yugoslavia. Through its cultural assemblage, the website links the literary, filmic, media, and military visions of the Balkans as a "staging ground for monstrous horror."[31]

Balkan Mediations cites the Internet's origins as yet another technology of the U.S. military to highlight the complicity between media and military technologies in justifications of contemporary U.S. violence. At the same time, Pomgrenade's use of the World Wide Web as a stage for activism opens a space for critical intervention against the dominant uses for new technologies. In a digital image entitled "Cockpit," which imagines a NATO bomber's view of the enemy in the seventy-four-day aerial campaign, Pomgrenade connects the destructive violence produced by extreme assertions of Western military superiority to the cultural production of vampiric and monstrous enemies. The image highlights the interdependence of war and the field of representation. In the very center of the digitalized cockpit, a caption indicts the NATO bomber and presumably the Western viewer: "You construct elaborate technologies to make your killing seem rational." The bomber's console consists of five animated screens that alternately display radar target-location systems and scenes from the ground view that portray the human destruction resulting from the bombing: refugees; debris from civilian buildings; and the enemy's media system, Radio Television Serbia, in flames. The ground views of the "targets" in Serbia and Kosovo are positioned alongside other "targets" of U.S. aggression in Iraq and in the United States itself. News footage of a rolling tank from U.S.

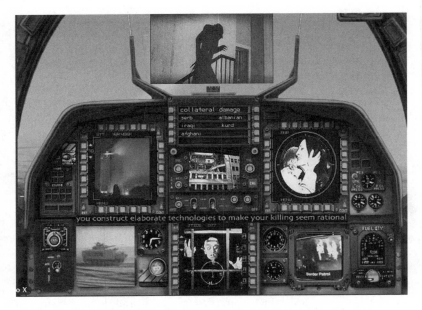

Figure 5. "Cockpit" from Pomgrenade's *Balkan Mediations* critiques the Gothic merging of military and media technologies in portraits of the "enemy."

Operation Desert Storm in Iraq implicates the U.S. media's construction of composite and interchangeable enemies. Meanwhile, images of U.S. officers "securing" the border by preventing undesired others from entering condemn ongoing U.S. racism, as exemplified in its immigration policy. Indeed, the technologies used to police U.S. minorities and immigrants by the U.S.–Mexico border developed after the U.S. military defeat in Vietnam as part of a program to "perfect electronic warfare" and tracking devices.[32]

The largest and most prominent screen in "Cockpit," which is positioned above the five smaller views of Western military destruction, frames the narrative of Western violence through a slide show of stills from F. W. Murnau's 1922 silent horror film *Nosferatu*, the first surviving screen adaptation of Stoker's *Dracula*. Since Dracula, the undead Transylvanian count, is the foremost figure of Balkan monstrosity in the Western imaginary, the *Nosferatu* film stills symbolize the cultural discourses and Gothic imaginary that mediated contemporary representations of "the enemy." The undead Count reemerges at the center of the war engine's console, yet the image of his looming shadow leaves ambiguous whether he is the one hunted or whether his shadow represents the fighter jet's own shadow. The "Cockpit" image suggests that the 1999 Gothic visions of "the enemy" were an instance of "Balkanism," a Western discourse that, according to the website, has produced the region "as a liminal space between Europe and orient, a zone of ethnic impurity, instability and irrationality, a staging ground for monstrous horror." As Maria Todorova has shown, the Balkans have never been viewed as totally other to the West because they are geographically in Europe. Instead, Western popular and political discourses have, over time, imagined the Balkans as the "incomplete self" that has yet to be enlightened.[33] In the Western imaginary, the distant and the more recent history of Balkan violence and hatred makes manifest the (im)possibility of transition from East to West, from primitive to enlightened, and from barbaric to benevolent. Like the looming shadow visible from "Cockpit," Western depictions of the Balkans reveal more about Euro-American self-perception than they do about the human landscape in the countries of the Balkan Peninsula. Indeed, inhuman geographies are necessary for the continued affirmation of Euro-American values and humanitarian ethos.

In Stoker's *Dracula*, vampirism is geographically rooted, emerging in the fault lines of the Balkan landscape. As the novel's Dr. Van Helsing explains to the vampire hunters in the Balkans, "there is something magnetic or electric in some of these combinations of occult forces which work for physical life in strange way."[34] Stoker's geological explanation for the origins of vampirism has hauntingly reverberated in the contemporary discourses about Euro-American humanitarianism and the ethnoreligious threat of "Balkanization." Pertinent to the instantiation of postsocialist imperialism is the fact that the count's vampirism originates in the violence of imperial conquest. Dracula tells the British solicitor Jonathan Harker that he had to redeem "that great shame of my nation, the shame of Cassova."[35] In his undeath, the count continually reenacts his redemption of Kosovo, which was lost to the Christian world when the Ottomans defeated the medieval Serbian Empire in the fourteenth-century Battle of Kosovo. Dracula's state of Balkan "undeath" only begins to threaten the "teeming millions" of London once his own landscape has become completely "barren of peoples" (what contemporary discourses have called "ethnically cleansed" landscapes).[36] The vanquishing of the count foreshadows the possibility of bringing modernity to the Balkans and making it truly European, which was a desire expressed by Western European politicians throughout the twentieth century. For this reason, the vampire hunters are necessarily a multinational group, representing Britain, the most powerful modern empire;

the Netherlands; and the United States, a rising empire allied with Western Europe through its origins in British colonialism.

The nineteenth-century Gothic production of the modern European human and the characteristics of humanity that came to be imagined against the horrors of Balkan inhumanity took shape in the cultural opposition between knowledge and superstition. In *Dracula*, the meaning of Europe at its outer limits was asserted through advancements in British technologies, particularly those of documentation and the law. Material documents of monstrosity, produced through scientific methods that include observation and representation, at once gave life to horrific otherness and sought to vanquish the evils of superstition and tradition. In this vein, new media technologies that could more quickly and accurately produce a record of monstrosity were portrayed as the foremost imperial weapons that could vanquish the evils of vampirism. The novel assembles a collage of journal entries originally written in shorthand, newspaper accounts, telegrams, and phonograph dictations, all of which are transcribed by the competent "new woman," Mina Harker, on her typewriter. Thomas Richards notes that textual archives were central for building and imagining empire in Britain.[37] He argues that because "in a very real sense, theirs was a paper empire," turn-of-the-century British fiction both (re)presented and (re)produced the unprecedented "alliance between power and knowledge."[38] Stoker's novel can be thus read as a paper archive that documents the vampire hunters' knowledge of Dracula in order to justify his destruction in the name of protecting Western modernity against past horrors. The documents exonerate the vampire hunters and legitimize their vigilantism.[39]

Without the new technologies of the Victorian era, such an extensive collection and preservation of textual evidence would have been impossible. For instance, shorthand notation used by both Mina and Jonathan Harker enabled a novel and more efficient method of notation; the Dictaphone into which their ally, Dr. Seward, dictated his journal entries represented the technological capability to record voices; and the typewriter allowed Mina, even when on the road, to speedily collate evidence of Dracula's existence, which ultimately legitimized his destruction. In addition to these technologies of documentation, the technologies of communication, such as the telegraph, and transportation, such as the efficient British rail system, emblematized the possibility of instantaneously transmitting knowledge and information that facilitated mastery over great distances. At the very end of the novel, even though Dracula had destroyed the original handwritten texts, Mina Harker's triplicate typescripts remain. Although Jonathan Harker doubts that these copies carry the same legitimacy as the originals or that anyone could believe the story told within their pages, the image of *Dracula*'s multiple copies with which the novel concludes invokes the reproductive power of Gothic horror and the reproductive capacities of modern technology.

Just as *Dracula*'s textual archive simultaneously produces monstrosity and legitimizes the Western right to vanquish the monstrous, modern law is also based on a system of textual citation that simultaneously produces the exception and establishes the rule. Dracula is initially able to establish himself in London and to acquire property there through his knowledge of British law. It is therefore important that the vampire hunters be able to reestablish their command over the metropole by asserting the spirit of the law over the letter of the law. As Carol Senf points out, it is ironic that Jonathan Harker and Dr. Van Helsing, who are both solicitors, "repeatedly violate the laws which they profess to be defending: they avoid an inquest of Lucy's death, break into her tomb and desecrate her body, break into Dracula's houses, frequently resort to bribery and coercion to avoid legal involvement, and openly admit that they are responsible for deaths of alleged vampires."[40] Within *Dracula*'s logic, however, it is only by operating outside the law that the vampire hunters can restore law and order to the imperial metropole. In spite of the fact that the count uses the letter of the British law, the vampire hunters establish evidence that he is fundamentally a criminal type who commits vampirism by turning the British law against itself. To do so, they contend that though Dracula is "not of nature" he must still "obey some of nature's laws."[41] By appealing to natural law as preceding contractual law, Van Helsing urges an understanding of the vampire hunters' vigilantism as superseding modern law. As Van Helsing says in preparation for the hunt, "What is to be done is not for police or of the customs. It must be done by us alone and in our own way."[42] In other words, since the count's actions are unnatural and outside the bounds of what modern law can account for, the vampire hunters' technically illegal actions are nevertheless represented as necessary for maintaining the law.

It is no coincidence that the Gothic frame proved so apt for narrating NATO's imperial military, media, and legal technologies as a humanizing force in the Balkans during the 1990s. Operation Allied Force was a war based in the extreme technological disparity between the NATO and Yugoslav militaries, which was evidenced in the fact that NATO ground troops were never deployed during the conflict.[43] Because NATO's campaign was exclusively aerial, in spite of flying over 31,000 missions, there was not a single Western-alliance casualty. While NATO pilots undertook minimal risk by maintaining a "safe distance" at 15,000 feet and deploying smart bombs and missiles, about 10,000 Yugoslav soldiers and 1,500 civilians were killed.[44] Additionally, NATO bombings so exacerbated the dire situation of the ethnic Albanian refugees in Kosovo that by May 1999 over half a million people were displaced.[45] NATO made use of the U.S. Department of Defense's Advanced Concept Technology Demonstration program, relying on remotely piloted unmanned surveillance aircraft such as the Predator, a system designed to detect camouflaged enemy targets through Precision Targeting Identification and Global Positioning System (GPS) satellites that guide missiles to designated enemy targets.[46] Even the indictment of Slobodan Milošević as a war criminal during the NATO campaign, the first such indictment of an active head of state in modern history, was justified by Western technology. While NATO continued to act as a warring party, the symbolism of Milošević's indictment refigured the alliance's military technologies as a benevolent surveillance mechanism used to "witness" human rights violations and to gather evidence against Milošević for the International Criminal Tribunal. As civilian casualties in Serbia and Kosovo mounted, Milošević's indictment legitimized the alliance's military operations through the very institutions of international law that NATO air strikes had bypassed by defying the United Nations' processes. Although the ideals defended by the U.S.-led NATO alliance were meant to represent nonracist and universal humanitarian values against the rogue Serbian state, as noted earlier, NATO was acting without the support of the United Nations. Because Russia and China had indicated their opposition to the air strikes, with the U.S.-led NATO bombing of Serbia and Kosovo, the United States was able to assert its military superiority, establishing a precedent for its right to global interventionism that excepts itself from the approval of the international community of nations.

U.S. exceptionalism in the realm of international law establishes the sovereign right of the United States to decide on, suspend, and maintain the international juridical order through its imperial sovereignty, which has continued to undergird the violent process of constituting the "new world order" that we see manifest in the contemporary U.S. occupation of Afghanistan and Iraq. Indeed, NATO's Operation Allied Force differed from earlier humanitarian interventions, such as those in Bosnia and Rwanda, in that, for the first time since the Third World independence struggles, the use of Western military force was explicitly understood to have imperialist objectives.

However, through multicultural rhetoric, the new imperial formation was distanced from eighteenth- and nineteenth-century imperial projects because it was enacted in the name of democracy, difference, and humanity. In his book *Empire Lite*, Michael Ignatieff, a Harvard professor of human rights and a prominent North American public intellectual, described empire as the necessary precondition for democracy in the contemporary global order.[47] Ignatieff's enthusiastic interpretation of war technologies, which, in his words, allowed "for the first time military means [to be] used to create a humanitarian space," validates Western violence as enlightened.[48]

Based on the tropes of technological progress and monstrosity in Bram Stoker's *Dracula*, the imperial Gothic continued to frame postsocialist fantasies of humanization inspired by Euro-American histories of slavery, imperialism, and institutionalized racism, whose legacies have not died out. Indeed, these histories are constitutive of modern Western epistemes through which the rest of the world is rendered legible. As Avery Gordon has suggested, "The post-modern, late-capitalist, postcolonial world represses and projects its ghosts or phantoms in similar intensities, if not entirely in the same forms, as the older world did."[49] Haunted by legacies of their racist "past," the United States and its Western European allies displaced ongoing racial anxieties by opposing their humanitarian presence in the Balkans to the premodern barbarism of "ethnic cleansing," for which the region came to be known. Yet even as Western politicians and the media "repressed" and "projected" their own past of racial violence and even the Holocaust onto the Balkans through their rationalizing political, media, and military technologies, the failure of these mechanisms to completely bury the memories of Western racial violence demonstrated that, to cite Stoker's *Dracula*, "the old centuries had, and have, powers of their own which mere 'modernity' cannot kill."[50]

The Holocaust Analogy, New Moral Imperatives, and the Racing of Religion

Of all the instances of horrific inhumanity produced by Western racial and technological modernity, none has a similarly privileged place in historical accounts as the Holocaust. As a complement to the Gothic frame, which provided a cultural repertoire of monstrosity through which U.S. media and political rhetoric portrayed Balkan atrocity and Euro-American technological imperatives, the Holocaust became an analogy for understanding "ethnic cleansing" in the region. Histories of genocide and attempted genocide, of course, do not begin or end with the Holocaust. The United States was itself founded on the attempted removal and mass killing of Native Americans at the hands of European settlers. However, by choosing the particular correspondence of World War II and the Holocaust with "ethnic cleansing," the U.S. media was able to foreground the U.S. role of first saving and then rebuilding war-torn Europe, then and now. The analogy seemed to suggest that Operation Allied Force was a reenactment of the moral imperatives from World War II. Though numerous historians criticized Clinton's appropriation of the Holocaust to justify the NATO campaign in Serbia and Kosovo, this particular historical comparison invoked the need to intervene militarily more clearly than any other could have.[51] Reenacting "saving the Jews" by "saving the Albanians," a unified West demonstrated to itself that it had, once and for all, come to embody a common multicultural humanity through the overcoming of its own past of prejudice and violence against racial and religious minorities.

Throughout the 1999 NATO campaign, numerous articles addressed the fact that for an American generation that had grown up opposing the Vietnam War, including Clinton, Kosovo was the first chance in which a clear moral choice between right and wrong presented itself—it was the baby boomers' turn to be heroes and to save the embattled Albanian minority in Kosovo. The NATO air strikes were therefore envisaged as the first just war since World War II. Clinton made the sweeping statement that "Sarajevo, the capital of neighboring Bosnia, is where World War I began. World War II and the Holocaust engulfed this region."[52] Indeed, according to Clinton, the United States and NATO were morally compelled to act because of the lessons taught by the Holocaust. Recalling the horrors of the civil war in Bosnia as the precedent for what was happening in Kosovo, Clinton argued in a presidential address that "this was genocide in the heart of Europe, not in 1945 but in 1995, not in some grainy newsreel from our parents' and grandparents' time, but in our own time, testing our humanity and our resolve."[53]

From the start of Operation Allied Force, U.S. network news alluded to the parallels between "ethnic cleansing" in Kosovo and the Nazi plan to eliminate all European Jewry. As soon as NATO air strikes began, U.S. televised news sources announced evidence of a growing human catastrophe in Kosovo, including forced marches and the dispossession of ethnic Albanians that had resulted from new "savage rounds of ethnic cleansing."[54] Though the pronouncement of the refugee crisis in Kosovo as the greatest human catastrophe since World War II implicitly invoked memories of the Holocaust, on March 28, NATO explicitly accused Serbian forces of "genocide."[55] News commentators were quick to urge the immediate documentation of war crimes, thus legitimizing NATO's aggression as a mission to gather evidence against Serbian war crimes that were assumed to exist prior to the fact of discovery.[56] As evidence of war crimes appeared to mount, the U.S. media broadcast images of streaming refugee columns, videos of burning villages, and personal testimonies. On April 10, the comparisons of the Kosovo crisis to the Holocaust became even more explicit. The German magazine *Der Spiegel* introduced evidence of a Serbian plan, entitled "Operation Horseshoe," which provided instructions for the Yugoslav military on how to annihilate the Kosovo Liberation Army and remove all Kosovar Albanians from the province. Though actual evidence of the plan has never been produced, rumors that these documents existed led to chilling comparisons between Nazi plans for the "Final Solution" to the Jewish "problem" and "Operation Horseshoe."

The U.S. media took these rumors as evidence that ever since the civil war in Bosnia, Milošević had been pursuing the goal of an ethnically pure, greater Serbia.[57] Disturbingly, *ABC News* announced a countdown to the moment when not a single Albanian would be left in Kosovo.[58] News cameras panned across the Kosovo landscape, which reporters described as "miles of emptiness." Kosovo was portrayed as a "country without people," a horrific image of what land looks like when it has been "ethnically cleansed."[59] While U.S. network news used the images of empty hillsides to show its viewers what a contemporary "final solution" looked like, televised reports of Albanian refugees that depicted people being crowded onto trains on their way to refugee camps in Macedonia alluded to the Nazi transport of Jews to death camps. *CBS News* coverage cut directly from the scenes of Albanian refugees to black-and-white footage of Jews being deported to death camps.[60] Through this insertion of historic footage of the Jewish Holocaust into the contemporary scenes of ethnic Albanian displacement from their homes, the U.S. media flattened history in order to evoke a clear distinction between "right" and "wrong" and "villain" and "victim."

Contemporary media and political discourses seamlessly refigured World War II history as the only analogy through which to grasp the evils of ethnic cleansing. Ironically, this occurred even though European modernity itself led to the horrors of the Holocaust. The recent history of Western European genocide should have served as a reminder for Operation

Allied Force that, in the words of Walter Benjamin, "there is no document of civilization which is not at the same time a document of barbarism."[61] However, NATO officials and Western leaders used the Holocaust as a touchstone to distinguish European humanity from Balkan barbarity. In order to construe NATO's militarism as part of a humanitarian ethics of intervention, European and U.S. foundations in racial and religious genocide were simultaneously rendered irrelevant to the present-day comportment of NATO nations, and significant only insofar as they became historical frameworks for understanding the Balkans as a contemporary site of inhumanity. Moreover, U.S. racism and European racism were framed as having been overcome in law and society long ago. Secretary General Javier Solana contrasted European values with Milošević's and argued that NATO was fighting to reverse Serbian crimes against humanity in Kosovo. Reporters echoed this logic, suggesting that Western leaders fought a war of "remembrance" as a "'never again' cry" to the Holocaust.[62] In her introduction of Holocaust survivor Elie Wiesel, who spoke on the perils of indifference at the White House, Hillary Clinton commented that Western values of "common humanity" stood opposed to the crimes of ethnic cleansing. During the same event, Bill Clinton suggested that it was only "natural" that Kosovo reminds us of the Holocaust.[63] He presented NATO's intervention in the region as an effort to preserve history, which the Serbs were trying to blot out in their campaign of ethnic cleansing. Thus while the United States and its allies engaged in a just war, defending Western values and spreading tolerance, the Serbs, according to one *Newsweek* reporter, lost all "norms of civilized behavior."[64] This reporter went on to argue that, unlike the Nazis, "the Serbs didn't need to load Kosovars into boxcars to look bad. This is the nation that invented the term 'ethnic cleansing.'"[65]

In their use of the Holocaust analogy, the media stirred U.S. audiences toward compassion by presenting NATO air strikes as an instance of benevolent intervention and implying that Western nations have the sovereign right to intervene because they use the lessons from past mistakes to fight racism and intolerance in the present. Although NATO did not put an end to "ethnic cleansing" in Bosnia for a number of years, quickly responding to "genocide" and stopping a second Holocaust in Kosovo became an ethical responsibility in what British prime minister Tony Blair called "a battle between good and evil; between civilization and barbarity."[66] Introducing the term *genocide* through which to interpret images of the conflict in Kosovo thus ascribed morality and good to the side of Operation Allied Force. After Milošević was indicted as a war criminal accused of genocide and eventually extradited to The Hague in 2001, the media again invoked a plethora of historical allusions to World War II and the Nuremberg Trials. These allusions definitively inscribed the West on the side of universal values and justice, giving it the juridical and moral authority to pass judgment for the second time in the twentieth century over extremist forms of racism and ethnic prejudice. If the Holocaust was evidence of Western humanity's past failures, then in acting to save the Kosovar Albanians "in time," the West was reaffirming its "humanity" by atoning for not acting in time to save the European Jews.

The Holocaust was useful not just as a moral referent and imperative for intervention in Kosovo but also as a frame through which to reimagine the role of racial and religious difference in postsocialist imperial projects. As Mick Hume has noted, the term *genocide* is fundamentally connected to conceptions of racial difference. He argues that in the case of the Balkans, the Holocaust analogy led to a misuse of this term, which "is not just another word for brutality, making people homeless, putting people on trains, or even murder. It means . . . [the] 'annihilation of a race.' "[67] Whether or not the term *genocide* was misused in this instance, its connotation, as evidenced through the privileging of the Holocaust in 1999, demonstrates the importance of religious conflicts in postsocialist racializing discourses of difference. The Holocaust emerged as a clear choice for a historical analogy through which to apprehend Balkan "ethnic cleansing," because the Nazi program occurred in Europe and served as an example of nationalist violence that conflated the religious and racial difference of the other. That U.S. and NATO intervention took place in Europe under the shadow of the Holocaust analogy precluded a critique of postsocialist imperialism, fought in the name of neoliberal principles of diversity and tolerance, as racist. Barnor Hesse has argued that since the end of World War II, the international concept of racism has privileged "the anti-fascist critiques of the Jewish Holocaust, while foreclosing subaltern and anti-colonial critiques centered on Western Imperialism."[68] The result of this imbalance, according to Hesse, has been that "the concept of racism is doubly-bound into revealing (nationalism) and concealing (liberalism), foregrounding (sub-humanism) and foreclosing (non-Europeanism), affirming (extremist ideology) and denying (routine governmentability)."[69] Hesse's framework helps elucidate what at first appears to be the incongruous equating of the Jewish Holocaust with the refugee crisis in Kosovo. In the U.S. media's emphasis on Serbian "nationalism," ethnic Albanian "sub-humanism," and Milosević's "extremist ideology," dominant discourses that favored "humanitarian" intervention concealed how U.S. liberalism and its multicultural ideology continued to privilege Euro-American modernity as a site of progress against non-European others. The favored circulation of the Jewish Holocaust as an analogy for Kosovo undergirded the racialization of religious difference in the postsocialist era that enabled U.S. humanitarian imperialism to be portrayed as multicultural and antiracist.

Because the Western media conflated ethnicity and religion in their analysis of violence between the Orthodox Christian Serbs and the ethnic Albanian Muslims, the coverage set a precedent for using "religious" and "ideological" difference to replace "racial" difference as the predominant mechanism for interpreting non-Western conflicts as irrational, premodern, and genocidal formations.[70] That this interchangeability enabled the comparison between "ethnic cleansing" in the Balkans and the Nazi genocide of the Jews in the Holocaust suggests the dehistoricizing effects of such representations that ultimately allowed the U.S.-led Western coalition to represent its militarism as a struggle for universal human values. Although the term "ethnic cleansing" that was used to describe monstrous violence in the Balkans was popularized in the English vocabulary in 1992 during the Bosnian civil war, it was not until NATO's Operation Allied Force that it came to be equated with "genocide."[71] Jean Seaton argues that the use of ethnicity to frame the civil wars in the 1990s was a depoliticizing mechanism that subsumed social and economic realities within the language of naturalized and essentialized differences.[72] In the aftermath of the Holocaust, ethnic and racial explanations for conflict became taboo, and the Cold War provided "the stable background framework for situating conflicts."[73] After 1989, "ethnicity" began to be used again by journalists who attempted to comprehend contemporary instances of global crises. As Cold War histories were buried, theories of primordial differences gained credence as referents through which to understand non-Western conflicts. The resurrected concept of ethnoreligious sectarianism was significant because it marked the reemergence of nineteenth-century essentializing explanations of difference that were used to conceive of European racial superiority and the right to imperial expansion.

The U.S. media's use of the Holocaust analogy displaced U.S. national foundations in genocide, slavery, and imperialism from the realm of Western "civilization" by contrasting the ideals of "common humanity" in the West with contemporary "ethnic cleansing" in the Balkans. Not only did the dehistoricized merging of the figures of the Nazi and the Serb, the Albanian and the Jew, and the conflict in Kosovo and the Holocaust conflate the different historical contexts, social complexities, and scales of violence but the use of the Holocaust analogy as the framing mechanism through which to understand Kosovo made it easy for the media to present a story of good and evil. Although both the U.S. media and the Clinton administration frequently invoked the Second World War's clear moral imperative in order to justify NATO's intervention in Kosovo, such instances of nostalgia also provided the opportunity for the West to rewrite its racist history, as it now presented a unified front against barbarity. With the United States and Germany no longer being the sites of genocide and Western Europe no longer the stage for the horrors of war, a unified West could finally symbolize its own redemption as it enacted its new imperial right to military aggression across the globe. While the West can recognize "racism" in contemporary instances of "ethnic conflict" by filtering it through the privileged frame of the Holocaust, it conceals its own context of domestic racial troubles, such as violent racism toward new immigrants, and new imperial ambitions, which unite Western capitalist states in the NATO alliance at present.

Media Technologies: Documenting the Horrors of a Humanitarian Crisis

The entrenchment of the Holocaust as a historical analogy for "ethnic cleansing" and the Gothic frame as a cultural repertoire for understanding humanitarian imperial technologies came together in media technologies rationalizing Operation Allied Force as a humanitarian and just war. A crucial task undertaken by the U.S. media was the humanization of NATO's military intervention. This had to do with the imperative to manage the contradiction between the images of high-tech warfare that U.S. audiences saw each day of the aerial campaign, and the accompanying rhetoric that this was a war fought in the name of a global humanity. The increased role of the media in postsocialist warfare, and the ways that Western journalism was portrayed in relation to the pursuit of human rights through militarism, became important for managing the paradoxical association between war and human salvation that underwrote the new humanitarian imperialism.

Attempts to redefine the U.S. media's role in the 1990s as an unbiased witness to humanitarian crises elided the collusion between media technologies that enable instant transmission of news and images, and new military technologies in the construction of modern wars. This was especially the case in Operation Allied Force, in which the Western media took on the role of documenting war crimes for use by the International Criminal Tribunal. The drive to document and therefore bring to light monstrous acts and horrific otherness through new media technologies, which affirms the objectivity and scientific authority of the Euro-American observer, is one of the central fantasies of the Gothic. In the present day, journalistic reports function similarly as a genre that documents and brings to light local and global developments. In instances of war, the scales of atrocity committed by the enemy, or in distant places embroiled in conflict, tend to be portrayed as unimaginable. Vivid images of suffering and death are circulated and reproduced, feeding the never-ending cycles of crisis and resolution produced by twenty-four-hour news networks. In spite of the sensational and spectacular composition and visual and narrative framing of such images, contemporary journalists emphasize objectivity in how information and news are transmitted to audiences. Especially in the reporting of distant horrors, the U.S. media insist on their independence from state control.[74] According to the Society of Professional Journalists,

> the history of journalism and the history of the laws of war are often intertwined. . . . Often, it is the journalists who are in the unique position of being able to combine reports from combatants and civilians, non-governmental organizations and government officials into a coherent and compelling account and to disseminate that account to a large audience. It is each journalist's responsibility to make that account as complete and as accurate as possible.[75]

In spite of the journalistic ideal of impartiality and fairness, the contradictions inherent in the concept of militaristic humanitarianism underscore the impossibility of unbiased media documentation.

Media coverage of the 1990s humanitarian crises cannot simply be seen as the objective documentation of horrors that worked to generate public empathy and urge governmental intervention. The crises themselves must be understood as media events that were produced in conjunction with Euro-American national and economic interests. Throughout the 1990s, academic considerations of the Western media's interaction with the state centered on the extent to which media documentation of humanitarian disasters influenced their governments to intervene in troubled regions. For instance, Piers Robinson's work on the "CNN effect" relies on Somalia, Iraq, Bosnia, Kosovo, and Rwanda as case studies for examining the extent to which the print and televised media's "attention to the human consequences of 'distant' civil wars" led to intervention.[76] Robinson concludes that "under conditions of policy uncertainty and critical and empathy-framed media coverage, the news media can be a factor in influencing policy-makers to use air power in pursuit of humanitarian objectives. No evidence was found that media coverage could cause policy-makers to pursue the more risky option of deploying ground troops during humanitarian crises."[77] Because Robinson's media-state model only considers the effects of the media on state intervention, his study ultimately reduces the state–media relationship to that of unidirectional influence. In contrast, the 1999 NATO campaign suggests that it is crucial to address media and military technologies as coconstitutive in managing humanitarian catastrophes. As Mirjana Skoco and William Woodger have shown, since the 1991 Gulf War, the U.S. military has strategically shifted its policy toward the media and has begun to share its operations' details with journalists in order to satiate the demands of twenty-four-hour news coverage. The military now provides the media with "good stories" but continues to exclude "sensitive" information from the public domain.[78] Relying on military publications and military academies' course descriptions, Skoco and Woodger conclude that since the end of the Cold War, the U.S. military has increasingly relied on the media to sell its policy to the public through "'compelling stories of human values.'"[79]

In spite of this trend, during Operation Allied Force the myth of an independent Western media that objectively documented the horrors of ethnic cleansing was crucial to justifying NATO's military aggression as a "humanitarian intervention" based in universal human values. Conversely, NATO demonized the Serbian media, arguing that it was a tool used by Milošević to indoctrinate his own people. On March 24, 1999, the day that NATO launched its air strikes against Serbia and Kosovo, the Serbian authorities arrested and expelled from the country most Western journalists. While the Milošević regime "assailed CNN as a 'factory of lies'" and accused the Western media of being a "part of the whole attack structure," U.S. journalists and media heads were not only frightened by the "harrowing experience" of "deportation" but also scrambling to find alternative intelligence sources in order to secure accurate reports from the war front.[80] The expulsion of Western journalists from Serbia and Kosovo was widely interpreted as Milošević's attempt to monopolize the global circulation of war images and to conceal the horror of Serbian war crimes from Western eyes. U.S. journalists argued that the action consolidated Milošević's totalitarian control through Radio Television Serbia (RTS). U.S. print and televised media thus contrasted themselves to RTS, whose headquarters were eventually demolished during the NATO air strikes, by presenting themselves as non-nationalist organizations and independent participants coming to the aid of hapless victims in the Balkans.

One of NATO's "humanitarian" aims, therefore, became installing a free and independent press in Serbia. Jamie Shea, NATO's primary spokesperson during Operation Allied Force, argued that Radio Television Serbia was "spreading hatred and creating this political environment of repression."[81] NATO's depiction of the Serbian media as illiberal and repressive legitimized its targeting of RTS in the middle of its campaign. On April 23, NATO bombed the RTS building in downtown Belgrade while there were at least 120 civilians working inside.[82] Even though sixteen civilians were killed in the attack, NATO officials insisted that RTS was part of the "national command network" and that "our forces struck at the regime leadership's ability to transmit their version of the news" by taking out the "source of propaganda."[83] By destroying RTS, the alliance affirmed that it recognized the media as a weapon during times of war—though, paradoxically, it only acknowledged it to be a weapon in the enemy's hands. In NATO's perspective, the Serbian media were turned into legitimate military targets because they were biased and therefore tools of Milošević's regime. Rather than expressing concern over NATO's destruction of a media network, as they had over being expelled from Yugoslavia, U.S. journalists echoed NATO's rhetoric that the destruction of RTS had hit the "heart of the propaganda machine."[84] By distinguishing propaganda from journalism, the U.S. media affirmed their supposed roles as independent and unbiased sources of news that documented global horrors for the Western public.

NATO's attempts to control information went beyond its cooperation with the Western media. When *Wired* magazine dubbed Operation Allied Force the "first internet war," it implied that in this war new media provided a forum in which different points of view could be expressed and that, at least to an extent, information flows were democratized. After the war, Jamie Shea acknowledged the influence of the Internet on warfare by positing that "in the future NATO needs to be 'more dynamic and creative' in obtaining access to enemy media in order to 'level the playing field.'"[85] In the context of Western technological might, however, leveling the playing field is only significant insofar as promoting the vision of Western warfare as humanitarian and moral remains a foremost concern. Goran Gocić suggests that in the case of Operation Allied Force, though the Yugoslav media's response to NATO bombings was much more sophisticated than

NATO's message, in a war in which "the technologically superior winner is known in advance, resistance significantly shifts in the realm of the symbolic."[86] Gocić concludes that since a pro-NATO stance was unthinkable during the bombing, far from liberating the Serbian media NATO in fact destroyed the widespread opposition to the Milošević regime that had been building in the 1990s. New media are not automatically democratizing forces; instead, media must be understood as instruments and technologies. As NATO's Operation Allied Force demonstrated, new technologies continually shift and redefine the mutually constitutive roles of the military and media in warfare.

In spite of being the "first internet war," the traditionally dominant forms of Western media (network and cable news, and major newspapers) continued to be the primary sources of news for Western audiences. During Operation Allied Force, the Western media tended to represent the war from the point of view of the new military technologies. Cable and network news sources broadcast cockpit scenes from fighter jets that deployed night vision technology and computerized target demolition, a common practice since the 1991 Gulf War. Unlike in the first Gulf War, images of NATO's airpower were regularly juxtaposed with images of refugee columns and mass graves. Viewed side by side, the violence of Western military might was refigured as a benevolent force in the service of conflict resolution. The aerial campaign provided a "war fit for Western eyes," in which NATO's mistakes and "collateral damage" were justified by footage of the Albanian refugees.[87] The media interpreted the scenes of burning villages and streaming refugees as evidence of the medieval warfare methods used by the Serbs. These scenes provided a contrast to NATO's technological warfare, which appeared to be enlightened and humanitarian. Although after the campaign it became evident that the majority of Kosovar refugees were displaced due to NATO air strikes, during the war, the images, which mostly focused on displaced women, children, and the elderly, provided "the visual alibi for U.S. and NATO intervention by establishing a national narrative about U.S. power and political good."[88] NATO's ambitions in Serbia and Kosovo were never simply, or even primarily, to stop Serbian violence against Kosovar Albanians. Rather, the U.S. media's adoption of NATO's military perspective, juxtaposed with scenes of the refugees, highlights the way in which the media contributed to the erasure of NATO's role as one of the warring parties with its own interests in securing economic and political control over the last "rogue" nation in Europe. By presenting NATO's military perspective of a benevolent intervention from the sky, the U.S.

OSTRUZNICA HIGHWAY BRIDGE, SERBIA
POST STRIKE

Figure 6. A repertoire of military images was used to represent the view of the aerial campaign. This one shows the successful destruction of a bridge in Serbia.

media confirmed President Clinton's rhetoric that this was a war of human values fighting the vestiges of Balkan barbarity and masked U.S. interest in "developing" Eastern Europe and pursuing its own economic interests there.

Ironically, the technologies of Western humanitarianism mirrored Milošević's own drive to "destroy," especially when it became evident that NATO bombings severely increased the number of refugees in Kosovo. The day after the air strikes began, NATO's Supreme Allied Commander, the American general Wesley Clark, declared:

> The military mission is to attack Yugoslav military and security forces and associated facilities with sufficient effect to degrade its capacity to continue repression of the civilian population and to deter its further military actions against his own people. We aim to put its military and security forces at risk. We are going to systematically and progressively attack, disrupt, degrade, devastate and ultimately destroy these forces and their facilities and support, unless President Milošević complies with the demands of the international community. In that respect the operation will be as long and difficult as President Milošević requires it to be.[89]

In Clark's assessment, it is humanitarianism that motivates NATO to "attack, disrupt, degrade, devastate and . . . destroy." NATO's "humanitarianism" seemed to need to give in to violence in order to force Milošević to comply.

Nonetheless, the U.S. media represented military technology not just as a technology of war but also as a technology of human rights that could gather evidence of ethnic cleansing. Just as Stoker's novel depicted new technologies of the Victorian era through which the vampire hunters documented Dracula's vampirism, so the Western media replayed images from satellite and reconnaissance photographs that revealed mass graves as evidence of Serbian war crimes. In her analysis of the satellite view of mass graves in Srebrenica photographed during the civil war in Bosnia, Lisa Parks argues that U.S. officials interpreted the images as objective and omniscient, claiming that they had "acquired evidence of genocide."[90] In the context of the international community's passivity during the war in Bosnia, Parks reads the satellite images as indicators of "distant technologised monitoring," passive voyeurism, and the "refusal to acknowledge (put into discourse) the complex political, socio-historical, economic and cultural conditions that have given rise to the recent conflicts in the former Yugoslavia."[91] Though in Operation Allied Force satellite technologies continued to function reductively, they no longer proved Western passivity, but instead the photographs of unconfirmed (and in many instances never confirmed) graves were used as evidence to fuel support for NATO's civilized humanitarianism against Serbian barbarity. Indeed, claiming that it is more difficult to argue with satellite and reconnaissance images than with eyewitnesses, the U.S. media explicitly recalled the Bosnia images to construct a time line of Serbian atrocities and to uphold the imperative for Western intervention.[92] As one reporter put it, "along the blood-spattered timeline of Slobodan Milošević, Kosovo is merely the hideous Now."[93]

Another strategy that the Western media utilized to bridge the distance between the highly technologized view of targets in Serbia and Kosovo and the purported humanitarian values of the military campaign was to personify the targets in the figure of Milošević. The Western media and military discourses about "degrading" Milošević's capabilities were based in the extreme gap between high-tech and low-tech war-waging potentials, since referencing the precision of high-tech weapons was crucial for developing metaphors about taking out targets located in the body of a single individual. Each time NATO took out "strategic" targets in Serbia and Kosovo, NATO spokespeople and the U.S. media represented the military acts as attacks on Milošević's "organism." In the prominent example of

NATO's demolition of RTS, which was viewed by the U.S. media as the heart of the Milošević propaganda machine, Jamie Shea set the precedent for the use of such metaphors connecting the vital systems of the human body with the vital systems constituting the state. He proposed that by demolishing RTS, NATO had struck at the "central nerve system of the Milošević regime."[94] The term "surgical" air strike, which was first used during the Gulf War, thus took on new meaning during Operation Allied Force. The spectacular showing of "overwhelming or decisive force," which was represented as being put to use against a single criminal, masked the damage to civilian life, including that done to the ethnic Albanians whom the technology was supposed to rescue from Milošević's tyranny.[95] In doing so, military and media technologies inscribed Western violence as just in contradistinction to individuated and pathologized religiously and racially motivated rogue forms of aggression.

In addition to humanizing NATO's militarized perspective on the war, the U.S. media refigured their own role in the war as that of war crime witnesses as they documented the refugee crisis and Serbian war crimes. The structure of most broadcast news reports during the seventy-four days of air strikes cut from images of NATO planes taking off and the digitalized images of targets to columns of refugees crossing the border into neighboring Macedonia and Albania. In this context, U.S. journalists saw their role in interviewing Albanian survivors as supplementing that of military technologies, since they argued that their interviews preserved evidence in a landscape that was emptied of people.[96] Indeed, "news organizations such as ABC . . . have willingly contributed documentaries, news reports and unbroadcast 'rushes' to the ICTY," the International Criminal Tribunal for the Former Yugoslavia.[97] Associating themselves with the ICTY and using familiar human rights genres, such as witness accounts and testimony, to frame their coverage of the war as an unbiased mode of documenting human rights atrocities, the U.S. media concealed their connection to and dependence on one of the warring parties—the U.S.-led NATO. Moreover, by depicting the war as being purely about human rights, it was implied that the United States and NATO were not participants in a war but, rather, benevolent interveners. The emergent conception of the U.S. media as an impartial technology documenting human rights violations through witness testimony thus elided the orchestration of Operation Allied Force as a coordinated media–military event. What is lost is that the U.S. media and the U.S.-led NATO used both visual and military technologies to shape the spaces of atrocity that they then "witnessed." The reconceptualization of postsocialist humanitarian imperial projects as nonracist and moral depended on such erasures.

In a special episode of ABC's *Nightline* about the difficulties of waging peace in Kosovo following the gradual return of Kosovar Albanian refugees to their homes, Ted Koppel, reporting from the scene, encapsulated the new role of the media as embodying the struggle for human rights and universal values.[98] Koppel and his team, who were riding through Kosovo in an armored vehicle, came across a group of Kosovar Albanian children who mistook them for NATO troops. As more and more children gathered, shouting "NATO! NATO! NATO!" Koppel explained to them that he and his crew were not NATO but, as the Western media, were the harbingers of liberation. The Kosovar children's confusion in their initial encounter with the *ABC News* crew, as well as Koppel's implication that the Western media's presence preceded the possibility of Western occupation or "liberation," demonstrates the need for media and military cooperation in framing contemporary U.S. wars. The distinction between media and military roles in times of war has only become more blurred in the current U.S. occupation of Iraq due to the practice of "embedding" journalists. The media police, collect evidence, and are upheld as impartial witnesses in contemporary warfare, neglecting the fact that it is ultimately media coverage that distinguishes between "collateral damage" and "victims." In this connection, U.S. journalists' upholding of NATO's militarism as humanistic and just, which removed NATO from consideration as one of the warring parties, belied the media's self-proclaimed role of objectively documenting atrocities and building a more "human" view of the conflict in Kosovo.

Postsocialist Imperial Sovereignty and International Law

The use of media and military technologies of documentation to apprehend war crimes, alongside the Holocaust analogy, facilitated NATO's invocation of international human rights law as justifying Operation Allied Force. The military operation explicitly referenced the Geneva Conventions, which established new regulations after World War II to prevent future wars and to outlaw war crimes, crimes against humanity, torture, and genocide in all instances of armed conflict. NATO itself, however, violated international law, the UN charter (by bypassing the Security Council), and its own founding charter (which established NATO as a defensive alliance). Like the early attempts at modernizing and codifying law during the time of Euro-American imperialist expansion, NATO's violation of international law opened up a space in which the West could create new law to justify its interventionism. The cultural invocation of Gothic inhumanity and monstrosity in the Balkans, which reaffirmed the U.S.-led West as a site of humanity and justice, was once again crucial for this shift. Through the opposition between the horrific monstrosity of ethnic cleansing and the ethical responsibility of Western humanitarian intervention, NATO militarism was portrayed as fighting on behalf of natural law and the rights of man, which preceded and trumped the letter of the international law. Following international law and charters, in other words, was represented as the choice that would have perpetuated the humanitarian catastrophe in Kosovo.

NATO's act of war established the sovereign right of the Euro-American powers to decide on the international juridical order. If, as Carl Schmitt famously argued in the context of Nazi Germany, the sovereign is the one who decides, then at issue is not just that Operation Allied Force violated Yugoslavia's sovereignty, as many scholars have pointed out. Rather, NATO's intervention established a new international juridical imperative in which (Euro-American) nations that establish themselves as spaces of rights, fighting against human rights violations in places marked by atrocity (the Global South and parts of Eastern Europe), need not follow the letter of the international law. In his work on the juridical and political constitution of modern governance, Giorgio Agamben builds on Schmitt's concept of "exception" and sovereignty to argue that the state of exception, in which the rule of law is suspended, undergirds a structure of sovereignty based in a juridical order that can only establish the norm in the suspension of the law.[99] In his most recent work, Agamben argues that "the state of exception increasingly tends to appear as the dominant paradigm of government in contemporary politics."[100] While Agamben's argument is based on the George W. Bush administration's suspension of the *national* juridical order enacted in the USA PATRIOT Act, NATO's Operation Allied Force can also be considered as the occasion and post–World War II precedent for the United States' suspension of *international* law. In other words, the "new" sovereign right to declare the state of exception in the international juridical order establishes the imperial sovereignty of the United States, a sovereignty that is based in its military and technological power. Since it went against the UN charter, Kosovo became a precedent for the United States to assert its sovereign right to decide on the exception to international law and its postsocialist imperial sovereignty.

Ever since Operation Allied Force set a precedent for deciding on the exception to international law, humanitarianism has become central to justifying each instance of U.S. interventionism that bypasses international approval. Indeed, the "new" imperial sovereignty claims to embody and spread human values. During the NATO air strikes, Jack Goldsmith, a professor of international law, argued that humanitarian emergencies provide an exception to international law "by custom and practice," though in the instance of U.S. interventionism the debates over legality remain largely theoretical because no nation-state or international organization can hold the United States accountable.[101] Because NATO's disregard for the UN charter raised critical questions about the force of international law and the legitimacy of the United Nations, those supporting the NATO air strikes quickly acknowledged that though technically illegal, NATO's cause was morally justified, and its military actions were therefore legitimate. Václav Havel, like President Clinton, argued that NATO's air strikes were the first war to fully privilege principles and values over national interests. He claimed that this war "did not happen irresponsibly, as an act of aggression or out of disrespect for international law. It happened, on the contrary, out of respect for the law, for the law that ranks higher than the law which protects sovereignty of states."[102] Any argument in favor of "just war," such as Havel's, demands closer consideration of who defines justice and decides on higher law. The report of the Brookings Institution, for instance, found that

> NATO had moral and strategic rectitude on its side in using military power in the Balkans. First, upholding human rights and alleviating humanitarian tragedy are worthy goals for American national security policy. Doing so reinforces the notion that the United States is not interested in power for its own sake but rather to enhance stability and security and to promote certain universal principles and values.[103]

The Brookings report tries to argue, as did Havel, that the universal principles of humanitarian law, which the United States and its allies were supposedly attempting to uphold, legitimized NATO's air strikes. In the end, however, the report has difficulty distinguishing between "universal principles and values" and U.S. national security and interests. The conflation between U.S. national interests and universal ideals forecloses the possibility that the United States itself would ever need to submit its actions to the judgment of an international court. By blurring the line between a higher moral law that suspends international law and Western national interests, the doctrine of humanitarian intervention legitimizes U.S. and Western global military presence.[104]

NATO's violation of the UN charter affirmed and upheld the U.S.-led West as a space that already embodies universal values and human rights and that therefore has the right to judge and punish the violators of the laws upon which it has decided. The Independent International Commission on Kosovo tried to account for the indeterminate space in international law opened up by Operation Allied Force. In its assessment of the war in Kosovo, the Commission concluded that because NATO's actions were legitimate but illegal, in cases of "genocide," the international community needs to recognize a "grey zone" that goes "beyond strict ideas of *legality* to incorporate more flexible views of *legitimacy*."[105] The Commission's proposal for a more "flexible approach" in instances of humanitarian crises raises a crucial point about the disjuncture between the law and the ideals of human rights and the principles of justice. Nevertheless, if NATO's violent humanitarianism is to be the precedent for a more "flexible approach" to international law, it has become clear that only the United States has the sovereign right to decide on the worthy values and the worthy crisis, and that it prevents other nations from doing so. As Nelson Mandela stressed in his introduction to the Kosovo Commission's report, "It has now become so customary to point to the failure of the international community to intervene and end the genocide in Rwanda that it is almost forgotten that this relative neglect of Africa in these matters is much more general than only the Rwanda case."[106]

The climax of NATO's Operation Allied Force was the criminal indictment of Slobodan Milošević. In this process, Milošević was identified with Hitler and Stalin, a composite figure of evil, like Stoker's Count Dracula. Like the vampire, who is described in the novel as a "criminal type," Milošević was the figure in the 1990s against whom the U.S.-led West established a new global order in which the West continually reimagines the face of the enemy and dubs it criminal. Diana Johnstone has argued that as the sole superpower in the post–Cold War era, the United States has devised a system of crime and punishment, underwritten by humanitarianism, which has become the justification for its global acts of military aggression.[107] Similarly, according to Alex Callinicos, the importance of the criminal in the new world order structures the dominant language of rights, justice, and law through which international affairs become depoliticized as the judicial order of crime and punishment (upon which the West has decided) becomes supreme.[108] The U.S. government's offer of a $5 million reward for the capture of Slobodan Milošević was one such highly publicized figuration of an outlaw dictator; the "Wanted" posters that circulated in the U.S. media refigured NATO's actions, ascribing to them the authority to police the international order and excluding the Euro-American alliance's actions from the scrutiny of international law. Like the packs of playing cards issued to U.S. soldiers in Iraq that featured Saddam Hussein and his officials, the poster of Slobodan Milošević provided a cultural reference through which the U.S. public could understand U.S. military action as an execution of justice.

Following his capture and extradition to The Hague in 2001, Milošević was put on trial for crimes against humanity in front of the International Criminal Tribunal for the Former Yugoslavia. Milošević's trial has been described as "the world's most closely watched criminal proceeding since the case of O. J. Simpson."[109] By removing the "last" Eastern European Fascist and Communist dictator—Milošević—and standing in judgment of what were depicted as his racially and religiously motivated crimes, the West was not only able to definitively add closure to the binaries of good and evil that constituted the Cold War framework but also able to establish new standards of morality for the "new world order." The emergent paradigm of humanitarian intervention and imperialism recognized Western capitalism as a system that provides for its citizens through "democracy," liberalism, and tolerance and opposes its system to the "horror" and barbarity of ethnic and religious conflict in non-Western and underdeveloped regions. The prominent journalist Roger Cohen described this opposition in his assessment that "modern American life is untethered to place, unlimited by distance, mostly untouched by horror. Not so in the Balkans, where real or imagined past Serbian suffering was the stuff of Mr. Milošević's invective."[110] According to Cohen, U.S. military aggression offers the Serbs democracy: "Communism promised equality. Hitler promised the 1,000-year Reich. Milošević promised glory. All the West offers, alongside the prosperity of this boardwalk, is the rule of law."

Authorizing the representational and legal systems of postsocialist humanitarian imperialism, political and media discourses recalled the narrative tropes of European imperialism, pointing to civilizational connections between Europe and the United States while at the same time underscoring the liberal democratic and antiracist nature of U.S. postsocialist power. To emphasize changes in Euro-American ideologies between the eras of European imperialism, the Cold War, and the postsocialist era, spaces like the Balkans had to be depicted as unchanging. In 1993, after the civil war in Bosnia had begun, the Carnegie Endowment for International

Peace republished its 1913 report on the Balkan Wars of 1912 and 1913 in the hope that it would shed light on the present situation. On the occasion of the report's reissue, the Carnegie Endowment engaged George Kennan, the architect of the U.S. Cold War policy of containment and ambassador to Yugoslavia in the 1960s, to write a new introduction. Kennan took the opportunity to explain the current conflict in the Balkans by drawing a connection between the Balkan Wars at the start of the twentieth century and at its end, concluding that we have today "the same Balkan World" that existed in 1913. [111] Tracing the beginnings of international peace movements and the development of "new legal codes of international behavior" to the Hague Peace Conferences of 1899 and 1907, which addressed "the Eastern question" and the Balkans, Kennan imagines the origins of the Euro-American alliance in the desire for peace, law, and justice against Balkan violence, that had ignited the First World War in Europe just as it had the 1999 war.

Contrary to Kennan's understanding that the Balkans interrupted the Euro-American progression toward global cooperation and peace, early attempts at codifying international law in the 1880s were rooted in the European "scramble for Africa" and in the imperialist nations' desire to create international laws that would legitimize their right to global expansion. Accounting for the divergent interests of the different European powers and the United States eventually culminated in the First World War. At the end of the twentieth century, the civilizational dilemmas of Western imperial power were once again at stake in the problem of the Balkans. Kennan's introduction to the reissue of the Carnegie Endowment report is striking in that although Kennan was himself a key figure in the formation of Cold War policy, his rhetoric in the report parallels the shift in U.S. policy from containment toward humanitarian imperialism justified in the name of international human rights law. The policy of containment maintained the United States' right to intervene in and protect its spheres of influence from Soviet "imperialism." In the "new world order," the U.S.-led West no longer struggles against a single site of evil, but it establishes its right to intervene in the name of human rights against multiple "rogue" states and dictatorships. Of major significance in the new doctrine of humanitarian intervention is that the United States conceives of its contemporary imperial projects as moral through ideas of freedom and tolerance, excluding itself from the scrutiny of international law, even as it decides when and where to punish rogue violators.

Operation Allied Force represented the first clear articulation and justification for postsocialist imperialism as the post–Cold War decade drew to a close. Opposing ethnic cleansing and human rights violations in the Balkans throughout the 1990s and, in 1999, finally battling Balkan prejudices with military force seemed to position U.S. force on the side of human rights and universal human good. This set the context for further U.S. militarism in the post-9/11 era, this time against non-European Muslim majority nations, to be read as continuing the struggle for liberal democratic values and tolerance already begun in the 1990s on behalf of Muslims. As new conceptions of "humanity" emerge from the violent mechanisms of humanitarian "empire lite," older imperial and Cold War notions of good and evil are both revived and reframed.

5 THE FEMINIST POLITICS OF SECULAR REDEMPTION AT THE INTERNATIONAL CRIMINAL TRIBUNAL FOR THE FORMER YUGOSLAVIA

THE 2009 THRILLER *Storm*, which dramatizes the political intrigues of the International Criminal Tribunal for the Former Yugoslavia (ICTY) in The Hague, frames the search for postwar justice in international courts of law as a story about faith.[1] The film begins at the moment a prosecutor at the Tribunal, Hannah Maynard, takes over a high-profile war crimes case against a Yugoslav National Army commander. During the trial, the defendant's attorney unexpectedly demonstrates that the prosecution's chief witness, Alen Hajdarević, has lied about seeing Serb forces loading Bosnian Muslims onto buses for deportation. In an early scene, Alen and Hannah have a conversation about his testimony outside of the courtroom. Alen, a Muslim, tells Hannah that he prayed before taking the stand, and he asks her how she prepares before a trial. Dismissing the notion of divine intervention in a secular institution, Hannah tells him, facetiously, that she eats chocolate. Later, when a trip to Bosnia definitively proves that Alen could not have seen the incident to which he claimed to be an eyewitness, he pleads with Hannah to continue to trust him that the commander on trial is indeed a war criminal. "I believe in this court," he proclaims. "It's all I have left!" Alen's faith in the Tribunal, and its function, differs from Hannah's. She tells him, brusquely, that this court deals in facts, not blind revenge, and she asks him to leave. Alen, reduced to his compromised and invalidated testimony, no longer has value as either a witness or, in Hannah's mind, a human being. The next morning he is found dead in his room, having committed suicide by hanging.

Unwavering in her assurance that a true accounting of war crimes can only occur through the procedural workings and authority of the Tribunal, Hannah becomes ever more invested in locating a living witness whose story can confirm, this time without perjury, the guilt of the accused. At

Alen's funeral, she meets his sister, Mira, whom she repeatedly presses for information. A young woman who has left Bosnia and her old life behind to start anew in Germany, Mira initially refuses to talk about the war, asserting that it will not lead to anything good. Eventually she gives in and provides the prosecutor with information not just about the deportation but about a hotel where she and many other Bosnian Muslim women were held captive and repeatedly raped by Serbian soldiers. Mira's new life begins to fall apart as she vividly recalls the sexual violence she suffered during her internment. Unfortunately, her evidence about the hotel, Hannah soon finds out, will be inadmissible because it is not part of the original charges. As Hannah's conviction that the Tribunal can lead to justice for victims falters, she finds it difficult to explain to Mira why she has been made to relive her trauma when her testimony will not be counted or become part of the official record. The recognition of the limits of international humanitarian and criminal law leads Hannah to reassess the Tribunal as the sole locus of hope for the Balkans, recognizing it instead to be a site that produces and consumes people for the sake of its own political and institutional ends. An outgrowth of violence in the former Yugoslavia, like the wars themselves, the Tribunal has the power to devastate and destroy lives, such as those of Alen and Mira and, ultimately, Hannah, who discovers that she herself is expendable in the political machinations of her superiors. Yet unlike the wars, in which lives were lost for the sake of nationalist fantasy, the Tribunal displaces those schemes and visions for the good life that refuse the modes of global humanization produced through the legislative and cultural technologies of the international court of law.

Rather than focus on postwar trauma and the politics of witnessing, two important axes of inquiry taken up in a number of studies of the Bosnian war, this chapter addresses feminist grammars of juridical faith and redemption.[2] The exhumation of dead, injured, and violated bodies by order of the ICTY, and the stories these bodies continue to tell, have become part of a global project of creating an authoritative historical accounting of humanitarian and human rights violations that affirms the need for an international rule of law. Administering and monopolizing ideas about justice in the Balkans, the ICTY calls on the postsocialist world to believe in and work toward becoming a part of a common humanity, which is defined through legislation that affirms the liberal principles of secularism and multicultural tolerance. During and after the 1993–1995 war in Bosnia and Herzegovina following the republic's secession from the former Yugoslavia, an emergent Euro-American humanitarian ethics developed through the consolidation of international juridical regimes of governance. Precisely because the international community saw itself as failing to stop the violence in Bosnia and Herzegovina as it was occurring, the growth and activity of the ICTY over the last two decades has emblematized the possibility for moral action in the region. International tribunals, established by the United Nations as fixtures of the new human rights regime, are simultaneously institutions in which peoples of different nations affirm their commitment to peace and reconciliation, and technologies through which landscapes of human waste are reproduced. Lives and geographies shattered by war, ethnic conflict, and tribalism authorize the continued existence of the Tribunal as the mechanism through which humanity can deliver itself from states of inhumanity.

Through the workings of the Tribunal, Bosnia has emerged as an investigational field within which feminist activists, jurists, politicians, and artists have made meaning of the postsocialist moral reordering of the world. Of the bodies that have figured as evidence of atrocity in the ICTY, as *Storm* illustrates, none have been as prominent as that of the raped and violated Bosnian Muslim woman. The issue of rape warfare in Bosnia, which has been conceived of as simultaneously historically and politically exceptional and exemplary, has been important for the convergence of feminist activism and the field of international law. Among its chief achievements, the ICTY cites novel developments in feminist jurisprudence. On February 22, 2001, six years after the official end to the violence in Bosnia, the Tribunal issued a groundbreaking ruling that three Bosnian Serb soldiers were guilty of crimes against humanity for raping and sexually enslaving Bosnian Muslim women. "This was the first time that rape [and sexual violence] have been [classified as torture] and prosecuted and condemned as crime[s] against humanity."[3] The ruling was important for feminist human rights activists in that, finally, women's embodied subjectivity stood for the abstract human of human rights.[4] However, constructing Bosnian Muslim women as victims of crimes against a universalized humanity not perpetrated by the supposedly patriarchal structures of Islam itself required that they first be portrayed as secular, modern, and European in contrast to dominant conceptions of Muslim women in the Middle East.

Building on the previous chapters' analysis of postsocialist humanitarian imperialism and the racialization of religious difference, I argue that the connection between the progress narrative of Euro-American feminism concerned with human rights and the discursive production of faith in the international institutions of law necessitated the secularization of Bosnian Muslim women. Tracing the relationship between the gendered discourses of ethnoreligious violence and juridical redemption, I map the co-articulation of the Tribunal and the camp. The international reaction to the war in Bosnia and the understanding that post–Cold War notions of humanity and morality would take shape through a stance against Balkan violence were fused in Euro-American feminist responses to the war, particularly in the outcry against what came to be known as the "rape and death camps." This response was further developed after the war through what can be thought of as the Tribunal's forensic investigations into the war in Bosnia in the postwar era, which have taken place continuously from 1993 to the present day. By forensic investigation, I mean not just the unearthing of mass graves but also the production of bodies (as witnesses, fictional characters, and ethnographic subjects) whose images, words, and stories become the fragments through which an "authentic" historical account is created as part of a therapeutic project that will bring the Balkans back into the fold of humanity following their wartime dehumanization in the 1990s.

The chapter begins with an overview of the scope and operations of the Tribunal, outlining the relationship between juridical humanization and the making of postsocialist humanity. Next I address how the new humanitarianism of the ICTY emerged at the epistemological juncture of multicultural and feminist progress narratives, making women's human rights the foremost symbol of juridical redemption for the Balkans. Because multicultural and feminist frames for humanitarian law necessitated the secularization of Bosnian Muslim women, I then analyze how Bosnian Islam was accommodated within a postsocialist imaginary of "new" Europe. To conclude, I discuss the relationship of the sacred and the secular in international human rights regimes. Proposing that the sacredness of human life through the institutionalization of liberal rights necessitates that modern global subjects profess their faith in the human rights regime, I analyze the Tribunal as a site of conversion in the new world order. Yet by disrupting and interrupting the narratives of justice produced by institutions such as the Tribunal, heterogeneous and different possibilities for the future continue to be imagined in the realm of culture. As this chapter concludes, fantasies and hopes that refuse to capitulate to the narrow yet universalizing definitions of freedom and democracy offered by liberal discourses of international human rights are important for conceiving of an alternative politics.

The Tribunal

In the history of humanitarian and human rights law that includes European imperial lawmaking and the post–World War II declarations of universal human rights, the ICTY marks the advent of juridical and institutional technologies underlying postsocialist imperialism. A counterpart to the humanitarian military violence discussed in previous chapters, the ICTY and other international tribunals use human rights and humanitarian law as modes of geopolitical governance that bring rogue nations and their inhabitants into the fold of postsocialist humanity. Like modern law in the colonial era, the expansive interpretation of humanitarian and human rights law establishes a temporal narrative in which not only individuals but nations and regions leave the past and become human in different historical moments (and at different rates).[5] Unlike colonial law, which bound its subjects to the authority of the state, international humanitarian law—institutionalized in courts of law whose authority some nations are obliged to recognize in order to receive international loans and aid, while others are not—establishes the new human rights regime as a way of acting on and enacting unequal sovereignties in the name of producing a common humanity.

A locus of juridical humanization for the non-Western world, the Tribunal recenters Euro-American procedural and moral norms of justice even as it claims to be mindful of cultural and contextual differences (particularly those of gender, race, and religion). Established as a court of law in The Hague, the Netherlands, by a United Nations Security Council mandate in 1993, the ICTY was the first war crimes court in existence since the Nuremberg and Tokyo post–World War II tribunals. With the Security Council's Resolution 827, the ICTY was formed "for the sole purpose of prosecuting persons responsible for serious violations of international humanitarian law committed in the territory of the former Yugoslavia."[6] During the debates on Resolution 827, it became clear that the ICTY would be conceived of as a different kind of tribunal, with the goal of engendering a new and more robust international concept of justice than did the Nuremberg and Tokyo Trials. The formation of the Tribunal prior to the conclusion of the wars over which the ICTY was to have primary jurisdiction framed the role of the United Nations, led by the Western European and U.S. nations, as that of chronicler of war crimes as they were occurring. Unlike the contained postwar trials of Nuremberg, which lasted from 1945 to 1949, and Tokyo, which took place from 1946 to 1948, the ICTY has been trying war criminals continuously from 1993 through the present.[7] In further contrast to the post–World War II tribunals, the ICTY's mandate is not to single out nations or ethnic or religious groups for punishment but, rather, to try those individuals accused of perpetrating crimes of war and crimes against humanity.[8] In this connection, former U.S. secretary of state Madeleine Albright stated, "This will be no victor's tribunal. The only victor that will prevail in this endeavor is the truth."[9] As evidence of fulfilling this primary mission, the ICTY is careful to point out that although the largest number of the accused are Serbs, "the Tribunal has investigated and brought charges against persons from every ethnic background."[10] Thus its principles and purpose are envisioned as having a more universal scope that will permanently influence the postsocialist geopolitical landscape.

The ICTY is explicit about being an activist institution, citing its cases as evidence that "efficient and transparent international justice is viable," and that it is possible to expand "the boundaries of international humanitarian and international criminal law, both in terms of substance and procedure."[11] Thus far "the Tribunal has indicted 161 [individuals] accused for crimes committed against . . . victims during the conflicts in Croatia (1991–1995), Bosnia and Herzegovina (1992–1995), Kosovo (1998–1999) and the Former Yugoslav Republic of Macedonia (2001)."[12] Over four thousand witnesses have testified. The Tribunal operates three trial chambers and one appeals chamber; maintains the divisions of the Office of the President, the Office of the Prosecutor, and the Office of the Registrar (which manages the witnesses and the accused); and runs the detention center. Employing nearly nine hundred staff members, the ICTY's operating budget has exceeded $200,000,000 each year since 2002, reaching $342,332,300 in 2008–2009.[13] As a long-standing and well-funded institutional fixture on the landscape of international justice in the postsocialist era, the ICTY is considered a model for other tribunals and international institutions of law, such as the International Criminal Tribunal for Rwanda (ICTR), founded in 1994, and the permanent International Criminal Court (ICC), established in 2002 through the ratification of the Rome Statute UN Treaty.[14]

The institutionalization of juridical activism in the development of an international human rights regime, of which the growth and importance of the ICTY is an example and a constitutive component, has largely been lauded as an actualization of a global humanitarian ethics. However, the growth of human rights as a framework outside of which it is increasingly difficult to conceptualize justice and transnational activism is a historically and culturally particular occurrence enabled by the demise of communism. First, in the geopolitical sense, the landscape of international relations has drastically changed since 1989. According to Rachel Kerr, the founding of the ICTY was made possible by an unprecedented "convergence of legal, political and diplomatic circumstances."[15] With the mandate to create the ICTY following the 1992 report on the war filed by the Commission of Experts, the UN Security Council expanded the previous Cold War–era understanding of the kinds of events and occurrences that constitute threats to peace and security in order to include intrastate as well as interstate conflicts. Kerr explains that this rearrangement of power was critical to the evolution of international humanitarian and international criminal law, leading to the transformation in the interpretation of the Security Council's authority that allowed for a juridical institution to be created through a political mandate.[16] Second, and more significant, the demise of communism has led to a narrowing of the range of visions of justice, particularly those that differ from the liberal democratic conception of juridical procedure and individual and minority rights.

For inhabitants of the former Yugoslavia, who had until 1990 lived under a system of socialist self-governance, the sort of justice resulting from the rulings of the ICTY has been perceived as limited. On the one hand, the emphasis on transparency and truth as the foundations for justice in the Tribunal tends to be opposed to the Communist regime's procedural obscurity and concealment. On the other hand, the legal reforms that have ushered in the postsocialist era (nationally and transnationally) have also been accompanied by neoliberal economic restructurings. These have exacerbated postwar poverty and inequality in much of the former Yugoslavia, which had been a relatively wealthy nation during the Cold War. Thus, as Isabelle Delpha shows, in Bosnia and Herzegovina, the achievements of the ICTY are viewed as distant and having little effect on day-to-day material hardships.[17] In this sense, the juridical and institutional framework obscures the possibility of economic and social welfare as an equal, if not a more important, site through which injustice and indignity can be apprehended on a global scale. The ICTY's parameters for determining guilt in the former Yugoslavia have also brought to the forefront the problem of unequal sovereignties.[18] Many Bosnians thus feel that the ICTY establishes a new hierarchy of humanity, distinct from the dehumanization of war, and that, as the ones being judged, the citizens of the former Yugoslavia have fallen in the rankings of that hierarchy since the demise of state socialism.[19]

The friction between distinct visions of justice suggests a need to investigate the Tribunal as a postsocialist mode of governance that uses and produces ex-Yugoslavia as a forensic and experimental field through which a postsocialist humanity born of the new international regime of human rights is normalized. In this broader sense, the work of the Tribunal far exceeds its stated mission of "bringing war criminals to justice, [and] bringing justice to victims." Rather, the Tribunal should be thought of as an institution, and as a culture, that displaces previous (socialist) modes of organizing nation and society. In the nations of the former Yugoslavia, these include, for instance, the principles of "brotherhood and unity" (*bratsvo i jedinstvo*), an anti-Fascist Partisan slogan from World War II under which the peoples of the former Yugoslavia united, and which became official policy on interethnic antinationalism in the Socialist Federal Republic of Yugoslavia, and workers' self-management (*radničko samoupravljanje*), a form of workplace decision making directed by workers themselves, pioneered in the former Yugoslavia after Tito's split with the Soviet Union. As socialist ideals are replaced by aspirations for European accession, economic liberalization, and human rights, inhabitants of the former Yugoslavia become postsocialist human beings, governed by the international rule of law.

As part of making new global subjects, the ICTY has been given the authority to confer humanity anew to the Balkans by producing an authoritative historical account of wartime atrocity as a way of reconciling former enemies. Numerous scholars have noted that the work of the ICTY has fundamentally altered the relationship between law and history in unprecedented ways.[20] According to the ICTY website, "The Tribunal has contributed to an indisputable historical record, combating denial and helping communities come to terms with their recent history. Crimes across the region can no longer be denied. For example, it has been proven beyond reasonable doubt that the mass murder at Srebrenica was genocide."[21] Indisputably, the work of accounting and accountability for the crimes of rape, mass murder, and genocide is crucial. However, considering the ICTY's primacy of jurisdiction over the former Yugoslavia, the mandate to produce a single historical narrative indicates that the expansion of international humanitarian and criminal law entails the engineering of individual and collective identities that can take shape only after contradictory and alternate accounts of the past are silenced. Central to the broader project of redeeming the Balkans from their recent inhuman acts, the singular historical narrative places the ICTY as a redemptive end point to the barbarous past. Through the workings of the Tribunal, the peoples of the former Yugoslavia enter the singular narrative of historical progress and are enfolded into universal (Euro-American) humanity. As the ICTY becomes the institutional seat of international juridical power in which Yugoslav barbarism, ethnic separatism, and violence are recounted and recorded as the historical record through the court archives and on the Internet, each recitation and record of inhumanity becomes the condition of possibility for rehumanizing the region through human rights law.

A "New Feminist Consciousness" of Juridical Redemption

The legislative activity of the ICTY over the last two decades, as well as its mission to produce a singular historical account of the wars, has dovetailed, overlapped, and been framed by liberal multiculturalist and feminist epistemologies and notions of progress. The Tribunal's decision to try rape as a crime against humanity for the first time has not just made new meaning of wartime sexual violence against women. More significantly, sexual violence against women has become foundational to the emergent political project of making women's human rights a normative postsocialist technology of moral governance. The hypervisibility of sexual injury in the new human rights culture is based on an evolutionary narrative of humanization, which leads to Euro-American liberal notions of difference and inclusion. After the Dayton Peace Accords, which brought an end to the violence in Bosnia and Herzegovina, feminist writing and activism surrounding the issue of rape warfare provided the groundwork that shaped, on an international scale, the mechanisms of international law mobilized on behalf of women's human rights. More than the other international courts and tribunals, the ICTY has become the locus in which the "new feminist consciousness" articulated its ambitions.[22]

From the start of the war in Bosnia and Herzegovina, U.S. and European feminists took up the issue of rape warfare as a foremost global feminist cause. Several prominent American feminists classified the violence in the former Yugoslavia as the first gendered genocide. In a 1993 opinion piece that appeared in the *New York Times*, Anna Quindlen called the war in Bosnia a "gynocide," while Catharine MacKinnon, that same year, argued in *Ms.* magazine that the rapes against the Bosnian women were a "postmodern genocide."[23] Reports of rape camps, which were sometimes affiliated with detention and exchange camps, and at other times devoted entirely to the captivity of women, came as shocking news. As in other wars, large numbers of women suffered rape or sexual assault during the Yugoslav wars—by some estimates, between twenty thousand and sixty thousand—and many of the rapes resulted in unwanted pregnancies.[24] While all of the warring parties claimed that women of their nationality were raped, Serbian soldiers committed the greatest number of rapes against Bosnian Muslim women. At the conclusion of the war, feminist investment in Bosnia was transferred to the ICTY as the institutional site that could restore the dignity of violated women and make it clear in future wars that crimes against women were war crimes.[25] As Beverly Allen wrote in the conclusion to her book *Rape Warfare*, if Walter Benjamin's angel could peer into and shape the postsocialist future, "it may well be through legal or juridical actions taken in regard to military aggression and war crimes."[26]

For Allen, as for other feminist scholars, the end of the Cold War led to an unprecedented opportunity to mold the institutionalization of global women's human rights.[27] In this respect, it is notable that feminists who are well known in U.S. women's rights struggles took up the issue of rape in Bosnia as the transnationalization of the issues they had fought over domestically in the 1970s and 1980s. Cynthia Enloe's afterword to *Mass Rape*, the most cited book on the wartime rapes in Bosnia, makes this quite explicit. She writes, "The very horror of the post–Cold War war in Bosnia has put rape on the international agenda."[28] Enloe suggests that "by the time Croatians, Serbs, and Bosnians were at war, there had been two decades of feminist work on rape."[29] Citing the history of antirape activism in North America and Western Europe dating back to the 1970s, Enloe proposes that these veteran activists were well prepared to take their struggle from the national courtroom to an international one. She outlines a transnational politics of hope modeled on the U.S. feminist progress narrative, which has led to the international-mindedness of Euro-American feminist publications, and she posits that the critique of Eurocentrism and ethnocentrism headed by Third World and women of color feminists, having made headway in these nations, produced a novel connection among women that is mindful of cultural and local differences. She writes, "These magazines [*Ms.*, *Off Our Backs*, and *Everywoman*] had become much more internationally minded by the early 1990s, thanks in large part to Third World feminists' 1980s critiques of European and North American feminists' parochialism. So it was not mere coincidence that Croatian feminist groups existed at the outbreak of the war and that they had personal contacts with the editors of *Ms*."[30] In this regard, Enloe views the efforts of *Mass Rape* as part of such a new transnational feminist network. Referring to Alexandra Stiglmayer, its editor, Enloe notes, "German feminists in the early 1990s perhaps have a special stake in figuring out just what it means for German women and Bosnian women to share 'Europeanness.' "[31]

A "new feminist consciousness," as Enloe puts it, was possible only when mainstream feminism, having undergone a racial and transnational self-critique, sought to shift the parameters of activism to reenter debates about universality. Fighting to expand the meaning of universal human rights through the rubric of women's rights, feminists working on behalf of rape victims during the war saw the Tribunal as a continuation of their efforts. Indeed, in its two decades of trying war crimes, the ICTY counts its decisions on wartime sexual violence to be among its chief successes, and as such it connects developments in humanitarian law to the successes of Euro-American feminism.[32] According to the ICTY website, "Almost half of those convicted by the ICTY have been found guilty of elements of crimes involving sexual violence. Such convictions are one of the Tribunal's pioneering achievements. They have ensured that treaties and conventions which have existed on paper throughout the 20th century have finally been put in practice, and violations punished."[33] As Patricia Sellers, a prosecution trial attorney and an adviser on issues of gender at the ICTY, noted about the prosecution of wartime sexual violence, "There has been more jurisprudence out of our Tribunal in five years than in the past five hundred years of international criminal courts."[34] For instance, Rule 96 of the Tribunal, enacted in 1994, was considered groundbreaking in facilitating the prosecution of rape. With the rule, victims' testimony requires no corroboration; consent is not an admissible defense, especially if women are subjected to threats or have reason to fear for their own or others' safety; and, finally, prior sexual conduct of the victim is not admissible into evidence.[35]

In addition to procedural developments, the ICTY's rulings provide crucial legal precedents for future courts dealing with cases of rape and sexual violence. In the ICTY's first major decision focusing exclusively on crimes involving sexual violence in 2001, Zoran Vuković, Radomir Kovač, and Dragoljub Kunarac, three Bosnian Serb soldiers, were convicted of crimes against humanity and violations of the laws of war. While a previous ruling by the Rwanda Tribunal was groundbreaking in its decision that rape could constitute a form of genocide, the 2001 ICTY ruling extended jurisprudence on sexual violence by deciding that sexual enslavement was a crime against humanity:

"What the evidence shows," said presiding judge Florence Mumba in a statement read in court, "are Muslim women and girls, mothers and daughters together, robbed of their last vestiges of human dignity. Women and girls, treated like chattels, pieces of property at the arbitrary disposal of the Serb occupation forces, and more specifically at the beck and call of the three accused."[36]

Sellers, elaborating on the significance of the ruling, explained that "for the first time since Nuremberg, [the Foča case] gave us modern jurisprudence under humanitarian law as to what enslavement meant—a person owning sexual access to a victim—which is very important in terms of the legal concept. . . . Enslavement wasn't dependent on being locked in a cell or working in a field with a ball and chains."[37] She also emphasized the universal import of these rulings, clarifying that "gender crimes" were not crimes against women but against "sexual integrity."[38]

Certainly, as some scholars have noted, it is dangerous to equate advances in jurisprudence with justice. Sara Sharratt, for instance, worries that the rulings only produce women as vulnerable, while portraying male victims as courageous survivors.[39] Wendy Hesford similarly warns that the ICTY and "legal remedies may inadvertently perpetuate the most powerful icon in the violent production of gendered identities—the spectacle of female victimization."[40] At the same time, there can be no doubt that the ICTY rulings signal an unprecedented merging of feminist and juridical notions of global progress. In this connection, Debra Berghoffen argues that the Tribunal has permanently changed the landscape of international human rights law and, more importantly, notions of humanity.[41] She proposes that with the creation of a new human right—the right to sexual self-determination—the ICTY validated the dignity of the vulnerable human body.[42] Because the ICTY identified rape as a crime against humanity and not a crime against women, the argument goes, following the 2001 ruling it is no longer possible to think of human rights offenses as an assault on the integrity of an imaginary invulnerable (male) body but, rather, as an attack against the "humanity of our embodied vulnerability."[43] The transformation of sexuality as a mark of human dignity thus demonstrates that vulnerability pervades all aspects of human life and, more importantly, it resignifies vulnerability from that of a feminine condition to that of a universal human condition.[44] Though she rejects the feminist and juridical developmental narrative espoused by the ICTY itself, Berghoffen nonetheless collapses the promise of the vulnerable body and the messianic promise of human rights. Thus while she distinguishes the notion of rights as the engine of the enlightenment from that of rights as a moral response to shared horror, she insists that it is necessary to keep faith in the present and future promise of juridical technologies as the defining essence of our common humanity.

The Secularization of Bosnian Muslim Women

In spite of the fact that the overrepresentation of the raped and violated Bosnian Muslim woman spurred an articulation of a postsocialist, global feminist consciousness capable of laying claims to the universality within the realm of human rights, feminist faith in the possibility of juridical redemption necessitated the secularization of the war's victims. Bosnian Muslims were portrayed as a religious group singled out for persecution within the former Yugoslavia, but Bosnian Islam was not viewed as a religion dictating a worldview distinct from that of secular modern notions of power, governance, and justice. Since Bosnian Muslims' religious subjectivity could not be the foundational difference around which the liberal progress narrative of Euro-American feminist consciousness was to develop, sexual vulnerability took its place as the foremost marker of Bosnian war crimes. For example, in MacKinnon's infamous article, "Turning Rape into Pornography," which prompted subsequent feminist interest in the Bosnian war, religion is reduced to a "cultural marker," which, like race and ethnicity but unlike sex, is not legible on Balkan bodies.[45] Although the Muslim woman was the hypervisible raped victim of war, as an unraced and secularized woman, she was able to stand for a universalized victim (woman) without particular religious or ethnic attachments.

In subsequent writings about Bosnia and the wars in Yugoslavia, MacKinnon makes the case explicitly that liberal notions of rights based on differences that can be accommodated within secular societies should be the foundation of a new international juridical order, modeled on U.S. and Canadian law. She writes, "In the received international human rights tradition, . . . equality has been more abstract than concrete, more transcendent than secular, more descended from natural law than admittedly socially based."[46] MacKinnon faults existing international human rights law for disregarding human difference and idealizing transcendence. Thus far, she argues, either women have been reduced to their gendered particularity, and therefore have not embodied universal humanity, or, when they have been included as victims in the realm of universality, their particularity as women has been erased. In contrast, a secular human rights regime would generate new principles "best approximated in North American equality law, pioneered by the Black civil rights movement in the United

States in the 1960s and 1970s and the women's movement in Canada in the 1980s and 1990s."[47] The tenets of a global women's movement and civil rights movement, according to MacKinnon, produce "a rich concept of equality not as sameness but as lack of hierarchy. . . . The movement provides a principled basis for sex equality as a human right."[48]

That MacKinnon explains the key distinction between a secular and a transcendent notion of human rights through North American models of "diversity" and "equality" grounded in the principles of civil rights speaks to the merging of U.S. racial and gender formations in law and culture and transnational regimes of justice and redemption in the contemporary world. Her formulation elucidates the particular representational modes through which Bosnian Muslim women were made to emblematize the need to shift and develop international human rights law in the postsocialist era. Secular differences are those differences that still enable the subject to place her faith in civil, liberal rights as the path to human equality and emancipation (and, therefore, what MacKinnon calls "relative universality"). Thus secular difference, such as culture, ethnicity, or sex, permits the subject of the postsocialist human rights regime to be folded into the story that MacKinnon and others tell of the global women's rights movement as leading, finally, to the recognition of gendered humanity as the new universal.

The meaning and value attached to secularism within Western Europe and the United States exceed the commonplace understanding of the concept of the secular as the separation of church and state. As an ideal for organizing religious belief in the modern world, secularism shapes the very notions of liberal democracy, tolerance, and fair governance, and as such it was crucial in conceptions of the proper development of the formerly socialist nations after 1990. The insistence on Bosnian Muslim women's secularism was essential to their ability to stand for feminist progress, facilitating the collusion between mainstream Euro-American feminism and humanitarian imperialism in the 1990s, and subsequent militarism in the post-9/11 era. Tracy Fessenden argues that whereas "an academic critique of the use of women as the marker of an imperial vision of civilization is now well established, this vision's reliance on a progress narrative of secularization has gone largely unremarked."[49] Historically, the "association between secularism and freedom . . . confers a special moral standing on those who share both secularism and its particular Protestant genealogy [of freedom of conscience], fueling imperial projects from nineteenth-century colonialism to contemporary international interventions."[50] For Fessenden, "special moral standing is frequently given in appeals to the treatment of women," and consequently, the "historical articulations between women's rights and U.S. imperialism are clearest in the realm of religion," even as the feminist progress narrative obscures this connection through its claims to secularism (liberating women from religious oppression).[51] That Bosnian Muslim women did not need to be liberated from religious oppression, supposedly unlike their Middle Eastern counterparts, fit with the claims of postsocialist imperialism as embracing diversity, as long as particular markers and modes of inhabiting difference could be accommodated within the liberal rule of law.

Of course, as a Muslim majority nation, Bosnia embodies the legacy of the Ottoman Empire on the European continent.[52] In this sense, the nation fits uncomfortably into notions of the properly European. According to Talal Asad, within the conception of Europe envisaged as not simply a continent but a civilization, Muslims are uniquely at once included and excluded within a mythology dependent on "notions of 'culture' and 'civilization' and 'the secular state,' 'majority,' and 'minority.' "[53] In his consideration of the shifting borders of postsocialist Europe, therefore, Asad proposes that "where European borders are to be drawn is also a matter of representing what European civilization is. . . . They reflect a history whose unconfused purpose is to separate Europe from alien times ('communism,' 'Islam') as well as from alien places ('Islamdom,' 'Russia')."[54] As European borders shift, even while the idea of Europe is reaffirmed, "the 'inside' cannot contain the 'outside,' violent cultures cannot inhabit a civil one— Europe cannot contain non-Europe. . . . And yet Europe must try to contain, subdue, or incorporate what lies beyond it, and what consequently comes to be within it."[55] It is not surprising, therefore, that the postsocialist temporality of social and economic transition, as well as of crisis, from the Bosnian war to the post-9/11 wars in the Middle East, has produced Muslim populations as the "problem" through which the borders and parameters of inclusion into the "free world" and new geopolitical divisions are determined. Building on existing literatures about the "problem" that Muslims represent for notions of Euro-American civilization and modernity, a number of scholars have noted that in commentaries on the Bosnian war, Bosnian Muslims were recognized either as European, and therefore not really thought of as Muslim, or, in cases where Bosnian Islam was seen as a nonsecular manifestation of faith, or as not really European.[56] Tone Bringa, for instance, argues that Bosnian Islam is either perceived as a remnant of the Ottoman past apart from European modernity or analyzed through the trope of Islamic fundamentalism threatening to encroach on Western Europe. Critical of both strands of reductive reasoning, Bringa urges a reconsideration of Islam in Bosnia that would emphasize Ottoman policies of religious tolerance. Because Bosnian Muslims challenge the "very ideas of Europe as a Christian entity," Bringa suggests that they can become a model for a new mode of religious open-mindedness on the Continent.[57]

Bringa's astute analysis of Europe's ambivalent relationship to Bosnian Islam, though incisive in its critique of the dual and contradictory mechanisms of exclusion, nonetheless misses the moments of inclusion and incorporation through which the United States and Europe rearticulate their own universality and progress. Bosnian prewar multiculturalism was in fact largely seen as a purview of Bosnian Muslims, since the Serbs were thought to have destroyed multiethnic coexistence and Bosnian cosmopolitanism in their genocidal quest for a "greater Serbia" cleansed of all Muslims and Croats. As such, in most wartime analyses, Bosnian Muslims became the bearers of any possible multiethnic and tolerant future in the region. The fact that Europe and the United States acknowledged and, indeed, foregrounded that the war's victims were Muslim was significant, showcasing the Western nations' commitment to religious freedom through their support of a non-Christian population. It was also imperative that Bosnian Muslims be portrayed as a secular people, whose values were aligned with the Western world in the sense that they did not let religion influence their commitment to liberal modes of governance. Keeping in mind that the breakup of the former Yugoslavia was not about ancient ethnic hatreds as described by the Euro-American media, but about the dissolution of socialist self-governance and the reorganization of the economy, society, and everyday life, the insistence on Bosnian Muslim secularism on the part of Western commentators and activists seemed to imply that they were already properly liberal subjects in contrast to the groups that were vilified during the conflict.[58] For example, ranking the extent to which antisecularism led to separatist nationalism and violence in the former Yugoslavia, Michael Sells proposes that unlike the mobilization of Serbian Orthodoxy, Bosnian Muslims "never achieved (or resorted to) a religious nationalist identity of any widespread acceptance."[59] Indeed, Sells emphasizes that any Islamic nationalism in Bosnia was not indigenous to the region but "imposed from the outside."[60] Only after the destructive power of Serbian "militant religious mythology" became evident did the Bosnian Muslims become vulnerable to the financial and religious influence of Saudi Islam, an implicitly nonsecular, militant mode of Islam in his line of argument.[61]

Throughout the 1990s, U.S. and European engagement with the Bosnian war resolved the contradiction between portraits of Bosnian Muslims as victims of Christian aggression and the collective Euro-American fantasy of dislodging Islam from the boundaries of New Europe through accounts that spotlighted Bosnian Islam's commitment to liberal multicultural values and religious tolerance. The seeming recognition of Bosnian Muslims as tentatively European, at least during the war years and, subsequently, within the ICTY, delinked the continued insistence that Muslim inhabitants living in Western nations were non-European (both in terms of geography and in terms of belief systems) from the critique that Europe itself was incapable of universality. Bosnian Muslims became the proof of Europe's capacity for religious diversity. Indeed, Europe was portrayed as the location of hope for Bosnian Muslims in the face of Balkan ethnoreligious "cleansing." It is not surprising, then, that most feminists writing about the plight of Bosnian Muslim women took pains to imagine the population as secular and, in this sense, already European in their outlook and way of inhabiting religious identity, confined to the private sphere. This was done through the ethnicization and culturalization of Bosnian Islam.[62] The idea that Bosnian Muslims were an ethnic minority sharing a cultural identity more so than a community of faith enabled Bosnian Muslims to be viewed as governable within and emblematic of the values espoused by the emergent human rights regime.

Throughout the Bosnian war, stories about prewar society drew attention to the fact that people lived side by side before the war. Commentators noted that Sarajevo was much more diverse than most cities in the United States and the West.[63] In her book on seeking justice after the war, one reporter who had been present during the violence explained how people in Sarajevo could still recall getting along. She describes how Bosnians remember the past: "See, we all got along, Muslim, Croat, Serb. . . . Our town had a mosque, but it also had an orthodox cathedral; we weren't religious, but we'd feast to celebrate the Muslim holiday of Bayram or the Serb holiday of Petrovdan; everyone went to Christmas Eve mass at the cathedral."[64] In this reporter's scenario of Bosnia's multicultural past, the mosques, churches, and religious holidays are depicted as *just* cultural symbols—manifestations not of faith but of ethnocultural diversity. In other words, they are signs that in the Balkans, the U.S. subject can recognize a *secular topography* of religious difference with which she can identify.

The discourse about Bosnian multicultural cosmopolitanism and of Bosnian Muslims as exemplifying the secular, cultural diversity that was uniquely Euro-American had a strong impact on feminist scholarship. Bosnian Muslim women were distinguished from the predominant stereotype of non-European Muslims as fundamentalist and misogynist. Former U.S. ambassador to Austria Swanee Hunt, who became interested in the Bosnian war during her time in Europe and continued working with a number of women's nongovernmental organizations in Bosnia after the war, published *This Was Not Our War: Bosnian Women Making the Peace*, a collection of interviews with Bosnian women. Hunt describes her informants as follows: "There is no dramatic Islamic tale to tell; few women in Bosnia look, act, or speak in some particularly Muslim way. They do not quote the Koran, nor do they see their choices limited by Islamic teaching. . . . Bosnian Muslim women are for the most part assimilated in a secularized society in which Islamic heritage provides traditions and values, but not dogma."[65] One of the women Hunt interviewed, Alma, is quoted as stating, "A Muslim woman—by religious rules—should be only a homemaker. But Bosnian women work. It's not like Algeria or some other place where they're fighting for basic rights. We should help the women of Kabul. Bosniak women are an inspiration for women all over the world."[66] In this interview excerpt, which frames an entire chapter as its epigraph, Bosnian women's universality (their "inspiration" for "the world") occurs only through their distancing from other non-European Muslim women. This is not to say that Hunt imagines Bosnians as non-Muslims. Rather, for Hunt, the women of Bosnia provide an occasion to spotlight the voices of "those who can distinguish between religion as a path to life and religion as a pretext for killing."[67] Religion, as the path to "life," involves an emphasis on traditions and values in the realm of the home and family rather than an association between piety and statecraft. Put otherwise, it is a secular conception of religion in the private sphere that offers a path to life after war.

Similarly, Beverly Allen's work on rape warfare makes the case for Bosnian women's secularism as a way to imagine Euro-American commitment to religious tolerance. In response to those scholars of rape warfare who "demonized" Muslim communities in Bosnia for maintaining patriarchal structures by ostracizing women who had been victims of wartime rapes, Allen writes that they "might be confusing racist clichés of Middle Eastern Arabs with the southern Slav heirs to the Bogomils," a pacifist sect of Christianity.[68] Though critical of "racist clichés" of Muslims, by distinguishing Bosnian Muslim women from their Middle Eastern counterparts, Allen herself racializes religious difference and replicates racist clichés. For Allen, Bosnian difference from the Middle East rests chiefly on their Slavic heritage. Descriptions of Bosnian Muslim women's whiteness that signifies their Europeanness are not new. For instance, in her renowned book from the 1930s, *Black Lamb and Grey Falcon*, Rebecca West wrote that among the Muslim Slavs of Sarajevo, she observed a veiled woman dressed in lilac silk, and then, catching a glimpse behind the veil, she saw a face "'completely un-Oriental, as luminously fair as any Scandinavian.'"[69] What is new in the postsocialist period is the association between the whiteness and the secularism of the Muslim women.

When Islamic fundamentalism or an antisecular tendency in Bosnia is addressed in Euro-American feminist scholarship, often it is in the context of laying blame for the moral failure of the Western nations to live up to their own secular commitment to religious tolerance by intervening in the conflict. In her research following up on *This Was Not Our War*, Swanee Hunt returned to Bosnia, where she found a nation increasingly turning to the Middle East. In her second book, *Worlds Apart*, Hunt proclaims that nonintervention by the United States leads to women on the streets veiling themselves.[70] Although, she argues, Bosnian Islam is about multiethnic tolerance and against veiling, when Iran funds cultural centers in the region, while the United States offers no aid for infrastructural rebuilding, fundamentalist values will win out.[71] In this perspective, because of U.S. and European shortcomings, the Bosnian way of being Muslim, that is, the secular, multiethnic, and tolerant way, came under danger from ultrareligious Serb nationalists and, later, Iranian and Saudi Muslim organizations. Western intervention, implicitly, would work to preserve secularism and diversity against the forces of the Middle East. In short, the United States and the West should see themselves as having a stake in the struggle between two ways of being Muslim. For Hunt, therefore, the blanket distrust of all of Islam becomes a "self-fulfilling prophecy" in which fundamentalism does indeed spread.[72] This lesson is also a feminist one. Had the women been in charge, she argues, the war would not have happened.[73] As evidence, she describes how women put on lipstick during the siege to get jugs of water. After the war, rather than delivering tractors, Hunt thus chooses to deliver tubes of lipstick to Bosnian women. As a ritual and recognition of universal womanhood, this exchange became for her the condition of possibility for local and global reconciliation, tolerance, and rebuilding.

That the Bosnian war became a feminist cause on a global scale, contributing to a feminization of peace and humanitarian action and a masculinization of war and violence, helps explain the gendered distinction that structured some Euro-American portrayals of Bosnian Muslims. Though

Bosnian Muslim men were seen as victims of Serbian violence, they none-theless were at times vilified with respect to Muslim women.[74] Ruth Seifert, for instance, suggests that the way to explain why Serbs raped Muslim women, while Muslim men did not rape Serbian women, is that societies with a low incidence of rape are the ones in which "male supremacy is com-pletely assured (an example would be most Muslim societies)."[75] Seifert, while reproducing the commonplace association between Muslim societies and rigid patriarchal structures, reinterprets the charge of traditionalism here to accommodate, and complete, the picture of Bosnian Muslim vic-timhood in this war. Thus, in spite of the charge that Muslim traditionalism and collective "shame" surrounding the issue of rape made stories and tes-timonies difficult to find, the accusation actually frames the testimony of those Muslim women willing to share their story as all the more important to the emergence of a new global feminist ethics and justice.[76] This new ethical vision produced the Euro-American woman (which could include Bosnian Muslim women) as the ideal multicultural and secular subject who breaks through the walls of patriarchy in her own society domestically as well as internationally.

Sacred Life, Common Humanity, and the Juridical Politics of Faith

The secularization of Bosnian Muslims during and after the war in Bosnia became the condition of possibility for the consolidation of a new global regime of humanitarian and human rights law—the mechanism for human salvation following the Dayton Accords.[77] The operations of the perpetual Tribunal, having coalesced with the project of postsocialist feminism, call on both the victims and the accused in the former Yugoslavia to place their faith not in religious narratives of deliverance but, rather, in the possibility of juridical redemption of their humanity. As Asad argues, human rights law can be thought of as "a mode of converting and regulating people, making them at once freer and more governable *in this world.*"[78] Through simultaneous emphasis on procedural "transparency" and historical "truth" as determined through forensic investigation, including the exhu-mation of mass graves, statements of victimhood and guilt, records of the hearings and testimonies, and documentary-style media outputs, the cul-ture of international humanitarian law increasingly monopolizes notions of justice. Creating a singular narrative of common humanity based in secular multicultural and feminist values, the Tribunal forces inhabitants of those regions marked by atrocity to declare their belief in its principles and procedures if they are to regain the world's recognition as properly human once again.

The ICTY website, which is organized as a public record of the Tribunal's chief accomplishments, simultaneously stages the spectacle of victims' violation and the condemnation and conversion of the guilty to demonstrate how a court of law can create a new social world in the Balkans. The Tribunal's digital archive prominently features excerpts from testimonies, categorized as "Statements of Guilt" and "Voice of the Victims." Both sets of narratives affirm the Tribunal as the locus where past atrocity can be overcome, and where former enemies embrace feminist, multicultural, and secular values. A statement taken from the testimony of Teufika Ibrahimefendić, a witness called before the court in 2000, encapsulates these goals: "All the victims . . . trust . . . that the people will muster enough courage, including victims, to tell the story of what happened. Those who did it, that they too will be able to speak out so that we all can have a basis for a common life together one day."[79] The "Voice of the Victims" page details the conditions of inhumanity through which international humanitarian law is acknowledged as a precondition for the future protection of human life as sacred. Within the historical narrative produced by the ICTY, the vulnerability of the victims' bodies takes precedence over particular bodies' ethnic, national, or religious affiliations. Victims of all ethnic groups thus become evidence of the Tribunal's project of sanctifying liberal notions of common humanity.

On the "Voice of the Victims" page, individuals tell their stories about how their lives will never be fully restored because of the extent of the horrors they have experienced, recounting their wartime torment and dehumanization as proclamations of psychic and social death. Witness DD, testifying with her name and identity withheld from the public, like a number of other victims, described the losses she suffered during the July 1995 genocide of Srebrenica, in which her husband and sons were killed. Next to her image, which is blocked out, a quote from her testimony reads, "This youngest boy I had, those little hands of his, how could they be dead? Every morning I wake up I cover my eyes not to look at other children going to school."[80] While Witness DD survived the Srebrenica genocide, her words imply that though she is alive, her life has not gone on, and that she does not wish to take part in the life that goes on around her (she shuts her eyes), as she states, "and then sometimes I also think it would be better if none of us had survived. I would prefer it." Many of the victims' quotes, excerpted from their testimonies on the "Voice of the Victims" page, echo Witness DD's sentiments—that

" ... It was systematic killing ... the organisers of that do not deserve to be at liberty."

Witness O, a survivor of the Srebrenica executions

▲ Video and Story

" ... He trampled on my pride and I will never be able to be the woman that I was."

Grozdana Ćećez, a rape victim at the Čelebići prison

▲ Video and Story

" ... He started speaking to us: 'Listen you guys, we are going ... to burn you all.' "

Emil Čakalić, a former detainee at Ovčara farm

▲ Video and Story

"Had it not been for this Omarska, my husband would probably be still alive, my nephew and many others."

Minka Čehajić, widow of an Omarska prisoner

"They continued to beat me until a policeman on duty entered and said: 'Leave the man alone. He's not going to survive.' "

Witness VV, a Bosnian army prisoner of war at Široki Brijeg, near Mostar

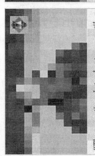

" ... He finished raping me ... and said that he could perhaps, do more ... but that I was about the same age as his daughter."

Witness 50, a teenage rape victim from Foča

Figure 7. "Voice of the Victims" envisions the Tribunal as a therapeutic space.

survivors are simply bodies emptied of their former lives. Habiba Hadžić, a Bosnian Muslim woman raped at the Serb-run Sušica camp, states, "I am a sick woman now. . . . I have nothing to hope for. . . . I would just like to ask . . . where they are. . . . I want to give them a proper burial . . . then I can go away myself."[81] The excerpt from Grozdana Ćećez, a Serbian woman raped at a detention camp in Bosnia, states, "He trampled on my pride and I will never be able to be the woman that I was."[82]

In spite of the testimonial declarations positioning the victims as the living detritus of the war, their words and physical presence at The Hague give life to the Tribunal. The victims' voices and scarred bodies and souls bear the traces of the horrific past, a reminder that the world needs the Tribunal as a humanizing mechanism to counteract the dehumanization of the detention, rape, and death camp. The "Voice of the Victims" page demonstrates the inextricable relationship between the spectacle of suffering and the rise of the global human rights paradigm in contemporary geopolitics. According to Wendy Brown, human rights activism

> generally presents itself as . . . a pure defense of the innocent and the powerless against power, a pure defense of the individual against immense and potentially cruel or despotic machineries of culture, state, war, ethnic conflict, tribalism, patriarchy, and other mobilizations or instantiations of collective power against individuals. More precisely, human rights take their shape as a moral discourse centered on pain and suffering rather than political discourse of comprehensive justice.[83]

While the ICTY continues to emphasize the suffering and pain of innocent victims of illiberal regimes, marked by practices of ethnic cleansing, tribalism, and patriarchy, its difference from human rights activism at large is that it has the institutional authority to create new modes of governance out of (and in response to) individual accounts of atrocity. As the official space in which individual "voices of victims" become part of a singular, authoritative historical account, the Tribunal turns testimonies of pain, suffering, and death into a collective global story of secular and juridical redemption through human rights. As the Tribunal home page notes, "Since its establishment in 1993 [the ICTY] has irreversibly changed the landscape of international humanitarian law and provided victims an opportunity to voice the horrors they witnessed and experienced."[84] Framing victims' testimony as an "opportunity to voice the horrors" constructs the Tribunal as a therapeutic space and, therefore, a transformative institution. Yet the transformation that the witnesses undergo is not individualized. Rather, it is portrayed as part of a broader transformation of justice on a global land-scape, the "landscape of international humanitarian law." Though the court cannot return psychic, social, or physical well-being to the victims, it can assign guilt for wrongdoing, remove guilty individuals from their societies, and institute the rule of liberal law in formerly despotic locales. On the ICTY website, next to the testimony of each victim is a summary of the prison sentence received by the guilty party—evidence of justice enacted by the Tribunal.

The ICTY's reproduction of inhumanity through testimony and visual spectacle calls for an exploration of how devastated, degraded, and dimin-ished lives are called on to sanction the institutionalization of a new human rights regime. The Tribunal, a permanent juridico-political feature of post-socialist governance that redraws the boundaries encompassing the land-scapes of humanity, cannot exist without the camp (including the rape and death camps exposed by feminist activists). Indeed, the images and testi-mony of violated bodies (the victims) serve as proof that the Tribunal must continue to exist if there is to be any justice. In his theorization of the politi-cization of bare life as the "decisive event in modernity," Giorgio Agamben addresses the intersections "between the juridico-institutional and the biopolitical models of power" through the body of homo sacer, the sacred man in Roman law, whose life cannot be sacrificed but who can be killed.[85] To contextualize the contemporary understanding of life as sacred, in the sense that today life is invoked as a fundamental right in the face of power, Agamben emphasizes that the notion of sacred life originally expressed "precisely both life's subjection to a power over death and life's irreparable exposure in the relation of abandonment."[86] For Agamben, the camps that came to light during the wars in the former Yugoslavia should be thought of as exemplary of the contemporary, "more extreme form" of the biopolitical paradigm he describes.[87] Referencing the feminist activist understanding of the rape in the camps as a tool of genocide, Agamben makes the case that "at issue in the former Yugoslavia is . . . an incurable rupture of the old *nomos* and a dislocation of populations and human lives along entirely new lines of flight."[88] At the end of *Homo Sacer*, Agamben thus puts forth the figure of "the Bosnian woman at Omarska" camp, among others, as repre-sentative of the "perfect threshold of indistinction between biology and politics."[89] He writes:

> The "body" is always already a biopolitical body and bare life. . . . In its
> extreme form, the biopolitical body of the West . . . appears as a threshold of

absolute indistinction between law and fact, juridical rule and biological life. . . . Today a law that seeks to transform itself wholly into life is more and more confronted with a life that has been deadened and mortified into juridical rule.[90]

Extending Agamben's analysis to conceive of the Tribunal and the camp as coconstitutive biopolitical spaces, through which the indistinctions between biology and politics, between law and fact, and between juridical rule and biological life become what Agamben calls the new "*nomos* of the planet," the transfer of the body, reduced by the camp to bare life, from the rape, death, and detention camps to the Tribunal, can be thought of as a moment of sovereign reordering. The new order heralds a messianic temporality, which declares that life has become sacred through the actualization of international human rights. As the very same bodies that were once subject to the camp become subjects of the Tribunal, their status as bare life in the camp is precisely what continues to constitute them as relevant to the Tribunal. Indeed, inhabiting the zone between life and death endows these particular bodies with unique value for the Tribunal, where their lives are redeemed not as individual living bodies but as part of common humanity. The imprecise zone between life and death is further blurred as the dead and the living alike are made to declare the distinction between global conditions of inhumanity and humanity, and between the law of the camp and humanitarian law, as part of the process of arriving at juridical redemption. The transfer from the camp to the Tribunal is thus the occasion when the sacredness of human life is asserted in the arrival of the human rights regime as the moment of human redemption from previous regimes that declared their power by taking life.

To make meaning of these bodies in the juridico-political realm of international human rights governance, the Tribunal takes possession of the dead and living victims previously subject to now-defunct or discredited sovereign political regimes. Even as the human rights regime puts into crisis the power of the sovereign state to take life with impunity, declaring life to be sacred, through the work of its tribunals it also asserts its power over bodies, enacted through its power to own rather than to kill. As dead bodies, and survivors and witnesses, are collapsed into the category of "evidence" in war crimes trials, that evidence comes under the temporary ownership of the Tribunal, which has primacy over survivors' desire to bury their dead. Bodies that become the property of the Tribunal are, in turn, given an afterlife as the foundation of postwar truth, healing, and humanitarian law.

Clea Koff, a forensic anthropologist who worked on the unearthing and identification of bodies found in mass graves in Rwanda, Croatia, Bosnia, and Kosovo, has chronicled the ambiguities inherent in the Tribunal's process of restoring human dignity by taking possession of human remains as evidence. She writes:

> My acute awareness of the Women of Srebrenica [an organization of widows and mothers] triggered the double vision. . . . I realized that the bodies belonged only temporarily to the Tribunal (as evidence of crimes against humanity), while they fundamentally belonged to the surviving relatives. In Rwanda, the double vision made me want to give remains back to relatives, regardless of protocol about bodies as Tribunal evidence. I even wanted to give the relatives just a bit of clothing, because their loss seemed so complete and was palpable to me.[91]

Koff's description of her "double vision" is in fact a realization that when bodies and remains are treated as Tribunal property, it deepens the already profound loss felt by survivors. However, for Koff, this is a necessary, secondary loss for the broader project of restoring not individual humanity but common humanity. As she argues elsewhere in the book, "despite the facts—whether religious, ethnic, or historical—that are supposed to differentiate places like Rwanda and Kosovo, their dead reveal their common humanity, one that we all share."[92] If, within the context of the war's production of bodies that could be killed and devastated with impunity, women's and men's bodies were reduced to their ethnicity, nationality, or religion, at the moment when the bodies became subjects of the Tribunal and the human rights regime in the postwar period, those same bodies, as Koff's book suggests, take on the meaning of universal (common) humanity.[93]

Like the victims, whose violated bodies and diminished lives are evidence of the need for juridical affirmation of the sacredness of common humanity in the face of national, ethnic, and religious violence, the "Statements of Guilt" section featured on the ICTY website highlights the fact that the humanization of landscapes scarred by sectarian violence requires a commitment to liberal multicultural values. Through declarations of repentance in front of the court, former war criminals demonstrate their enlightenment as human beings, making the ICTY a theater of redemption upon whose stage public conversion occurs. The Tribunal provides an institutional platform for the guilty to voice their feelings of remorse and for war crime perpetrators to pronounce their submission to the rule of humanitarian law. Conversion narratives demonstrate that for the Balkans to reenter

Figure 8. "Statements of Guilt" produces the International Criminal Tribunal for the Former Yugoslavia (ICTY) as a theater of conversion.

global humanity, their view of right and wrong must come into alignment with that of the human rights regime and the principles of tolerance. It is important that the idea of a common humanity in which the postsocialist world order places its faith is undergirded by a secular morality that the ICTY is seen to legislate and defend. Statements of repentance for actions undertaken during the war, and expressions of a desire for reconciliation, thus often articulate a longing for multiethnic and multireligious friendship to be enabled by the ICTY's process of establishing an authoritative truth.

Stevan Todorović's confession provides an example. His crimes are described in terms of his role as the "Police Chief and a member of the Bosnian Serb Crisis Staff in Bosanski Šamac, Bosnia and Herzegovina in 1992–1993. He persecuted non-Serb civilians on political, racial and religious grounds. Over a period of eight months, Todorović beat and tortured men, and ordered and participated in the interrogation of detained persons ordering them to sign false statements. He issued orders and directives that violated the rights of non-Serb civilians to equal treatment under the law." In his statement of guilt, Todorović articulates his recognition that the principal cause of inhuman acts is ethnic and religious intolerance. Through his professed desire for reconciliation, he announces his conversion to liberal personhood, and thus he positions himself as someone who can build a postsocialist and postwar future.

> Before the war, I had not planned ethnic cleansing or persecution, nor was I aware of any such plan. Two weeks into the war, I realised that a large number of non-Serbs had left and were continuing to leave the territory of Šamac municipality. I realised but I lacked courage to prevent the *illegal and inhuman activities* that were going on and that such treatment of non-Serbs, due to which those people left the territory of Šamac municipality. . . . I am ready to testify, to cooperate, and to say everything I know in the interests of truth and justice. My wish and hope is, and that depends on you, Your Honours, to go back to the wonderful prewar times that we had when all the people of Bosnia lived in unity and happily together. Unfortunately, I cannot change history. I would wish and am ready, if you give me such a chance, to try and improve the future. . . . I'm also ready to invest every effort in the new multiethnic Bosnia, to have a positive effect on the surroundings so that the interethnic wounds should heal as soon as possible and that peoples and nations should live in mutual respect and harmony and thereby to atone for my sins up to a point, *my sins towards men and to God.*[94]

That Todorović should describe acts of ethnic intolerance and ethnic cleansing as inhuman and a sin against both men and God is telling of the new status of multiculturalism as the secular moral order in which human beings must place their faith in the postsocialist era.

Like Todorović, most of the guilty express their ardent wishes for multiethnic togetherness and for the people of Yugoslavia to be as they were before the war (the "Brotherhood and Unity" model). While the statements initially seem to parallel the ICTY's mandate for multicultural tolerance as the path for reconciliation and peace, the multicultural ideal within the human rights regime differs in the kind of social world it seeks to produce for the future Balkan nations. In the progress narrative of the rule of liberal law emphasizing minority rights, tolerance, and economic reform, the emphasis is on the protection of the individual or the "minority" from the state rather than on a collective political vision like, for better or worse, the model of socialist self-governance in ex-Yugoslavia. This is not to say that the human rights project is an apolitical one. Unlike the guilty pleas that profess a desire to turn back the clock and express regret that they cannot bring back the past, the ICTY's undertaking of reconciliation is not about bringing back a socialist past but, rather, about making a different kind of social and political future for the Balkan republics within an expanded Europe. As an institutional organ of the human rights regime, the Tribunal creates a new postsocialist human, a rights-bearing individual, who has faith in the principles of tolerance and minority rights as well as in the rule of international humanitarian and criminal law.

The human rights regime that is given jurisdiction over the former Yugoslavia through the ICTY thus enacts judgments and new laws that go hand in hand with other economic and social mechanisms of liberal development and reform. As Wendy Brown explains, human rights are ultimately "a politics" that organize "political space, often with the aim of monopolizing it. It also stands as a critique of dissonant political projects, converges neatly with the requisites of liberal imperialism and global free trade, and legitimates both as well."[95] The process of monopolizing justice, I would argue, is tied to the universalizing secular narrative of human redemption in this world, inherent in the concept of rights. Put otherwise, for a global human rights regime to truly monopolize social justice discourses and activism, people must place their faith in the concept of "rights" as the defining essence of humanity, rendered sacred through a belief in international law and domestic liberal reforms. To place one's faith in the notion that as a human being one has certain rights (particularly those spelled out in the Universal Declaration of Human Rights and subsequent UN documents) is to produce an imaginary of international human rights as a messianic engine of global progress that continually expands the bounds of humanity to include previously excluded others, such as women and religious and racial minorities, as rights-bearing subjects. The fact that these rights can be, and usually are, violated in instances of crisis or war simply furthers a notion that victims must maintain faith in the principles of human rights, which define the fundamental, irreducible quality of their humanness. This faith, in turn, gradually replaces and even criminalizes other possible systems of faith and notions of humanity and justice, as well as human desires and needs that might define the good life otherwise.

Seeing Otherwise and the Politics of Refusal

In light of the overwhelming enfolding of conflicting notions of the good life within human rights and humanitarian techniques of governance, it is important to ask whether it might be possible to see social worlds in those spaces that come to prominence in the global imaginary as spaces of atrocity without the spectacle of the devastated, injured body as the condition of possibility for redemption. Can life after war be materialized without taking recourse to therapeutic justice, healing, and rights as modes of redemption that require always returning to the camp? How might Bosnia itself refuse its geopolitical status as a forensic site and perpetual crime scene through which European and U.S. nations make meaning of postsocialist morality and humanity? A short 2003 Bosnian documentary entitled *Slike sa ugla* (*Images from the Corner*) is a powerful visual statement about the texture of ordinary life in postwar Bosnia that refuses the international humanitarian conceptions of justice, futurity, and body politics.[96] The director, Jasmila Žbanić, a Bosnian artist who founded the independent production company Deblokada, makes documentary and feature films that attempt to capture the enmeshment of the war in the everyday lives of Bosnians. Conceiving of Sarajevo as a city whose complexity is a manifestation of the past, present, and future, coexisting in a multifaceted and often conflicted temporality, her films are saturated with the legacy of the war, while rejecting the messianic promises of international humanitarian governance that seek to freeze Bosnia in crisis as the birthplace of the camp in the new biopolitical era.

Not strictly a documentary, *Slike sa ugla* is a portrait of the kinds of fantasies that can take shape through absences, remembrances, and storytelling in the mode of seeing otherwise. The film's images are of unremarkable landscapes and occurrences in present-day Sarajevo—soccer matches, nighttime streets, a vegetable market. There is no footage of the war, the dead, or the injured. The visual absence of wartime violence within contemporary Sarajevo is accompanied by a voice-over and interviews that focus almost exclusively on the legacies of war. Through the juxtaposition of scenes of ordinary postwar life with memories of violence and loss that are inescapable, the film asks how to talk about, represent, and live with the past without reinstating hatred and the fear of others. The first images in *Slike sa ugla* are those of the director at a circus with her young daughter. The cheerful music, bright costumes, and trained animals remind Žbanić that she has not been to the circus in ten years—not since the war started. As the camera zooms in on the face of the woman in the center of the ring, Žbanić's voice-over tells us that she looks like Bilja, one of the most beautiful girls in Sarajevo, who lived in the director's neighborhood. Bilja was badly injured in 1992, becoming one of the first to be wounded in Žbanić's generation. As the scenes of white horses dancing around the circus performer continue, the voice-over informs us that though Žbanić and Bilja were not close, Bilja's fate stayed with her, and her injury has continued to be one of the most painful and difficult images of the war.

The concept of one person's fate remaining within another person frames the rest of the film as an ethics of recollection and fantasy that refuses to reduce an individual to her devastated, injured body. Bilja's story, and Žbanić's search for what happened to Bilja after the war, is also a story about Žbanić herself and about postwar life in Sarajevo. From the scenes of the circus, the film winds its way to the corner of Magribija Street, where an eighty-millimeter mortar shell injured Bilja. Nineteen pieces of shrapnel hit her, and she lost her arm. Her father and dog were killed on the spot. In the current day, the scene from the corner is uneventful. A gray residential building stands on the quiet street. A young boy speeds by on his bike. Filming the empty street corner, Žbanić tells a story of a French reporter who materialized out of nowhere just as the shell hit in 1992. As Bilja lay in a pool of blood, he did not help. He just kept snapping photos, using up three rolls of film. Bilja was evacuated from Sarajevo later that year, and no one knows exactly what happened to her afterward. The film then begins piecing together the story of what became of Bilja in the ensuing ten years through a series of conversations with friends and former neighbors. Some

Figure 9. The corner of Magribija Street, where Bilja was injured. From *Slike sa ugla* (2003).

remember Bilja from her stay in the hospital. Others talk about catching a glimpse of her riding a bicycle on the street after being released. One friend even claims that he saw her walk by him at a café in Paris. These sightings and fantasies of Bilja's life stand in contrast to the image of her injury that has traveled the world. The film does not just search for Bilja but also for the photograph of Bilja taken by the French reporter, which Žbanić's friend tells her won the World Press Photo Award in 1992.

Throughout *Slike sa ugla*, Žbanić contrasts the images of war that Sarajevans continue to live with every day, and from which they cannot free themselves, with the images of the war taken by foreign reporters for the world to consume. During the war, she tells us, the people of Sarajevo became sensitive to the presence of cameras, which mercilessly photographed them without their permission. Returning to the corner where Bilja was injured, Žbanić admits to finding the famous photograph of Bilja on the Internet. The photo made her feel the same way she did when she first saw it—humiliated, angry, and insulted. Refusing to show the photograph in the film, she explains that it would be wounding Bilja all over again by exposing her to the gaze of strangers. Instead, Žbanić goes to the famous Holiday Inn where all the foreign reporters used to stay. The images of the now-empty hotel lobby are accompanied by the telling of a story rumored to be true in the old neighborhood about how Bilja walked over to that hotel after leaving the hospital. As the story goes, Bilja found the French photographer and asked him how he could just stand there, taking pictures of her without helping. He responded that he was just doing his job. Ever since she heard that story, Žbanić admits to being curious about just how long it would take to use up three rolls of film. The film cuts to a shot of the empty corner of Magribija Street, and the scene is re-created through the sounds of a clicking camera and the noise of the roll of film being rewound and replaced with a new one. Though it takes less than a minute to use up three rolls, it feels endless. Nevertheless, that minute does not encompass Bilja's life or personhood. The man who claims to have seen her in Paris tells Žbanić that Bilja is now working on a screenplay for her own film. She is the one behind the camera in France. Žbanić wonders whether it is a coincidence that both she and Bilja decided to work in film after the war. She asks herself whether by making this film about her search for Bilja she will be able to see Magribija Street differently. Can she create new images that will free her of the old ones? The film ends with Žbanić standing at a train station. A voice, which audiences are meant to presume belongs to Bilja, speaks in French. We hear that, finally, after a decade, she is preparing to visit Sarajevo. As a train pulls out of the station, leaving Sarajevo, Žbanić remains standing on the platform—Bilja has not arrived. In a final voice-over, Žbanić muses that as new wars entice journalists to move on to new places, making new images of violence and death (the news), Sarajevans remain at home, left to live with the old images, all the while seeking to make new ones.

Slike sa ugla proposes that to see otherwise requires a politics of refusal. The most important refusal is the film's visual denunciation of the image of Bilja's injured body. Rather than reproduce this image as evidence of Bosnians' wartime inhumanity, stories about the image represent the inhumanity of Euro-American modes of documentation and the sedimentation of the other. Slike sa ugla does not forget Bilja's pain but neither does it reinflict the moment of injury and loss. Instead, it replaces the World Press photo with fantasy images of Bilja constructed through hearsay, rumor, and remembrance. Like the photographers criticized in Slike sa ugla, the Tribunal, a cornerstone of the new human rights regime, needs to continually reproduce the devastated body, though rather than through images it does so through the authority of the word (testimony) and the law. In doing so, it freezes Bosnia and the former Yugoslavia in a moment of atrocity, legible on the body, like the moment of Bilja's wounding. In this sense, the absence of Bilja's body throughout Žbanić's film becomes a radical politics and ethics of rejecting the role of the other against which Euro-American morality and humanity are affirmed. Bilja's absence is productive of stories and fantasies about the continuation of her life and the life of Sarajevans and Bosnians. In other words, her absence is not a sign of emptiness but of richness. These stories are part of a heterogeneous temporality in which the past, present, and future are superimposed on each street corner and in each individual. Constructing new images does not replace the old ones with which Sarajevans coexist on a day-to-day basis. Rather, the film suggests, if the new images are to be ethical, they must not attempt to encompass entire worlds in a single moment, nor to displace or erase the past in a temporality of messianic redemption. An ethical image, as well as an ethical politics, is rather that which actively struggles with the complexities of everyday living, remembrance, fear, and fantasy, for all the discomfort, possibility, silence, and contradictions to which it may lead.

EPILOGUE

Beyond Spectacle: The Hidden Geographies
of the War at Home

IN THE INTRODUCTION to her book on the impact of the Yugoslav wars of secession on Bosnian women, *Worlds Apart,* former U.S. ambassador Swanee Hunt expresses serious concerns about the state of American democracy in the post-9/11 era. Presuming that it is the geopolitical responsibility of the United States to advance ethnic, religious, and women's rights abroad, she contrasts the Clinton administration's humanitarian aid to Muslims in Bosnia with George W. Bush's wars in Afghanistan and Iraq. Hunt writes that while 9/11 could have been turned into an opportunity for Americans to empathize with and "understand what the people in Bosnia felt," the Bush administration instead decided to "flagrantly disregard" human rights and use American resources for an unjustified war at the critical moment when "America could have solved most of the humanitarian crises in the world and become the friend of billions."[1] She conjures up the figure of the Bosnian Muslim woman as a symbolic victim and survivor, whose story can lead to a politics of diversity and tolerance as the basis for humanitarian action. Recovering the now-forgotten image of the violated body that had less than a decade ago led to moral outrage on the part of the U.S. public, the book's introduction suggests that Americans can emerge as humanitarian political actors even after 9/11 if they reinvest in liberal ideals. I end with this example that calls for reviving 1990s humanitarianism to propose that the imagined break between U.S. policy in the post-9/11 period, conceived as a moment of crisis for American democratic ideals, and during the conflict in Bosnia, portrayed as its moment of possibility, obscures the ideological continuities between Cold War racial liberalism, postsocialist humanitarian imperialism, and post-9/11 militarism. U.S. intervention on behalf of human rights during the 1990s wars in the Balkans continues to serve as proof of the nation's willingness to aid properly reformed Muslims when they are figured as objects of humanitarian intervention. As such, it undergirds contemporary U.S. warfare in the Middle East as an ongoing, democratic, and egalitarian struggle for religious tolerance and women's rights.

The racialization of ideological and religious differences in late twentieth-century U.S. geopolitics underlying the entrenchment of postsocialist imperialism, which this book has traced through analyses of how media, military, and juridical technologies are deployed to morally underwrite U.S. militarism, continues to justify post-9/11 interventionism as being about democratization. However, the contradictions inherent in claims to U.S. democratic transparency, manifest in the many modes of documentation used to expose hidden human rights abuses in the 1990s, have come to the forefront in unprecedented ways. From the USA PATRIOT Act, passed in 2001 to reduce restrictions on the government's ability to collect intelligence in its war on terror, to the military technologies and methods of waging war in Afghanistan and Iraq, it is increasingly impossible to imagine U.S. governance as self-evidently transparent in contrast to the opacity of tyrannical rule elsewhere.

For instance, a 2011 episode of *Frontline* traces the emergence of what journalist Dana Priest calls "Top Secret America," a product of "9/11's unprecedented yet largely invisible legacy: the creation of a vast maze of clandestine government and private agencies designed to hunt terrorists and prevent future attacks on the U.S."[2] According to the program, the aftermath of 9/11 led to the waging of a new kind of war in which U.S. presidents have access to continuing funding with indefinite limits and which is, even more importantly, "shrouded in secrecy." In 2001, under the guidance of Cofer Black, President Bush signed a far-reaching finding permitting the Central Intelligence Agency (CIA) to engage in a covert war in Afghanistan against al-Qaeda. Priest argues that this launched the largest undercover operation since the height of the Cold War. "Fighting in the shadows," CIA operatives saw on-the-ground combat for the first time since the Second World War, and the Taliban regime quickly fell. The victory in Afghanistan was then folded into a broader U.S. geopolitical strategy that has come to be known as the "war on terror." Indeed, as *Frontline* explains, even as the victory in Afghanistan was being celebrated, the CIA was already active in other wars spread across at least a dozen countries.

The perpetuation of the globalized war on terror has necessitated the usage of novel military and intelligence technologies, which in turn created an entirely new infrastructure, both within the United States and abroad.

Frontline's "Top Secret America" shows how "Unmanned Aerial Vehicle" rooms, located in places such as Tampa, Florida, became locales from which predator missiles could be launched with the click of a button against such potential "targets" as individual vehicles driving along a dirt road in Yemen. For Priest, drones were just one of the extraordinary technologies indicating that the rules had been completely overhauled. The secret authorization of "enhanced interrogation techniques" for use on suspected terrorists legalized what had until then been considered torture. Priest uncovered a network of nearly twenty-four "black sites," secret prisons funded and run by the CIA located throughout the world, constructed to accommodate the ever-growing number of suspected terrorists. These facilities, as part of an international network of prisons sanctioned by the White House, characterize the unprecedented development of what Priest terms a U.S. "secretly run government."

Meanwhile, as the more "conventional" war that followed in the footsteps of Special Operations Forces began the Shock and Awe campaign in Iraq in 2003, on the home front the "war to protect the homeland" was in full swing. The National Security Agency (NSA) started intercepting phone calls and e-mail communiqués of U.S. citizens. With the advent of what came to be known as the Terrorist Surveillance Program, a warrant was no longer needed for such actions. The NSA created a "global electronic dragnet" that captures 1.7 billion intercepts from computer networks, phone calls, and radio broadcasts from around the world, every day. To sort through the tremendous amount of data collected, the NSA solicited the help of nearly 480 private contractors, spending billions of dollars. The war over information is now fought from office parks scattered all over America, "hidden in plain sight."[3] As places from which to launch drone strikes, engage in cyberconflict, and collect information, unremarkable commercial buildings sprung up in suburban areas. According to Priest and her associates, many are only a few stories high, but they extend deep underground, complete with shops and places to eat—a secret "underworld" that, as *Frontline* documents, most Americans do not know exists. Priest calls this an "alternative geography of the United States," which supports the newfangled, invisible bureaucracy. The "secret geography" is both hidden from the public and proximate, dotting the map of the entire nation.

Even after one of the most public failures of U.S. national intelligence— the failure to find the purported weapons of mass destruction in Iraq—"top secret America" has only continued to grow under the direction of the recently created position and office of the Director of National Intelligence.

Figure 10. An office building, part of the everyday geography of "Top Secret America."

As a presidential hopeful, Barack Obama promised to work for a return to "transparency." However, almost all of the undisclosed operations have been reauthorized by the new administration, which in fact increased the usage of lethal drone attacks and other covert actions. Priest posits that funding for "top secret America" was expanded in spite of the economic crisis, as was the war against al-Qaeda and the Taliban in Afghanistan and Pakistan. Employing nearly one million people, "top secret America" has produced a shadow army that performs jobs about which most U.S. citizens cannot know.

As *Frontline*'s "Top Secret America" demonstrates, the opacity of the post-9/11 mode of warfare is interwoven into the everyday, familiar landscapes of U.S. life. The very ordinariness of office parks inhabited by security and intelligence employees enables the underground world to remain undetected. A very extraordinary form of clandestine and long-distance warfare is thus fought from edifices that conjure up normality. Indeed, the new war, because it blends into the texture of commonplace American geographies, is not felt as a war by most of the U.S. public. Many U.S. citizens never directly experience or need to give much thought to the destructive impact wreaked by the new military and surveillance technologies, in terms of both lost lives and destroyed infrastructures abroad. As prisoners, victims of torture are kept out of sight (barring, of course, exceptional instances, such as when the Abu Ghraib abuses came to light). Abu Ghraib, however, seems to be no exception. Meanwhile, even as exposés, such as the *Frontline* episode, periodically gesture to the secrecy and antidemocratic tendencies of the war on terror and the war for homeland security, simultaneously a barrage of images and discourses justifies the machineries of concealment. For instance, although the stealth techniques of the homeland protection programs explicitly infringe on civil liberties, they are nonetheless understood as fundamentally being about the protection of U.S. democratic ideals (the American way of life) against the terrors wreaked by religious extremists. In this sense, the principles of U.S. democracy are upheld even as its procedural and juridical rules are overturned.

Portraits of atrocity in the part of the world seen to generate terror and terrorists are also used to justify U.S. secrecy as being, at its core, about the spread of democracy. In this sense, the new war is a continuation of the 1990s humanitarian interventions of postsocialist imperialism. While shadow domestic geographies that enable the perpetuation of the U.S. war on terror are hidden in suburban buildings, and black sites keep prisoners out of the U.S. public view, images of spectacular deaths caused by religious extremism proliferate.[4] Even as I write this epilogue, the Boston Marathon bombing of April 15, 2013, in which three people were killed and 264 others were injured, looms large as a tragedy that seemingly justifies the need for the nation's ongoing vigilance against what has come to be broadly termed "Islamist terrorism." Indeed, the imperative to expose religious motivations for violence stands in stark contrast to "top secret America's" networks of concealment made defensible by nationalist discourses of securitization. Yet the drive to lay bare religious violence as simultaneously not of the here and now, and as the ultimate threat to the spread of modernity and universal human values through its use of contemporary communications and networking technologies, is about more than the post-9/11 ossification of the composite figure of the "Muslim Terrorist" as a new enemy *par excellence.*

Depictions of Islamic radicalism, extremism, and terrorism both constitute and exceed the contemporary racialization of Arabs and Muslims, the effects of which are palpable in anti-Muslim acts of reprisal and discrimination that led U.S. Arab and Muslim communities to a collective plea in the wake of the Marathon bombings, summed up by Khaled Beydoun as, "Please don't be Arabs or Muslims."[5] Yet what is at stake is not just the designation of ethnic "Arab or Muslims" as the enemy but rather the discursive construction of a religiously fanatical and dogmatic Muslim or Arab perpetrator. The other is no longer simply knowable through his or her racial exteriority, but rather, it has become imperative to uncover and expose his or her interiority. The U.S. secular media and politicians' imperative to know whether violence is caused by perverse religious beliefs (although, of course, designations of faith gone awry are almost exclusively conflated with fundamentalist Islam in the U.S. public imaginary), and ensuing classifications of violent acts as terroristic or not based on motive, demonstrate the extent to which liberal democracy (and the operations of global capital) authorize U.S. militarism to discover, isolate, and eliminate those who have failed to convert or reform their beliefs, using any means necessary to do so. What is important to emphasize is that not all Muslims are singled out for exclusion and disciplining in this frame. It is, rather, that U.S. technologies of governance, including surveillance, policing, and military technologies, are vested with the power to tell radical, extreme, and fundamentalist Muslims apart from properly reformed Muslims fitting into the fabric of a secular, global ethos supporting the rule of law, free markets, and liberal democracy.

The fact that the so-called Boston bombers, once captured, turned out to be from the postsocialist world is one productive example through which to apprehend and untangle some of the complicated new imbrications of race and religion, interiority and exteriority, and concealment and revelation underpinning contemporary U.S. enactments of imperial violence. The two brothers implicated in the crime, Dzhokhar and Tamerlan Tsarnaev, are ethnic Chechens who immigrated to the United States in 2002 and 2003 respectively. As the U.S. media attempted to piece together a coherent narrative about the making of terrorists, an organizing theme and anxiety underpinning many of the stories circulating on television and in print revolved around how difficult it is to uncover and spot religious extremists before they turn to acts of terror. The *Washington Post* described the Tsarnaev brothers thus: "With their baseball hats and sauntering gaits, they appeared to friends and neighbors like ordinary American boys. But the Boston bombing suspects were refugees from another world—the blood, rubble and dirty wars of the Russian Caucasus. . . . Hidden behind the lives they had been leading in Massachusetts is a biography containing old resentments that appear to have mutated into radical Islamic violence."[6] According to this article, the brothers' performance of their Americanness was quite convincing. From their hoodies, to their active participation in boxing and wrestling, they easily blended into the texture of everyday life in the United States. Yet, as this article opines, their "blood," which chained them to a landscape of atrocity, and "biography," which formed their persons out of ancient ethnic hatreds, predetermined their surrender to the forces of radical Islam—their hidden "mutation." Put otherwise by CNN, "they might have fulfilled every immigrant's dream" had it not been for their radicalization that led to the nation's "nightmare."[7]

The brothers' ambiguous whiteness and Europeanness, contextualized as it is through Cold War racializing discourses about Eastern Europe, makes evident why revealing perverse religious beliefs, or "mutated" ones, has become the imperative of the day. The radical difference that matters is no longer simply visible, grafted onto the skin and legible as phenotype. As Sarah Kendzior has written,

> After wild speculation from CNN about a "dark-skinned suspect," on Thursday the *New York Post* published a cover photo falsely suggesting a Moroccan-American high school track star, Salah Barhoun, was one of the bombers. . . .
>
> Later that Thursday, the FBI released photos of two young men wearing baseball caps—men who so resembled all-American frat boys that people joked they would be the target of "racial bro-filing." The men were Caucasian, so the speculation turned away from foreign terror and toward the excuses routinely made for white men who kill: mental illness, anti-government grudges, frustrations at home. The men were white and Caucasian—until the next day, when they became the wrong kind of Caucasian, and suddenly they were not so "white" after all.[8]

Kendzior is quite right to point out that the unearthing of Islamic religious extremism as the motivation for the bombing, which the media has supported through numerous accounts of Chechnya's radicalization over the last two decades, shifted the terms through which the crime was discussed and through which it will be prosecuted. The surviving suspect, Dzhokhar Tsarnaev, has in fact been charged with using a weapon of mass destruction—a charge that surely would not have been made had the suspect been American born or a non-Muslim. Moreover, in spite of the fact that the use of drones by the U.S. government has killed nearly 4,700 people, in contrast to the 3 killed by the bombs placed by the Tsarnaev brothers, Islamist motivation in and of itself is enough to collapse an act of violence into an act of mass destruction.[9] As is well known, drones are not classified as weapons of mass destruction, in large part because they are framed as a necessary technology used to uncover the destructive acts planned by radical Others unsuitable for thriving in a secular liberal world. *If* one takes whiteness to be associated with U.S. belonging, Kendzior is also right to argue that the bombers, once identified as Chechen, were deemed to be "not so 'white' after all." Indeed, some U.S. politicians called for trying Dzhokhar Tsarnaev as an enemy combatant in spite of his legal status as a U.S. citizen.[10]

Yet given my argument throughout this book about the development of multiculturalism as a racial and secular value attributing morality to U.S. violence as a global humanitarian and humanizing process, I suggest that it would be a mistake to read media portraits of Dzhokhar Tsarnaev as "not so 'white' after all." As the news reports cited previously demonstrate, the press continually read his external appearance as normatively white. Rather, it might be more accurate to conclude that the press figured Dzhokhar Tsarnaev as being not so *American* after all, and this precisely because through his association with religious extremism he proved himself to be not tolerant enough of diversity. In a sense, the fact that he is from a part of the world formerly under Soviet rule, a region marked in the U.S. imaginary as intolerant, illiberal, and monocultural, makes him a likely candidate (within the frame familiar to U.S. audiences) to fall prey to Islamic "extremism." As radical Islam takes the place of communism in U.S. depictions of radical alterity that threatens liberal notions of normative (non-threatening, cultural) diversity that can be allowed to flourish, what remains from the Cold War era is the understanding that it is interiority/belief that signifies the differences that matter. As the Tsarnaev brothers' uncle proclaimed to the media by way of asserting his own belonging to the U.S. nation, " 'Anything else to do with religion, with Islam, it's a fraud, it's a fake,' he said. He described the family as peace-loving, ethnic Chechens."[11] What the suspects' uncle's statement reveals is that even as the historic association of whiteness with value continues to structure inequities and injustices within the United States, the value attributed to the proper U.S. citizen increasingly has to do with espousing the correct sort of beliefs, including tolerance and respect for cultural diversity, through which the nation recognizes itself in contradistinction to extremism, fundamentalism, and terrorism.

As emerging communications technologies that constitute our "intelligence" about the world simultaneously support and vindicate our own government's secrecy and violation of the rule of law and enable the real-time exposure of others' atrocities, we must continue to pay attention to how and where our gaze is elicited and directed across media and political discourses. This includes thinking about the ways in which languages of juridical rights and humanitarian intervention reproduce the injury and devastation they seek to oppose, reaffirming our humanity. It may also entail envisaging and pursuing a politics of refusal, like Bosnian director Jasmila

Žbanić, whose films reject the imperative to replicate spectacles of the violated body. As part of seeing otherwise, it is important to reexamine the concept of liberal rights (individual rights, minority rights, and human rights) as the only path to social justice and democracy, an assumption that emerged with the United States' mythologizing of the civil rights movement and the ossification of multiculturalism as the hallmarks of U.S. racial progress narratives. By foregrounding the cultural mythologies through which claims to rights, tolerance, and diversity have led to violence, we can begin to conceptualize and reclaim alternative formulations for justice.

ACKNOWLEDGMENTS

This project was conceptualized in the years immediately following 9/11. The urgent need to critique the ways in which the United States wages war and stakes its claims to empire in the post–Cold War era has motivated me over this last decade. My political investments and interdisciplinary approach to thinking about U.S. humanitarian militarism, race, and imperialism have been profoundly shaped by ongoing conversations with faculty and friends in UC San Diego's (UCSD) literature department, where I was a graduate student. As my adviser there, Lisa Lowe was, and continues to be, an inspiration for the kind of intellectually rigorous yet compassionate scholar and teacher I hope to become one day. My admiration and appreciation for Lisa as a politically committed thinker, and for her unique generosity of spirit that lifts up young scholars, have only grown with the passage of time. I am deeply indebted to her ongoing mentorship, and thankful for her steadfast belief in my scholarship. Her advice to me to think nonintuitively centrally informs this work. At UCSD I was also fortunate to work with an incredible committee: Winnie Woodhull, Shelley Streeby, Judith Halberstam, and Martha Lampland. I additionally want to thank Denise da Silva, who organized a reading group that raised questions with which I continue to struggle in my scholarship, as well as Emily Cheng, Chris Guzaitis, and Heidi Hoechst.

Since leaving UCSD, my research and writing has benefited from the support and guidance of remarkable colleagues at a number of institutions and departments. I am grateful to Lisa Parks for serving as my mentor during a postdoctoral fellowship year in UC Santa Barbara's film and media studies department, and for introducing me to an innovative group of scholars working on Central and Eastern European culture. At the State University of New York (SUNY) Stony Brook's Department of Comparative Literature and Cultural Studies, I am especially thankful to Ira Livingston, Krin Gabbard, and Jackie Reich. Saba Mahmood, who was my mentor for the President's Postdoctoral Fellowship at UC Berkeley, helped me to develop my thinking on religious difference as I began the long process of turning my dissertation into a book. My year at UC Berkeley would not have been the same without the input of my writing group members, Kalindi Vora, Kim Tallbear, and Elly Teman.

I was able to complete this book thanks to the generosity of friends and colleagues at UC Santa Cruz, which has been an intellectually stimulating institutional home for me these last five years. Felicity Schaeffer is an exceptional comrade in the feminist studies department. Her keen insights and willingness to read drafts at the last moment have helped me many times. Anjali Arondekar and Gina Dent organized a manuscript workshop that pushed me to reconceptualize the project in productive ways at just the right time. I am grateful to Amelie Hastie and Wlad Godzich for their participation and comments during that workshop. I also want to thank the rest of my feminist studies colleagues, Bettina Aptheker, Karen Barad, Carla Freccero, Lisbeth Haas, and Marcia Ochoa, who inspire me through their scholarship, activism, and teaching, and my feminist studies students, for their commitment to making a better world. Outside of feminist studies, Mayanthi Fernando, Caetlin Benson-Allott, and Meghan Moodie, who began their careers at UC Santa Cruz the same year I did, helped me to orient myself. Our ongoing friendships and work together continue to be meaningful. My participation in the UCSC Human Rights working group was critical for my thinking in the final chapter. I especially thank Rosa-Linda Fregoso, Shelley Grabe, and Sylvanna Falcon for inviting me to join. I am also grateful to have friends in the film and digital media department, especially Shelley Stamp, Irene Luzstig, and Soraya Murray.

A number of grants and fellowships provided me with the time and resources to write this book. Funding in 2010–2011 from the UC Humanities Research Institute to form a working group, "Imperial Legacies, Postsocialist Contexts," proved crucial as I developed a frame for the research I had gathered. Conversations with Kalindi Vora, the group's coconvener, and Kristie Dorr, Vera Fennel, Grace Hong, Julietta Hua, Anita Starosta, and other members reminded me that collaborations tend to produce the most innovative writing and thinking. At UC Santa Cruz, the Faculty Research Grant made it possible for me to return to the TV News Archive at Vanderbilt University, while the Institute for Humanities Research Faculty Fellowship offered invaluable course relief that enabled me to complete revisions. I am also thankful to the Hellman Fellows Program and the Center for New Racial Studies for funding research for this book.

My experience at the University of Minnesota Press has been a rewarding one. It was a pleasure to work with Danielle Kasprzak, who is a fantastic editor and an engaged guide at the press. I appreciate her commitment to interdisciplinary and unconventional work. I am also grateful to Grace Hong and Roderick Ferguson for seeing the book's potential in the broader field of race and ethnic studies, and for including me in their series *Difference Incorporated*. Grace has been an amazing interlocutor as she steered the book toward publication. Her discerning advice and encouragement enabled me to remain enthusiastic about the project as I completed revisions. I am exceptionally fortunate to have benefited from Fatima El-Tayeb's brilliance as a reader. Her incisive suggestions motivated me to reenvision the manuscript's trajectory and provided a blueprint for making this a much better book than it would have been otherwise. Katarzyna Marciniak also carefully read and commented on the manuscript, and I am thankful to her for believing in my work.

I could not have finished this book without the friendship of Julietta Hua and Kalindi Vora. I cannot thank them enough for thinking and talking with me about the ideas contained within it over these many years, and for staying in good humor in spite of reading multiple drafts of this manuscript. Julie's keen ability to see the big picture—and to make any revisions, no matter how big or small, seem manageable—helped me tremendously. Her talents for working with a project on its own terms are unparalleled. Kalindi's gift for reminding me to keep imagination, fantasy, and "dreaminess" alive in our work continually revitalizes my intellectual and political commitments. I look forward to continuing our collaborations in the years to come.

I am lucky to have an amazing network of friends who provided emotional support, including Liz Boschee Nagahara, Elizabeth DeWitt, and Kathryn Eigen. A special thanks goes to Kathryn, who patiently read through all of the chapters. Finally, I want to thank my family for their love and humor, for reading and asking the hard questions about numerous incarnations of the manuscript, and for helping me to reimagine what this work might mean in the wider world: Ljiljana, Radoslav, Vesna, Gordana, and Nikki.

NOTES

Introduction

1. "About the ICTY," http://www.icty.org/sections/AbouttheICTY (emphasis added).
2. A number of studies have theorized the relationship between "race" and "culture" in the twentieth century. See, for instance, Etienne Balibar and Immanuel Wallerstein, *Race, Nation, Class: Ambiguous Identities*, trans. Chris Turner (New York: Verso, 1991); Pierre-André Taguieff, "The New Cultural Racism in France," trans. Russell Moore, in *Telos* 83, Spring 1990, 118–22; Richard T. Ford, *Racial Culture: A Critique* (Princeton, N.J.: Princeton University Press, 2005).
3. Looking at a variety of representational sites, I build on Lisa Lowe and David Lloyd's definition of culture. They argue, "Rather than adopting the understanding of culture as one sphere in a set of differentiated spheres and practices, we discuss 'culture' as a terrain in which politics, culture, and the economic form an inseparable dynamic" (1). See their "Introduction," in *The Politics of Culture in the Shadow of Capital* (Durham, N.C.: Duke University Press, 1997), 1–32.
4. Among the proponents of empire, this book addresses in some detail the writings of Robert Kaplan (in the first chapter) and Michael Ignatieff (in the first and fourth chapters).
5. Jodi Melamed, *Represent and Destroy: Rationalizing Violence in the New Racial Capitalism* (Minneapolis: University of Minnesota Press, 2011), 11.
6. Talal Asad, *Formations of the Secular: Christianity, Islam, Modernity* (Stanford, Calif.: Stanford University Press, 2003), 147.
7. Ibid., 145.
8. This, of course, is a myth. Puritans sought to form a religious state, expelled heretics, and certainly do not fit the mold of religious tolerance attributed to them today.
9. David Sehat, *The Myth of American Religious Freedom* (New York: Oxford University Press, 2011), 6.
10. Asad, *Formations of the Secular*, 241.
11. See Tracy Fessenden, *Culture and Redemption: Religion, the Secular, and American Literature* (Princeton, N.J.: Princeton University Press, 2008).
12. As Asad notes in *Formations of the Secular*, secularism is not just about the separation of church and state or tolerance; rather, it produces a narrative

of transcendence, "an enactment by which a political medium (representation of citizenship) redefines and transcends particular and differentiating practices of the self" (5).

13. Writing about the Philippine context, Neferti Tadiar contrasts Spanish imperialism and U.S. imperialism in terms of their differing Christian conceptions of redemption: "Under Spanish colonialism, God may have already been the white Father, but under U.S. imperialism, he gains a benevolent countenance. In contrast to the distant Spanish God, the Protestant God of U.S. imperialism is benevolent, close, and 'humanly near.'" See *Things Fall Away: Philippine Historical Experience and the Makings of Globalization* (Durham, N.C.: Duke University Press, 2009), 236.

14. W. E. B. Du Bois's history of the Reconstruction era powerfully demonstrated that slavery determined "the whole social development of America," and that "black labor became the foundation stone not only of the Southern social structure, but of Northern manufacture and commerce, of the English factory system, of European commerce, of buying and selling on a world-wide scale." See *Black Reconstruction in America, 1860–1880* (New York: Simon and Schuster, [1935] 1992), 13, 5. Du Bois argues that more than simply exemplifying the contradictions in U.S. democracy, the legacy of slavery has continued to determine "the limits of democratic control" (13). While the project of Reconstruction that followed the Civil War held the revolutionary promise of accomplishing democracy in the United States, Du Bois shows that ultimately the needs of Northern industry and Southern planting reproduced the system of racialized exploitation and disenfranchisement. Nearly a century later, the civil rights era seemed to once again represent an opportunity for radical social, economic, and racial change.

15. Mary L. Dudziak, *Cold War Civil Rights: Race and the Image of American Democracy* (Princeton, N.J.: Princeton University Press, 2000), 13 (emphasis added).

16. Nikhil Pal Singh, *Black Is a Country: Race and the Unfinished Struggle for Democracy* (Cambridge, Mass.: Harvard University Press, 2004), 5.

17. Ibid., 17.

18. See, for instance, Lisa Lowe, *Immigrant Acts: On Asian American Cultural Politics* (Durham, N.C.: Duke University Press, 1996); Robert Lee, *Orientals: Asian Americans in Popular Culture* (Philadelphia: Temple University Press, 1999).

19. Melamed, *Represent and Destroy*, xvii. Melamed argues that post–World War II and post–Cold War racial logics can be divided into three racial systems of knowledge and governance: first, racial liberalism (mid-1940s to 1960s), the era corresponding to the civil rights movement; second, liberal multiculturalism (1980s to 1990s), the era of "repressive incorporation of the post-1964 race-based social movements," which were contained and managed through an emphasis on identity, recognition, and representation; and, finally, neoliberal multiculturalism (2000s), which "has created new privileged subjects, racializing the beneficiaries of neoliberalism as worthy multicultural citizens and racializing the losers as unworthy and excludable on the basis of monoculturalism, deviance, inflexibility, criminality, and other historico-cultural deficiencies" (xv, xix, xxi). Like Melamed, I am interested in the strands of multiculturalism associated with the U.S. state, although there are

certainly modes of multicultural thought that are not in line with the liberal and neoliberal incorporation of difference. For instance, Ella Shohat proposes that a "polycentric multiculturalism entails a profound reconceptualization and restructuring of intercommunal relations within and beyond the nation state. It hopes to decolonize representation." See Shohat, "Introduction," in *Talking Visions: Multicultural Feminism in a Transnational Age* (Cambridge, Mass.: The MIT Press, 1998), 1–12, 2.

20. A number of interesting studies have been done on the racial categorization of Muslims in U.S. law. Among these, Moustafa Bayoumi's "Racing Religion" does a particularly good job of tracing this process in the law. In contrast, I am interested not in the racing of a religion but in the racing of a religious belief system—that is, how modes of religious life that do not conform to the individual freedom of conscience model are racialized. See Bayoumi, "Racing Religion," *CR: The New Centennial Review* 6, no. 2 (2006): 267–93.

21. Asad, *Formations of the Secular*, 11.

22. On race and technology, see, for instance, Lisa Nakamura, Beth Kolko, and Gilbert Rodman, eds., *Race in Cyberspace* (New York: Routledge, 2000); on technology and conflict, see selections from Lisa Parks, *Cultures in Orbit: Satellites and the Televisual* (Durham, N.C.: Duke University Press, 2005).

23. Wendy Hesford, *Spectacular Rhetorics: Human Rights Visions, Recognitions, Feminisms* (Durham, N.C.: Duke University Press, 2011), 7.

24. Ibid., 9. Unlike Hesford, I do not necessarily see legal and humanitarian constructions of human rights as separate. As chapter 5, which focuses on the ICTY, demonstrates, legal developments in the postsocialist era are very much tied to humanitarian initiatives.

25. Julietta Hua, *Trafficking Women's Human Rights* (Minneapolis: University of Minnesota Press, 2011), 10. The coarticulated relationship between racial/cultural particularity and universality in the human rights regime reflects developments in capitalism. For instance, Grace Hong argues that "late twentieth-century capital has its own universal mode: paradoxically, a universalized fetishization of difference," most evident in the realm of consumerism. See *The Ruptures of American Capital: Women of Color Feminism and the Culture of Immigrant Labor* (Minneapolis: University of Minnesota Press, 2006), xiv.

26. Randall Williams, *The Divided World: Human Rights and Its Violence* (Minneapolis: University of Minnesota Press, 2010), xx (emphasis in original).

27. Ibid., xiv.

28. Ibid., xviii.

29. See Amy Kaplan, "Where Is Guantanamo?" *American Quarterly* 57, no. 3 (2005): 831–58; John Carlos Rowe, "Culture, U.S. Imperialism, and Globalization," in *Exceptional State: Contemporary U.S. Culture and the New Imperialism*, ed. Ashley Dawson and Malini Johar Schueller (Durham, N.C.: Duke University Press, 2007), 37–59; Jasbir K. Puar, *Terrorist Assemblages: Homonationalism in Queer Times* (Durham, N.C.: Duke University Press, 2007), which analyzes contemporary U.S. imperial nationalism through what Puar terms *sexual exceptionalism*.

30. For instance, Ashley Dawson and Malini Johar Schueller critique Elaine Tyler May, who saw "post-9/11 policies and rhetoric as a continuation of Cold War ideologies." See *Exceptional State*, 1–33, 8.

31. "Who Are Americans to Think That Freedom Is Theirs to Spread?" *New York Times Magazine*, June 25, 2005, 45.

32. Ibid., 44.

33. Ibid., 45.

34. "How Communists Operate: An Interview with J. Edgar Hoover," *U.S. News and World Report*, August 11, 1950, http://www.usnews.com/news/national/articles/2008 /05/16/how-communists-operate-an-interview-with-j-edgar.

35. Similar shifts did not occur in Western Europe. Indeed, as Fatima El-Tayeb argues, "racelessness" is the predominant ideology in Western Europe, whereby "racial thinking and its effects are made invisible" (xvii). El-Tayeb demonstrates how the ideology of racelessness enables the ongoing externalization of raced populations, including Muslims, from European nations. See El-Tayeb, *European Others: Queering Ethnicity in Postnational Europe* (Minneapolis: University of Minnesota Press, 2011).

36. Of course, most theorizations of European modernity and race presume a unified conception of Europe that scholars of Eastern and Central Europe have contested. Western European racial and national identities were not exclusively consolidated against others whose bodily appearance came to signify race difference in modernity. Since the time of the European Enlightenment, Eastern Europe, similar to the Orient, has been produced as a constitutive other to "the West." A crucial distinction, however, is that Eastern Europe's difference was imagined through its proximity to the West rather than its distance. Historian Larry Wolff has proposed that Western Europe invented Eastern Europe "as its complementary other half in the eighteenth century, the age of Enlightenment" (4). Wolff demonstrates that between the Renaissance and the Enlightenment, the French *philosophes*, most importantly Voltaire and Rousseau, led the philosophical and geographic "conceptual reorientation of Europe," so that the significant axes of trade, travel, and culture underwent a shift from North to South and West to East (5). The result of this reorientation was significant: Eastern Europe came to stand as an intermediary link, as Balzac observed, "between Europe and Asia, between civilization and barbarism" (13). See Wolff, *Inventing Eastern Europe: The Map of Civilization on the Mind of the Enlightenment* (Stanford, Calif.: Stanford University Press, 1994). Maria Todorova's work on the Balkans furthers Wolff's analysis of Eastern Europe's in-between position in Western imaginative geographies. She argues that the Western discourse of "Balkanism," which she distinguishes from Orientalism, has historically constructed the Balkans as Europe's "incomplete self" (18). With its implication that the region can become complete with time, Todorova's formulation of Balkan "incompleteness" adds a temporal dimension to theorizations about the way in which Eastern Europe has been conceived. Through an understanding of Eastern Europe as an "incomplete self," it is possible to address the region's discursive production as an anachronistic reflection in which the Western subject could imagine a recent European past. See Todorova, *Imagining the Balkans* (New York: Oxford University Press, 1997).

37. Denise Ferreira da Silva, "Towards a Critique of the Socio-logos of Justice: The *Analytics of Raciality* and the Production of Universality," *Social Identities* 7, no. 3 (2001): 421–54, 422–23 (emphases in original).

38. Other scholars have made similar arguments. As David Theo Goldberg explains, "Just as spatial distinctions like 'West' and 'East' are racialized in their conception and application, so racial categories have been variously spatialized . . . into continental divides, national localities, and geographic regions." See Goldberg, *Racist Culture: Philosophy and the Politic of Meaning* (Malden, Mass.: Blackwell, 1993), 185. Building on theories about the racialization of non-European continents, Sara Ahmed argues that European whiteness was consolidated in relation to racially conceived global geographies. Ahmed proposes that "racial others become associated with the 'other side of the world' . . . they come to *embody distance*. This embodiment of distance is what makes whiteness 'proximate,' as the 'starting point' for orientation." See Ahmed, *Queer Phenomenology: Orientations, Objects, Others* (Durham, N.C.: Duke University Press, 2007), 121 (emphasis in original).

39. Borstelmann observes that during the Cold War, "parallels between political totalitarianism and racial totalitarianism [in the American South] could occasionally be striking." Although Borstelmann attempts to show that contrary to the image of racial harmony that dominant political discourses were trying to project, racism continued to plague the United States in the early stages of the Cold War, U.S. Cold War rhetoric in fact exploited and reproduced parallels between the U.S. South and the U.S.S.R. Such comparisons worked to regionalize the problem of racism in the United States, depicting racism as a black–white issue and eliding considerations of racial problems in the nation as a whole. In addition, equating institutionalized segregation with political totalitarianism imagined racism as an "ideology" in a nation that was supposed to embody the "end of ideology." The racialization of the U.S.S.R. and the U.S. South thus projected the U.S. illiberal racist "past" onto spaces that were constructed through public discourse as needing to be modernized. See Borstelmann, *The Cold War and the Color Line: American Race Relations in the Global Arena* (Cambridge, Mass.: Harvard University Press, 2001), 4.

40. The opposition between U.S. freedom and communism through which racial progress in the United States has been narrated covers over the extensive involvement of working-class Americans, African Americans, and other U.S. minorities in Marxist and Communist organizations that opposed racism and oppression in the United States.

41. Sharad Chari and Katherine Verdery, "Thinking between the Posts: Postcolonialism, Postsocialism, and Ethnography after the Cold War," *Comparative Studies in Society and History* 51, no. 1 (2009): 6–34, 18.

42. As Edward Said famously argued, European empires mapped a coherent idea of Western civilization by producing and reproducing an authoritative discourse about the East and the Oriental other. While Said's focus is on the Middle East as the site of Orientalist imperial fantasies, after World War II America's map of the free world produced the U.S.S.R., the predominant emblem of Communist ideological alterity, as an important marker of "the East." At this time, the United States further

refigured Orientalist discourses, which imagined a homogeneous West, by contrasting domestic racial diversity and anti-imperialist benevolence toward the Third World with Soviet "imperialism." See Said, *Orientalism* (New York: Vintage Books, 1979).

43. For instance, Melani McAlister's *Epic Encounters* demonstrates that in the second half of the twentieth century, U.S. cultural representations of the Middle East "have been consistently obsessed with the problem of racial diversity." See McAlister, *Epic Encounters: Culture, Media, and U.S. Interests in the Middle East, 1945–2000* (Los Angeles: University of California Press, 2000), 11. Christina Klein similarly discusses American Cold War modifications to the European Orientalist paradigm in her analysis of middlebrow culture and East Asia. Klein argues that the United States "became the only Western nation that sought to legitimate its world-ordering ambitions by championing the idea (if not always the practice) of racial equality" (11). She concludes that this facilitated "a global imaginary based on connection" that "legitimated U.S. expansion while denying its coercive or imperial nature" (13). See Klein, *Cold War Orientalism: Asia in the Middlebrow Imagination, 1945–1961* (Berkeley: University of California Press, 2003).

44. Kate Baldwin's *Beyond the Color Line and the Iron Curtain: Reading Encounters between Black and Red, 1922–1963* (Durham, N.C.: Duke University Press, 2002) reconceptualizes theorizations of the black Atlantic to take into account the importance of the Soviet Union for understanding black transnationalism. Jodi Kim's *Ends of Empire: Asian American Critique and the Cold War* (Minneapolis: University of Minnesota Press, 2010) critiques U.S. imperialism in Asia by addressing Asian American literature and film in the context of Cold War geopolitics, with Asia triangulating U.S.–Soviet relations in the second half of the twentieth century. Penny Von Eschen's *Satchmo Blows Up the World* (Cambridge, Mass.: Harvard University Press, 2004) explores how the U.S. State Department sent jazz musicians as part of foreign policy strategy. Von Eschen explains how the United States showcased itself as a racially diverse nation through cultural exports.

45. Prior to the Cold War, the U.S. imaginary of Eastern Europe was primarily linked to the patterns of immigration from Eastern Europe to the United States. As scholars have noted, Eastern Europeans, along with the Jews, Italians, and Irish, were among the various European immigrant groups to be eventually incorporated into an American category of "whiteness" that initially included only northern Europeans. According to David Roediger, in the late 1800s, immigration from Western and northern Europe far outstripped immigration from Central and Eastern Europe, with the number of immigrants from the "other" Europe, or "new immigrants," beginning to rise toward the end of the nineteenth century and far outstripping northern and Western European migration by the 1910s. See Roediger, *Working Towards Whiteness: How America's Immigrants Became White: The Strange Journey from Ellis Island to the Suburbs* (New York: Basic Books, 2005), 146. In spite of the "new immigrants'" initially precarious position in the American racial landscape, where many were discriminated against through hiring and labor practices and racist nativist attacks, they always held a position "in-between" racialized populations, such as black and

Asian Americans and the older immigrant groups that constituted white Americans already enjoying the full privileges of citizenship. In other words, Eastern European immigrants were always viewed as having the potential to be assimilated into whiteness (as Theodore Roosevelt predicted, within two generations) (64). In fact, a wide variety of factors, including the great migration of African Americans to the North in the 1920s, housing laws and restrictions, and antimiscegenation laws, contributed to the gradual incorporation of southern and Eastern European immigrants into American whiteness by the 1940s and 1950s. The gradual assimilation of new immigrants in the United States has provided a model through which "ethnicity" is distinguished from race. According to Omi and Winant, for instance, ethnicity is a category that is mutable, allowing for assimilation, while race "was equated with hereditary characteristics" (see Omi and Winant, *Racial Formations*, 15). That is, in U.S. nation formation, racial difference is understood as the difference that always remains visible, while ethnic difference is viewed as cultural, a difference that can be shed. For more on Eastern European immigration in relation to the domestic consolidation of whiteness in the United States, see David Roediger, *The Wages of Whiteness: Race and the Making of the American Working Class* (London: Verso, 1991); Matthew Frye Jacobson, *Whiteness of a Different Color: European Immigrants and the Alchemy of Race* (Cambridge, Mass.: Harvard University Press, 1999); Noel Ignatiev, *How the Irish Became White* (New York: Routledge, 1996); George Lipsitz, *The Possessive Investment in Whiteness: How White People Profit from Identity Politics* (Philadelphia: Temple University Press, 2006); Omi and Winant, *Racial Formations*.

46. Kim, *Ends of Empire*, 42–43.

47. Cited in Trevor B. McCrisken, *American Exceptionalism and the Legacy of Vietnam: U.S. Foreign Policy since 1974* (New York: Palgrave, 2004), 22.

48. Vladislav M. Zubok, *A Failed Empire: The Soviet Union in the Cold War from Stalin to Gorbachev* (Chapel Hill: University of North Carolina Press, 2007), 46 (emphasis added). In spite of this predominant characterization, Francine Hirsch's study has demonstrated that Sovietization was not a homogenizing process but one that involved "an interactive and participatory process" of vastly multiethnic peoples of the former Russian Empire, of which the Soviet Union was an inheritor (5). Although the ideal of recognizing nationalities did not prevent the Soviet Union from abolishing certain cultural, religious, and linguistic practices, the ideology behind the formation of the Soviet Union nevertheless contradicts the dominant Western Cold War perspective that Sovietization was an official policy of homogenization. Thus although American racial diversity was celebrated against the negative example of the Soviet Union during the Cold War, the Soviet Union itself actually functioned as a kind of multicultural entity. See Hirsch, *An Empire of Nations: Ethnographic Knowledge and the Making of the Soviet Union* (Ithaca, N.Y.: Cornell University Press, 2005).

49. Cited in Raymond Pearson, *The Rise and Fall of the Soviet Empire* (New York: Palgrave, 2002), 45–46. There were, however, a variety of books making similar arguments in the 1960s, including Robert Conquest's *The Last Empire: Nationality and the Soviet Future* (Stanford: Hoover Institution Press, 1986) and Walter Kolarz's *Communism and Colonialism* (New York: Macmillan, 1964).

50. Pearson, *Rise and Fall*, 46. Seton-Watson distinguished between an "inner" empire, that is, the Soviet Union itself, and an "outer" empire constituting the satellite nations.

51. See Madina Tlostanova, " 'Why Cut the Feet in Order to Fit the Western Shoes?': Non-European Soviet Ex-Colonies and the Modern Colonial Gender System," presented at the Symposium on Gender, Empire, and the Politics of Central and Eastern Europe, Central European University, Budapest, May 17–18, 2007. Also see Stephen Velychenko, "The Issue of Russian Colonialism in Ukrainian Thought: Dependency, Identity and Development," *Ad Imperio* 1 (2002): 323–67.

52. Hirsch, *An Empire of Nations*, 3 (emphasis added).

53. Ibid., 15. While prior to the 1917 revolution the Bolsheviks condemned all forms of imperial exploitation and called for national self-determination, after the revolution it became clear that Soviet Russia could not survive without the natural resources of the non-Russian provinces in Europe and Asia (5). According to Hirsch, "In an effort to reconcile their anti-imperialist position with their strong desire to hold on to all of the lands of the former Russian Empire, the Bolsheviks integrated the national idea into the administrative-territorial structure of the new Soviet Union. . . . They placed all of the peoples of the former Russian Empire into a definitional grid of official nationalities—simultaneously granting these peoples 'nationhood' and facilitating centralized rule" (5–6).

54. According to Shu-mei Shih, "The apparent inapplicability of the postsocialist framework to the West (i.e., Western Europe and the United States) is the major reason for the general lack of interest in the topic in American academia, where the discussions of postsocialism are largely confined within the now nominally debunked but actually existing area studies, the assumption being that it lacks universal significance" (28). See "Is the *Post-* in Postsocialism the *Post-* in Posthumanism?," *Social Text* 30, no. 1 110 (Spring 2012): 27–50. For another argument in favor of addressing postsocialism as a global condition, see Zsuzsa Gille, "Is There a Global Postsocialist Condition?,"*Global Society* 24, no. 1 (2010): 9–30.

55. Of course, postcolonial theorists have used the term to describe and critique ongoing legacies of imperial rule in the postcolonial world.

56. See, for instance, Agens Heller, "Between Past and Future," in *Between Past and Future: The Revolutions of 1989 and Their Aftermath*, ed. Sorin Antohi and Vladimir Tismaneanu (Budapest: Central European University Press, 2000), 3–13.

57. Edward Said, *Culture and Imperialism* (New York: Knopf, 1993).

58. Chad Thompson, "Postcolonialism, Postsocialism, and Multiple Remembrances," *Socialist Studies* 6, no. 1 (2010): 1–10, 9.

59. Shih, "Is the *Post-* in Postsocialism the *Post-* in Posthumanism?," 42.

60. Ibid., 31.

61. Ibid., 29.

62. Ibid., 29.

63. Chari and Verdery, "Thinking between the Posts," 10.

64. Ibid., 11.

65. Ibid., 12.

66. Among these, particularly incisive studies include Elizabeth Dunn's *Privatizing Poland: Baby Food, Big Business, and the Remaking of Labor* (Ithaca, N.Y.: Cornell University Press, 2004) and, outside of the context of Central and Eastern Europe, Lisa Rofel's *Desiring China: Experiments in Neoliberalism, Sexuality, and Public Culture* (Durham, N.C.: Duke University Press, 2007).

67. Excellent examples of such an approach, focusing on the cultures of Central and Eastern Europe, include Katarzyna Marciniak's *Streets of Crocodiles: Photography, Media, and Postsocialist Landscapes in Poland* (Chicago: Intellect, 2011) and Aniko Imre's *Identity Games: Globalization and the Transformation of Media Cultures in New Europe* (Cambridge, Mass.: The MIT Press, 2009).

68. As Katherine Verdery shows, understanding communism as a mode of totalitarianism is largely wrong. Throughout the Eastern Bloc, opposition movements constantly undermined the Communist regimes. See Verdery, *What Was Socialism, and What Comes Next?* (Princeton, N.J.: Princeton University Press, 1996), 20.

69. Verdery argues, for instance, that it was socialism's articulation with capitalism that ultimately led to its demise. See Verdery, *What Was Socialism*, 33.

70. Numerous critics have already addressed the importance and adaptation of *Heart of Darkness* in Vietnam War films such as Francis Ford Coppola's *Apocalypse Now* (1979) and Oliver Stone's *Platoon* (1986).

1. Racial Time and the Other

1. Arthur Schlesinger Jr., *The Disuniting of America: Reflections on a Multicultural Society*, revised and enlarged ed. (New York: Norton, 1998). Speaking about the work, Schlesinger stated, "I am all for multiculturalism when that means teaching our kids about other continents, cultures, creeds, colors; when that means giving proper recognition to the role of minorities in the history of the United States; when it means seeing things from different viewpoints. But when multiculturalism is carried to the point of promoting and perpetuating separate ethnic and racial communities, I find that alarming." Cited in Joan Sutton Strauss, "The Alarming Rise of Ethnicity: Bosnia a 'Murderous Portent' of Future: Arthur Schlesinger," *Financial Post* (Toronto), September 14, 1992, 17.

2. Strauss, "The Alarming Rise of Ethnicity," 17.

3. Schlesinger, for instance, in *The Disuniting of America* (52), argued that history, or how we know and teach the past, became an unparalleled "weapon" in the post–Cold War global and national reordering of things.

4. Ibid., 11.

5. Fukuyama, "The End of History?," *National Interest*, Summer 1989, www.wesjones .com/eoh.htm.

6. In the article, Fukuyama briefly addresses, and dismisses, nationalism and religious fundamentalism as serious ideological threats to parliamentary democracy.

7. See Benjamin Barber, "Jihad vs. McWorld," *Atlantic Magazine*, March 1992, http:// www.theatlantic.com/magazine/archive/1992/03/jihad-vs-mcworld/3882/. Also see Samuel P. Huntington, "The Clash of Civilizations?," *Foreign Affairs*, Summer 1993, http://www.foreignaffairs.com/articles/48950/samuel-p-huntington/the -clash-of-civilizations.

8. As Schlesinger puts it, "The United States is the only large-scale multi-ethnic society that has worked, and that is because it developed a notion of an American identity which transcends, absorbs, changes and is changed by, the subcultures which newcomers bring to this country" (cited in Strauss, "The Alarming Rise of Ethnicity," 17). In other words, the United States uses diversity as a resource of change. Other nations and regions, those mired in conflict over race and religion, by implication, refuse change, choosing instead to violently pursue ancient conflicts.

9. Michael T. Kaufman, "The Dangers of Letting a President Read," *New York Times*, May 22, 1999, B11, late edition.

10. Johannes Fabian, *Time and the Other: How Anthropology Makes Its Object* (New York: Columbia University Press, 1983), 7.

11. Numerous studies of European imperial travel literature have observed that travel writing, in its historical function of culturally mapping European empires, worked to consolidate European national identities as embodiments of modernity and civilization and to justify European dominance over their racialized colonial peripheries. Mary Louise Pratt's seminal work, *Imperial Eyes*, examines European travel and exploration writing since 1750 in connection to European imperial—political, economic, and geographic—expansion. Her work elaborates on the power dynamics inherent in the Western traveler's field of vision, which she explains through the figure of the "seeing-man," her label for "the white male subject of European landscape discourse—he whose imperial eyes passively look out and possess" (9). Building on Pratt's work, Inderpal Grewal argues that by the nineteenth century, observation and travel were aligned to develop a "visualization of experience" as part of a racialized and gendered Western subject formation (1). In the moment of high European imperialism, travel narratives thus functioned to consolidate European whiteness over and against their racialized exteriority. See Inderpal Grewal, *Home and Harem: Nation, Gender, Empire, and the Cultures of Travel* (Durham, N.C.: Duke University Press, 1996); Mary Louise Pratt, *Imperial Eyes: Travel Writing and Transculturation* (New York: Routledge, 1992).

12. See Larry Wolff's *Inventing Eastern Europe: The Map of Civilization on the Mind of the Enlightenment* (Stanford, Calif.: Stanford University Press, 1994).

13. Of course, even before the Cold War, when travel became a privileged symbol of capitalist subjects' mobility, travel narratives were important to Western European views of Eastern Europe. Historians of Eastern Europe, such as Larry Wolff and Maria Todorova, have demonstrated that between the eighteenth century and the start of the Cold War, the travel narrative served as the predominant cultural form through which the West has imagined Eastern Europe. Yet while, according to Wolff, "the invention of Eastern Europe" in the eighteenth century did not require Enlightenment thinkers to physically travel to Eastern Europe in order to imagine its physical and moral landscapes, in the Cold War period Western travelers had to penetrate the Iron Curtain in order to demonstrate their freedom to move. See Wolff, *Imagining Eastern Europe*; Maria Todorova, *Imagining the Balkans* (New York: Oxford University Press, 1997).

14. As Caren Kaplan shows, "Travel is very much a modern concept, signifying both commercial and leisure movement in an era of expanding Western capitalism." See Kaplan, *Questions of Travel: Postmodern Discourses of Displacement* (Durham, N.C.: Duke University Press, 1996), 3.

15. Henry Luce, "The American Century," in *Culture and Containment: 1929–1945*, ed. Warren Susman (New York: George Braziller, 1973), 324.

16. Fabian, *Time and the Other*, 6.

17. J. M. Degérando, cited in Fabian, *Time and the Other*, 7.

18. Ibid., 7, 11–12 (emphasis in original).

19. Ibid., 2.

20. Ibid., 26.

21. Ibid. (emphasis in original).

22. Ibid., 27, 146. In *Time and the Other*, Fabian further contrasts secular and natural time, an important distinction for the emergence of anthropological knowledge. For my purposes here, however, I am limiting my discussion to his elaboration of secular time and its relation to the trope of travel.

23. Ibid., 144.

24. Anita Starosta, "Eastern Europe, Literature, and Post-Imperial Difference" (PhD dissertation, UC Santa Cruz, 2009), 31 (emphasis in original).

25. Thomas Borstelmann, *The Cold War and the Color Line: American Race Relations in the Global Arena* (Cambridge, Mass.: Harvard University Press, 2001), 258.

26. Melani McAlister's chapter "Iran, Islam, and the Terrorist Threat, 1979–1989," in *Epic Encounters: Culture, Media, and U.S. Interests in the Middle East, 1945–2000* (Los Angeles: University of California Press, 2001), extensively explores "the cultural and political work that the representation of terrorism did in mapping certain moral geographies, and the role of that mapping in supporting U.S. expansionist nationalism" (201).

27. On the domestic front, emphasis on the Soviet threat abroad obscured the Reagan administration's racist policies and destruction of social welfare networks throughout the 1980s. Borstelmann, for instance, explains that "Reagan rode to victory in 1980 on a wave of unhappiness with inflation, unemployment, and the seizure of American hostages in Teheran. His defeat of Carter carried racial significance. . . . His political ascendancy built from the Watts riots of 1965, as he was elected governor of California a year later as a proponent of law and order. His opposition to civil rights bills in the 1960s is well known. In 1980 Reagan continued the Republican strategy of appealing to disaffected white Southern voters, in particular by rejecting affirmative action. . . . The Justice Department opposed affirmative action, narrowed its definition of racial discrimination, and supported federal tax exemptions for racially discriminatory schools. The administration's economic policies favoring wealthier Americans and cutting social spending disproportionally hurt nonwhite citizens" (Borstelmann, *The Cold War and the Color Line*, 259–60). While in office, the Reagan administration's trickle-down economic policies thus widened the gap between poor and wealthy Americans, and the burdens of his cuts to social spending fell disproportionately on nonwhite citizens.

28. James Kyung-Jin Lee, *Urban Triage: Race and the Fictions of Multiculturalism* (Minneapolis: University of Minnesota Press, 2004), xiv.

29. Peter McLaren, "White Terror and Oppositional Agency: Towards a Critical Multiculturalism," in *Multiculturalism: A Critical Reader*, ed. David Theo Goldberg (Cambridge, Mass.: Blackwell, 1994), 51.

30. Lee's book was broadly circulated and well received, gaining a nomination for the National Book Award and winning the Jean Stein Award.

31. Andrea Lee, "Double Lives," in *They Went: The Art and Craft of Travel Writing*, ed. William Zinsser (Boston: Houghton Mifflin Company, 1991), 57–74, 57.

32. Ibid., 58.

33. Her work was excerpted in the June 30 and July 7 editions of the *New Yorker*.

34. December 3, 1979, 120–40.

35. *New Yorker*, February 18, 1980, 25.

36. "Talk of the Town," *New Yorker*, July 14, 1980, 22.

37. Ibid., 120.

38. Ibid., 133.

39. Kate Baldwin, *Beyond the Color Line and the Iron Curtain: Reading Encounters between Black and Red, 1922–1963* (Durham, N.C.: Duke University Press, 2002), 3–4.

40. Lee, "Double Lives," 59.

41. Ibid., 60.

42. Ibid.

43. Ibid., 61.

44. Ibid., 65.

45. Ibid., 66.

46. Ibid., 70.

47. Ibid., 73.

48. Ibid., 71.

49. *New York Times,* October 6, 1981, C9.

50. In Pratt, *Imperial Eyes*, 78.

51. Susan Jacoby, "One Year in Moscow," *New York Times*, October 25, 1981, BR3.

52. Allison Blakely, in his historical look at Russian representations of blackness, argues that it is Lee's light skin that allows her to observe racism in the U.S.S.R. He writes, "Andrea Lee, a black American who accompanied her husband during his ten months as an exchange student in Russia, . . . elicited the following comment from an Ethiopian she met: 'Most of my African classmates hate it here. . . . The Russian narod, the masses, call us black devils and spit at us in the streets.' Lee was apparently not recognized as black by Russians because of her light complexion. She observed several clear signs that strong negative racial feelings toward blacks as well as other non-Russian nationalities persist in Soviet society" (141). At the same time, there is no indication in *Russian Journal*, or in Lee's later consideration of her time spent in the U.S.S.R., that her light complexion allowed her a more whole or unbiased view of the U.S.S.R. In fact, Lee paints a very negative portrait of the Ethiopian students' attitude toward black Americans—an attitude that the Russians she

encounters do not seem to possess. See Blakely, *Russia and the Negro: Blacks in Russian History and Thought* (Washington, D.C.: Howard University Press, 1986).

53. Patricia Williams, *Seeing a Color-Blind Future: The Paradox of Race* (New York: Farrar, Straus, and Giroux, 1997), 4.

54. This chapter was part of the excerpt included in the June 30, 1980, issue of the *New Yorker*.

55. *Russian Journal*, 67.

56. Ibid., 68.

57. Ibid., 183.

58. Ibid., 184.

59. Ibid., 183.

60. Ibid., 183–84.

61. Ibid., 234.

62. Ibid.

63. Ibid.

64. Ibid., 8.

65. Yelena Khanga, with Susan Jacoby, *Soul to Soul: The Story of a Black Russian American Family, 1865–1992* (New York: W. W. Norton & Company, 1992). Most reviewers of *Soul to Soul* praised the memoir for addressing the complicated connections between U.S. racial history and Cold War history. Eric Foner's review in the *New York Times*, "Three Very Rare Generations," was the only one to suggest that Khanga's book fell flat in relation to the radical history of the black diaspora that it told (December 13, 1992, 14, late edition, East Coast).

66. James McBride, "Yelena Khanga's Voyage of Discovery: A Black Soviet Journalist, Learning—and Teaching—in the Land of Her Grandparents," *Washington Post*, February 4, 1998, B1.

67. Gary Lee, December 20, 1992, X2.

68. Karima A. Haynes, "How a Black/Jewish/Polish/Russian/African Woman Found Her Roots," *Ebony*, December 1992, 44.

69. V. R. Peterson, "Review of *Soul to Soul*," *Essence*, December 1992, 42.

70. Shortly after Yelena's birth, in 1962, her father was assassinated in Tanzania.

71. *Soul to Soul*, 27.

72. Dale Peterson, *Up from Bondage: The Literatures of Russian and African American Soul* (Durham, N.C.: Duke University Press, 2000), 11.

73. *Soul to Soul*, 229.

74. Ibid., 252.

75. V. R. Peterson, "Review of *Soul to Soul*," 42.

76. *Soul to Soul*, 297.

77. Ibid., 114.

78. Ibid., 115.

79. Ibid., 271.

80. Ibid.

81. Quoted in Diane E. Lewis, "A Black Journalist from Russia Dreams of Cooperative Effort," *Boston Globe*, November 30, 1992, 52.

82. Kate Baldwin, *Beyond the Color Line*, 253.

83. Valerie Bunce, "Postsocialisms," in *Between Past and Future: The Revolutions of 1989 and Their Aftermath*, ed. Sorin Antohi and Vladimir Tismaneanu (New York: Central European University Press, 2000), 122–152, 136–37.

84. See the organization's mission statement and history on its website, freedomhouse .org.

85. Robert D. Kaplan, *Balkan Ghosts: A Journey through History* (New York: St. Martin's Press, 1993), xxi.

86. Ibid., 48.

87. This argument was first outlined in *Balkan Ghosts* and developed in more detail in Robert Kaplan, *Eastward to Tartary: Travels in the Balkans, the Middle East, and the Caucus* (New York: Random House, 2000), 12, 32.

88. Cynthia Simmons, "Baedeker Barbarism: Rebecca West's *Black Lamb and Grey Falcon* and Robert Kaplan's *Balkan Ghosts*," *Human Rights Review*, October–December 2000, 109–24, 109. Kaplan himself has ardently denied wanting to influence policy in the Balkans in favor of isolationism. Responding to reports that Clinton used his book as an excuse against intervention, having "inferred that the region's peoples had never lived together peacefully very long," Kaplan writes, "This sort of report wouldn't bother me had I been, like so many others, opposed to intervention. Unfortunately . . . I wasn't. From late 1992 to the present . . . I have been an unambiguous, public interventionist." Kaplan's response was published as the opinion piece "Reading Too Much into a Book," *New York Times*, June 13, 1999, republished in *Balkan Ghosts: New Edition* (New York: Picador, 2005), xxix.

89. Simmons, "Baedeker Barbarism," 110.

90. Ibid., 113.

91. Ibid., 114, 116.

92. Kaplan, "Reading Too Much into a Book," xxix.

93. Ibid., xxxi.

94. Ibid.

95. Kaplan, *Balkan Ghosts*, xxiii.

96. Ibid., xvi.

97. Ibid., xv.

98. Ibid., xvi, xvii.

99. Ibid., xvi.

100. See Vesna Goldsworthy, *Inventing Ruritania: The Imperialism of the Imagination* (New Haven, Conn.: Yale University Press, 1998). Goldsworthy argues that Kaplan "ensures that Central Europe's most monstrous creation of modern times, Hitler, can be unburdened on the Balkans" (7).

101. Kaplan, *Balkan Ghosts*, xxiii.

102. Ibid., xxxvi.

103. Ibid.

104. Ibid., 97.

105. Ibid., 76.

106. Ibid., xxiii.

107. Ibid.

108. Ibid., 175.

109. Ibid., 108.

110. Ibid.

111. Ibid., 108, 122.

112. Ibid., 16 (emphasis in original).

113. Ibid., 25.

114. Ibid., 169.

115. Ibid., 174.

116. Ibid., 179–80.

117. Ibid., 122–23.

118. Ibid., 38.

119. Ibid.

120. Ibid.

121. Ibid., 149–50.

122. Ibid., 58.

123. Kaplan, *Eastward to Tartary*, 33.

124. Ibid., 6.

125. Ibid., 26. In *Eastward to Tartary*, the sequel to *Balkan Ghosts*, Kaplan further expands on the distinctions between the Hapsburg and Ottoman Empires, arguing that the difference in development between those nations, like Hungary, Poland, and the Czech Republic that had been affected by Hapsburg rule, and those like Romania and Bulgaria that had been under Ottoman rule, remains profound in spite of the fifty years of communism throughout the Eastern Bloc (6).

126. Ibid., 285.

127. Ibid., 287.

128. Shu-mei Shih, "Is the *Post-* in Postsocialism the *Post-* in Posthumanism?," *Social Text* 30, no. 1 (Spring 2012): 27–50, 29.

129. See Robert Kaplan, *Surrender or Starve: The Wars behind the Famine* (Boulder, Colo.: Westview Press, 1988), and *Soldiers of God: With the Mujahidin in Afghanistan* (Boston: Houghton Mifflin, 1990).

130. "The Coming Anarchy" was published in 1994 in *Atlantic Monthly* magazine and has caused much debate. In the piece, Kaplan takes a Malthusian perspective that nature and resources, rather than imperial legacies, cause Africa's problems. Republished in *The Coming Anarchy: Shattering the Dreams of the Post Cold War* (New York: Random House, 2000).

131. Kaplan's critique of liberal humanitarian impulses is most clearly articulated in *The Coming Anarchy*, while his post-9/11 *Imperial Grunts: The American Military on the Ground* (New York: Random House, 2005) is ardently supportive of an aggressive U.S. imperial policy.

132. See Patrick Brantlinger, "Kipling's 'The White Man's Burden' and Its Afterlives," *English Literature in Transition* 50, no. 2 (2007): 172–91, 185.

133. Cited in Brantlinger, "Kipling's 'The White Man's Burden' and Its Afterlives," 185.

2. The Vietnam War and the Ethics of Failure

1. *An Unlikely Weapon,* directed by Susan Morgan Cooper, Morgan Cooper Productions, 2008.

2. See Patrick Hagopian, "Vietnam War Photography as a Locus of Memory," in *Locating Memory: Photographic Acts,* ed. Annette Kuhn and Kristen Emiko McAllister (New York: Berghahn Books, 2005), 201.

3. See, for instance, Michael Griffin, "Media Images of War," *Media, War & Conflict* 3, no. 7 (2010): 7–41.

4. Luciano explains that in the nineteenth century, grief as the affective time of feeling became a compensatory mechanism for the perceived mechanization and fast pace of a modernizing nation. See *Arranging Grief: Sacred Time and the Body in Nineteenth-Century America* (New York: New York University Press, 2007), 6.

5. Edward Said, *Culture and Imperialism* (New York: Vintage Books, 1993), 428.

6. As a number of scholars have noted, Conrad's *Heart of Darkness,* a novel that addresses multiple and overlapping imperial projects and critiques the brutality and horror embedded in European civilizational discourses, became a dominant narrative frame through which the Vietnam War was dramatized in the U.S. imaginary. See, for example, Margot Norris, "Modernism and Vietnam: Francis Ford Coppola's *Apocalypse Now,*" *Modern Fiction Studies* 44, no. 3 (1998): 730–66. Also see Said, *Culture and Imperialism,* xix.

7. Joseph Conrad, *Heart of Darkness,* ed. Paul B. Armstrong (New York: Norton, 2006).

8. "Address of Senator John F. Kennedy Accepting the Democratic Party Nomination for the Presidency of the United States—Memorial Coliseum, Los Angeles," July 15, 1960, *The American Presidency Project,* ed. John T. Woolley and Gerhard Peters, http://www.presidency.ucsb.edu.

9. Ibid.

10. Ibid.

11. Dipesh Chakrabarty, *Provincializing Europe: Postcolonial Thought and Historical Difference* (Princeton, N.J.: Princeton University Press, 2000), 15.

12. "Address of Senator John F. Kennedy."

13. Ibid.

14. According to Richard Slotkin, throughout U.S. history, the frontier has symbolized the possibility of the nation's spiritual regeneration through violence. See *Regeneration through Violence: The Mythology of the American Frontier, 1600–1860* (Middletown, Conn.: Wesleyan University Press, 1973); *Gunfighter Nation: The Myth of the Frontier in Twentieth-Century America* (New York: Harper-Perennial, 1993).

15. Slotkin writes that Thomas Jefferson's and Frederick Jackson Turner's conception that U.S. democratic principles regenerate in the frontier and Andrew Jackson's principle of territorial conquest in the frontier all have at their foundation the Puritan idea that spiritual regeneration occurs in the New World frontier (*Gunfighter Nation,* 11).

16. Slotkin, *Gunfighter Nation,* 77.

17. Ibid., 14.

18. This included an argument for promoting diversity. As Kennedy explained in a 1962 speech, "We must reject over-simplified theories of international life—the theory that American power is unlimited, or that the American mission is to remake the world in the American image. We must seize the vision of a free and diverse world— and shape our policies to speed progress toward a more flexible world order." Address given at the University of California at Berkeley, March 23, 1962, John F. Kennedy Presidential Library and Museum, http://www.jfklibrary.org/Research /Ready-Reference/JFK-Speeches/Address-At-The-University-Of-California-At -Berkeley.aspx.

19. In Slotkin, *Gunfighter Nation*, 527.

20. Ibid., 585.

21. William Spanos, *America's Shadow: An Anatomy of Empire* (Minneapolis: University of Minnesota Press, 1990).

22. James Clifford, *The Predicament of Culture: Twentieth Century Ethnography, Literature, Art* (Cambridge, Mass.: Harvard University Press, 1988), 105.

23. These are named as the three primary causes for criticism in the addendum to the 1910 *Encyclopedia Britannica* entry on the Congo Free State (in Conrad, *Heart of Darkness*, 113). The collapse of humanitarian concerns into non-Belgian free-trade interests in Africa abounded in British reformers' writing on the subject of the Congo Free State. In particular, ideas about "freedom" depended on the European nations' negotiations regarding their sovereignty in colonial holdings, and through respect for these agreements certain forms of imperial rule were deemed principled and just. Edmund Morel, the founder of the Congo Reform Association, a group that publicized the atrocities in the Congo Free State, explained it thus: "A European Government may be justified in evolving theoretical paper rights of sovereignty over land which—and such land does exist in many parts of tropical Africa—is, through pestilence, inter-tribal warfare, emigration, or some such cause, really and truly 'vacant.' . . . But to treat native land-tenure as a factor of no account in Afro-European relationship . . . is merely an attempt to cover spoliation, robbery, and violence under legal formulae (see "Property and Trade versus Forced Production," in Conrad, *Heart of Darkness*, 164). According to Morel, beyond the claiming of "vacant lands," once imperial sovereignty is established there is a correct and an incorrect way to deal with native populations. In contrast to the Congo Free State's abuses, Morel cites the positive example of "voluntary labor of the natives" in French Senegal and British Gambia to prove the "commercial proclivities of the Negro" and to argue for their participation in the principles of free labor and free trade (170). Morel concludes that what would be a proper humanitarian and moral project for Europeans to undertake is thus one that would lead to the development of capitalist principles in Africa. He writes, "In helping him to develop his property on scientific lines; in granting him internal peace; in proving to him that he is regarded not as a brute, but as a partner in a great undertaking from which Europe and Africa will derive lasting benefit—Europe will be adopting the only just, right, and practical policy" (171). The limits of the liberal critique, launched within a framework that took as a priori the

justice of European capitalist, scientific, and civilizational principles in Africa, were made manifest in the inadvertent association between humanitarian action in Africa and European profit from African "voluntary labor" that, as Morel noted, "supplied Europe with £100,000 worth of high-class cocoa, and they and their relatives on the French Ivory Coast sent us £500,000 worth of mahogany" (170).

24. Conrad, *Heart of Darkness*, 22.
25. Alan Simmons, "Conrad, Casement, and the Congo Atrocities," in Conrad, *Heart of Darkness*, 187, 189.
26. Adam Hochschild, "Meeting Mr. Kurtz," in Conrad, *Heart of Darkness*, 177–78.
27. Chinua Achebe, "An Image of Africa," Special Issue on Literary Criticism, *Research in African Literatures* 9, no. 1 (Spring 1978): 1–15.
28. Ibid., 8.
29. Ibid., 3.
30. Ibid., 9.
31. Ibid., 13. Hunt Hawkins, for instance, writes in response to Achebe that "the lasting political legacy of *Heart of Darkness*, more than any confirmation of racism, has been its alarm over atrocity. Its title has entered our lexicon as code for extreme human rights abuses, usually those committed by whites in non-Western countries but also those committed in Europe" (quoted in Conrad, *Heart of Darkness*, 375). Of course, Achebe's point is that the metaphysical production of Africa as object enables the formulation of atrocity to begin with.
32. "To Roger Casement," in Conrad, *Heart of Darkness*, 270.
33. Conrad, *Heart of Darkness*, 33.
34. Ibid., 36.
35. Ibid., 95.
36. Ibid., 95–96.
37. Ibid., 70.
38. Marita Sturken, *Tangled Memories: The Vietnam War, the AIDS Epidemic, and the Politics of Remembering* (Berkeley: University of California Press, 1997).
39. Norris, "Modernism and Vietnam," 731.
40. Ibid., 735.
41. From *Hearts of Darkness: A Filmmaker's Apocalypse*, written and directed by Fax Bahr and George Hickenlooper, Cineplex-Odeon Films, 1991.
42. Amy Kaplan, "Left Alone in America: The Absence of Empire in the Study of U.S. Culture," in *Cultures of U.S. Imperialism*, ed. Amy Kaplan and Donald Pease (Durham, N.C.: Duke University Press, 1993), 18.
43. Ibid., 19.
44. *Hearts of Darkness* even suggests that previous failures, such as that of Orson Welles, to translate Conrad's novel successfully for the big screen represent a sort of filmmakers' curse. The "curse" is made manifest in Francis Coppola's individual, creative journey into darkness and the obstacles beyond the crew's control encountered during the production process, such as the typhoon that stopped production for two months and Martin Sheen's heart attack.

45. As Kim Worthy argues, in spite of the documentary representation of Francis Coppola as a Hollywood outsider and underdog who suffers great losses throughout the filming process, *Hearts of Darkness* is not about a loss but about a victory at Cannes. See "Emissaries of Difference: Conrad, Coppola, and *Hearts of Darkness*," *Women's Studies: An Interdisciplinary Journal* 25, no. 2 (1996): 153–67.

46. Bahr and Hickenlooper, *Hearts of Darkness*.

47. According to an interview with Hagedorn, both stories are inspired by actual events that took place in the Philippines. The first is based on an alleged hoax about the Tasaday tribe from Mindanao, in the southern Philippines. The second is about Francis Ford Coppola's filming of *Apocalypse Now* in the Philippines beginning in 1976. See http://us.penguingroup.com/static/rguides/us/dream_jungle.html.

48. Jessica Hagedorn, *Dream Jungle* (New York: Penguin, 2003), 305.

49. Ibid., 85–86.

50. "A Conversation with Jessica Hagedorn," http://us.penguingroup.com/static/rguides/us/dream_jungle.html.

51. Hagedorn, *Dream Jungle*, 219.

52. Ibid., 247.

53. Ibid., 248.

54. Ibid., 248 (emphasis in original).

55. During the Vietnam War, journalistic reports critical of U.S. warfare and even imperialism often objectified Vietnam as a peasant nation, which was outside of modernity until it was violently brought into Cold War politics through U.S. militarism. As Hagedorn's *Dream Jungle* insightfully demonstrates, fictions about war, even those that strive for an antiwar message, do not necessarily step out of dominant national and imperial frames and might replicate the very violence they propose to critique. Indeed, they often depend on existing imperial worldviews and thus re-create temporalizing fictions of prehistory and premodernity through which to envision the possibility of national recovery.

56. Sara Ahmed, *The Cultural Politics of Emotion* (New York: Routledge, 2004), 21.

57. Ibid., 101–2.

58. Ibid., 106.

59. The association between the camera as weapon and the violence of representation is, of course, well established. Barthes and Sontag both draw on this association. Recently, Judith Butler elaborated on Barthes's and Sontag's theorizations, arguing that the camera's agency is a technology of war rather than an extension of the person holding the camera. See Butler, *Frames of War: When Is Life Grievable?* (New York: Verso, 2010).

60. Butler, *Frames of War*, 76–77.

61. Ibid., 49–50.

62. This is, for instance, the main logic of Philip Jones Griffiths's antiwar book of photography, *Vietnam Inc.* (New York: Phaidon, 2001), originally published in 1971. The text accompanying the images posits that the village system in Vietnam, unchanged for thousands of years, has made the Vietnamese impossible to defeat, and that the

nation is incompatible with the ideologies that the United States wants to export through war.

63. David Grosser, "American Hearts and Minds," in *From Hanoi to Hollywood: The Vietnam War in American Film*, ed. Linda Dittmar and Gene Michaud (New Brunswick, N.J.: Rutgers University Press, 1990), 276.

64. As John Carlos Rowe points out, even documentaries that attempt to tell alternate histories are often normalized in their reception. He cites *Hearts and Minds* as one example. Rowe argues that in a war in which reality seemed illusive amid the chaos and irrationality, realist aesthetics helped satisfy the desire to explain and rationalize horrific events. In this sense, the documentary form functions as an "idea weapon" in that it furthers the illusion of realism. Thus even though, as I am suggesting here, the still image of horror, which Davis's documentary incorporates into its form, functions as a punctum to rationalizing discourses about the war, the "real" that is seen as the defining feature of the documentary form and photojournalism also served an alternate function of restoring reason. See Rowe, "Eyewitness: Documentary Styles in the American Representations of Vietnam," in *Cultural Critique* 3 (Spring 1986): 126–50.

65. Roland Barthes, *Camera Lucida: Reflections on Photography*, trans. Richard Howard (New York: Hill and Wang, 1981), 90. On the relationship between the still photograph and docudramas depicting the Vietnam War, see Sturken's *Tangled Memories*.

66. Ibid., 92.

67. See, for instance, Susan Sontag's discussion in *Regarding the Pain of Others* (New York: Picador, 2003), 59, and Barbie Zelizer's *About to Die: How News Images Move the Public* (New York: Oxford University Press, 2010).

68. Sylvia Shin Huey Chong, *The Oriental Obscene: Violence and Racial Fantasies in the Vietnam Era* (Durham, N.C.: Duke University Press, 2012), 77.

69. Sontag, *Regarding the Pain of Others*, 42.

70. Ibid., 53, 74.

71. Ibid., 71–72.

72. *Eddie Adams: Vietnam*, ed. Alyssa Adams (New York: Umbrage Editions, 2008).

73. Vivian Sobchack, cited in Chong, *The Oriental Obscene*, 89.

74. Ibid., 11.

75. Ibid.

76. Ibid., 12.

77. Ibid., 17.

78. Ibid., 16.

79. Ibid., 16. In contrast, Adams's own view of his photography emphasized the process of framing war over the idea that photographers convey a transparent access to reality. In the collection of photos, Adams is quoted as stating, "I think all war should be shot in black-and-white. It's more primitive. Color tends to make things look too nice. It makes the jungle in Vietnam look lush—which it was. But it wasn't nice" (42). Unlike the contemporary mythologizing of Vietnam as accessible and transparent and, therefore, open to moral action, Adams's perspective emphasizes that he

self-consciously depicted Vietnam as primitive to convey a message about the evils of war. For him, it was necessary to portray Vietnam carefully so that the lush setting did not exceed its intended message—about war, about suffering, and about death. This conception of the Vietnamese landscape articulated by Adams as symbolic of the United States' descent into chaos and brutality is echoed in countless portrayals of the jungle as leading to savagery and making victory for the United States impossible. For instance, Larry Burrows's well-known 1963 *Life* magazine photo essay, which portrays death and devastation, is subtitled, "We Wade Deeper into the Jungle."

80. Robert Hariman and John Lucaites, *No Caption Needed: Iconic Photographs, Public Culture, and Liberal Democracy* (Chicago: University of Chicago Press, 2007), 2.

81. Ibid., 2.

82. Ibid., 183.

83. Cited in Noam Chomsky, "Visions of Righteousness," in *The Vietnam War in American Culture*, ed. John Carlos Rowe and Rick Berg (New York: Columbia University Press, 1991), 22.

84. Ibid., 21.

85. Conrad, *Heart of Darkness,* 61–62.

3. Restoring National Faith

1. *Charlie Wilson's War,* directed by Mike Nichols, Universal Studios, 2007.

2. Cited in Mark Graham, *Afghanistan in the Cinema* (Urbana: University of Illinois Press, 2010), 51.

3. Graham proposes this reading in *Afghanistan in the Cinema*, 53.

4. On Christian iconography and the frontier myth, see Richard Slotkin's *Regeneration through Violence: The Mythology of the American Frontier, 1600–1860* (Middletown, Conn.: Wesleyan University Press, 1973) and *Gunfighter Nation: The Myth of the Frontier in Twentieth-Century America* (New York: Harper-Perennial, 1993).

5. For conceptualizations of Afghanistan as the "graveyard of empires," see, for example, Milton Bearden, "Afghanistan, Graveyard of Empires," in *Foreign Affairs* (November–December 2001), http://www.foreignaffairs.com/articles/57411/milton-bearden/afghanistan-graveyard-of-empires, and Seth Jones, *In the Graveyard of Empires: America's War in Afghanistan* (New York: Norton, 2009).

6. Stephen Vlastos, "America's 'Enemy': The Absent Presence in Revisionist Vietnam War History," in *The Vietnam War in American Culture*, ed. John Carlos Rowe and Rick Berg (New York: Columbia University Press, 1991), 55.

7. "Text of the Reagan Message to Congress on Foreign Policy," *New York Times*, March 15, 1986, 4.

8. *ABC News*, February 19, 1981.

9. *ABC News*, November 18, 1985.

10. Interview, *ABC News*, November 22, 1983.

11. "Transcript of Reagan's State of the Union Message to Nation," *New York Times*, January 26, 1988, A16.

12. "Text of the Reagan Message to Congress on Foreign Policy."

13. Interview with Mark Palmer of the State Department, *ABC News*, November 18, 1985.

14. Cited in Graham, *Afghanistan in the Cinema.*
15. Leslie H. Gelb, "The Doctrine/Un-Doctrine of Covert/Overt Aid," *New York Times*, February 21, 1986, A14.
16. Cited in Gelb, "The Doctrine." For a critique of the Reagan Doctrine as vague, see John R. Wallach, "Reagan Misuses History in Seeking Aid for the Contras," *New York Times*, April 13, 1986, E25.
17. "Excerpts from the President's Speech in California on U.S.-Soviet Relations," *New York Times*, August 27, 1987, A8.
18. Ibid.
19. CBS, special broadcast, January 4, 1980.
20. "Renewing the Compact," *New York Times*, July 18, 1980, A8.
21. *NBC Nightly News*, January 14, 1982.
22. Robert Pears, "Arming Afghan Guerillas," *New York Times*, April 18, 1988, A1.
23. "America: Where Do We Go from Here?" *CBS News*, February 1, 1980.
24. Pat Mitchell and Jeremy Isaacs (producers), *Cold War* "Soldiers of God," narrated by Kenneth Branagh, CNN, September 29, 2001; original air date 1998.
25. *CBS Evening News*, April 4, 1980.
26. *CBS Evening News*, December 15, 1982.
27. "Inside Afghanistan," CBS, *60 Minutes*, April 1, 1980.
28. *NBC Nightly News*, June 11, 1984.
29. "Red Star over Khyber," PBS, *Frontline*, narrated by Judy Woodruff, December 13, 1984.
30. Ibid.
31. Rosanne Klass, "The New Holocaust," *National Review* 4 (October 1985): 28–29.
32. Orrin G. Hatch, "Don't Forget the Afghans," *New York Times*, November 22, 1985, A35.
33. Cited in Jean-Francois Revel, "The Awful Logic of Genocide," *National Review* 4 (October 1985): 22–28.
34. Ibid. In line with the emphasis on Soviet brutality against civilians, numerous news reports cited the practice of planting land mines, masked to look like children's toys, so that when a young child picks up what he or she thinks is a toy, the mine detonates, maiming the child but not killing him or her. A representative report is Dan Rather's "Inside Afghanistan," CBS, *60 Minutes*, April 1, 1980.
35. A number of news reports used the phrase "hidden war" to describe the Soviet invasion, for example, *NBC Nightly News*, June 11, 1984.
36. Revel, "The Awful Logic of Genocide," 22.
37. Klass, "The New Holocaust," 29.
38. *NBC Nightly News*, July 19, 1980.
39. *CBS Evening News*, December 15, 1982.
40. *ABC News*, September 10, 1985.
41. Reagan made this comment on March 21, which he proclaimed to be Afghan Day, dedicating an upcoming space shuttle launch to the people of Afghanistan (*NBC Nightly News*, March 10, 1982).
42. Cited in Hatch, "Don't Forget the Afghans."
43. *CBS Evening News*, April 5, 1983.

44. Interestingly, and possibly to show their own transparency of journalistic practice, Dan Rather introduced the third part of Durschmied's "Under the Soviet Gun" with a report that the Soviet state news agency critiqued the CBS special as justifying undisguised U.S. interference in Afghanistan, *CBS Evening News*, April 7, 1983.

45. Interview with Frank Anderson of the CIA, in *Soldiers of God*.

46. "Afghanistan: Scenes from a Secret War," 1984, http://www.documentaryfree.com /watch/afghanistan-1984-scenes-from-a-secret-war.

47. *Soldiers of God*.

48. *ABC News*, December 27, 1984.

49. "The Face of Afghanistan's Pain: An Anonymous Portrait Echoes a Nation in Turmoil," NPR, *The World*, September 24, 2001.

50. Rae Lynn Schwartz-DuPre, "Portraying the Political: *National Geographic*'s Afghan Girl and U.S. Alibi for Aid," *Critical Studies in Media Communication* 27, no. 4 (2010): 336–56, 344.

51. Ibid.

52. Ibid., 347.

53. Ibid., 348.

54. Ibid., 351.

55. "Search for the Afghan Girl," National Geographic Channel, *Explorer*, 2002.

56. Wendy Hesford and Wendy Kozol offer an insightful reading of the famous 1985 *National Geographic* image of an Afghan girl juxtaposed with the 2002 image of the same girl as a grown woman wearing a veil. They write, "The 1985 *National Geographic* Afghan girl cover image that features the girl's apparent beauty and innocence appeals to Western viewers' sensibilities about who deserves and needs rescue" (6). In contrast, on the 2002 cover, the veil "functions as a symbol for Third World Women—secrecy, obscurity, and silence. . . . The veil has been configured in much of Western discourse as exemplifying the Other's imprisonment—a configuration upon which the United States has been dependent in its nationalist discourse of military intervention" (6). Adding to Hesford and Kozol's argument, I suggest that these two images also testify to the ways in which religion, as an increasingly important category in geopolitics, has been gendered. In 1985, the cover featuring the unveiled girl represented Afghanistan's need to be rescued from "godless" Soviet imperialism; after 9/11, the cover with the veiled woman represents Middle Eastern women in need of rescue from Islamic fundamentalism. Both visual calls to rescue, however, justify U.S. military presence. See *Just Advocacy? Women's Human Rights, Transnational Feminisms, and the Politics of Representation* (New Brunswick, N.J.: Rutgers University Press, 2005).

57. Chengzhi Zhang, "The Eyes That Will Make You Shiver," trans. Chee Keng Lee, *Inter-Asia Cultural Studies* 5, no. 3 (2004): 486–90.

58. Zhang discusses the technological "dazzle" in the episode as providing a verdict on the true identity of the Afghan girl, just as weapons technologies determine the outcome of the U.S. war in Afghanistan.

59. Greg Zoroya, "National Geographic Tracks Down Afghan Girl," *USA Today*, March 13, 2002, www.usatoday.com/news/world/2002/03/12/afghan-girl.htm.

60. Rose Capp, "The Quiet American," *Senses of Cinema*, 24, www.sensesofcinema.com
/2003/24/quiet_american/.

61. Cited in Joe Wiener, "Quiet in Hollywood," *Nation*, December 16, 2002, 6–7.

4. *Dracula* as Ethnic Conflict

1. *Van Helsing*, directed by Stephen Sommers, Universal Pictures, 2004.

2. "In the President's Words: 'We Act to Prevent a Wider War,' " *New York Times*, March 25, 1999, A15, late edition.

3. Samuel P. Huntington, "The Clash of Civilizations?," in *The Globalization Reader*, ed. Frank J. Lechner and John Boli (Malden, Mass.: Blackwell, 2000), 27–33.

4. Cited in Inderpal Grewal, *Home and Harem: Nation, Gender, Empire, and the Cultures of Travel* (Durham, N.C.: Duke University Press, 1996), 26.

5. Although it has been debated whether Romania can be considered a Balkan nation, it generally falls under this classification in the Euro-American popular imaginary. My use of moral geographies builds on Edward Said's elaboration of imaginative geography in *Orientalism* (New York: Vintage Books, 1979), which he develops to explain how space and time, as history and geography, attain meaning in cultural, political, and academic formations. He was particularly interested in the emergence of the concept of "the West" through the imagining of "the Orient." According to Said, "Space acquires emotional and even rational sense by a kind of poetic process, whereby the vacant or anonymous reaches of distance are converted into meaning for us here. The same process occurs when we deal with time" (55).

6. "In the President's Words."

7. Branka Arsić, "On the Dark Side of the Twilight," *Social Identities* 7 (December 2001): 551–71, 551.

8. Tomislav Longinović, "Vampires Like Us: Gothic Imaginary and 'the serbs,' " in *Balkan as Metaphor: Between Globalization and Fragmentation*, ed. Dušan Bjelić and Obrad Savić (Cambridge, Mass.: The MIT Press, 2002), 45.

9. Ibid., 51. I wish to be more than clear that I am not proposing to exonerate Milošević as a chief player in the destruction of Yugoslavia, nor am I suggesting that the world should have passively observed the conflict in the region escalate. Instead, I am attempting to assess the media and military technologies and the political and legal narratives through which the U.S.-led West of the post–Cold War order has been able to establish its often violent imperial interests as universal, benevolent, and humanitarian.

10. Ibid., 55.

11. Tim Allen, "Perceiving Contemporary Wars," in *The Media of Conflict: War Reporting and Representations of Racial Violence*, ed. Tim Allen and Jean Seaton (New York: Zed Books, 1999), 11–42.

12. See Tomislav Longinović, *Vampire Nation: Violence as Cultural Imaginary* (Durham, N.C.: Duke University Press, 2011).

13. John Bowen, "The Myth of Global Ethnic Conflict," *Journal of Democracy* 7, no. 4 (1996): 3–14, 3.

14. "Speech: 'I'll Leave the Presidency More Idealistic,'" *New York Times*, January 19, 2001, A24, late edition, East Coast.

15. I cite the term "blood and belonging" from the title of Michael Ignatieff's book on the "new" nationalisms of the 1990s, which exemplifies the essentializing logic in dominant explanations of ethnicity and conflict. See *Blood and Belonging: Journeys into the New Nationalism* (New York: Farrar, Straus and Giroux, 1993).

16. Jasminka Udovicki and Ivan Torov, "The Interlude: 1980–1990," in *Burn This House: The Making and Unmaking of Yugoslavia*, ed. Jasminka Udovicki and James Ridgeway (Durham, N.C.: Duke University Press, 1997), 83 (emphasis added).

17. Susan Woodward, "International Aspects of the Wars in Former Yugoslavia," in Udovicki and Ridgeway, *Burn This House*, 217.

18. The Socialist Federal Republic of Yugoslavia, founded in 1943, consisted of six republics (Slovenia, Croatia, Bosnia, Serbia, Montenegro, and Macedonia) and two autonomous provinces within Serbia (Vojvodina and Kosovo).

19. "Clinton on Kosovo: 'We Can Make a Difference,'" *New York Times*, February 14, 1999, 1:8, late edition, East Coast.

20. Clinton, cited in "War and Analogy," *New York Times*, April 18, 1999, 4:18, late edition, East Coast.

21. Clinton, "In the President's Words."

22. Ibid.

23. Clinton, "A Just and Necessary War."

24. Michael Ignatieff, "The Next President's Duty to Intervene," *New York Times*, February 13, 2000, 4:17, late edition, East Coast.

25. "Clinton, Saluting Kosovo Albanians, Urges Forgiveness," *New York Times*, November 24, 1999, A1, late edition, East Coast.

26. Ibid.

27. Serge Schmemann, "From President, Victory Speech and a Warning," *New York Times*, June 11, 1999, A1, late edition, East Coast.

28. See Longinović's discussion of "the failure of universal humanism" predicated on the "ceaseless return of the desire for survival at the expense of the blood of the other" (95) in *Vampire Nation*.

29. See Nina Auerbach and David Skal's preface to the Norton Critical Edition of Bram Stoker's *Dracula* (New York: Norton, 1997), xii.

30. www.pomgrenade.org/BM/.

31. Since NATO's Operation Allied Force is remembered as the "first internet war," Pomgrenade's web art can be read as a form of activism that repurposes wartime media technologies to intervene in the dominant modes of U.S. militarism since the end of the Cold War.

32. Paul Virilio, *War and Cinema: The Logistics of Perception* (New York: Verso, 1989), 85.

33. Maria Todorova, *Imagining the Balkans* (New York: Oxford University Press, 1997), 18.

34. Stoker, *Dracula*, 278.

35. Ibid., 34.

36. Ibid., 277.

37. Thomas Richards, *The Imperial Archive: Knowledge and the Fantasy of Empire* (New York: Verso, 1993).

38. Ibid., 4, 5.

39. As Judith Halberstam has pointed out, "Dracula is not simply a monster, but a technology of monstrosity." She makes the case, therefore, for the "productivity of gothic fiction" (106). See *Skin Shows: Gothic Horror and the Technology of Monsters* (Durham, N.C.: Duke University Press, 1995).

40. Carol Senf, "*Dracula*: The Unseen Face in the Mirror," reprinted in Stoker, *Dracula*, 425.

41. Stoker, *Dracula*, 211.

42. Ibid., 277.

43. In 1990, the Federal Republic of Yugoslavia consisted of Serbia and its two provinces, Vojvodina and Kosovo, and the republic of Montenegro.

44. "Hit Smarter, Not Harder?," CNN.com, 2001, http://www.cnn.com/SPECIALS/2001/gulf.war/legacy/airstrikes/.

45. See Michael Mandel, "Illegal Wars, Collateral Damage, and International Criminal Law," in *Yugoslavia Unraveled: Sovereignty, Self-Determination, Intervention,* ed. Raju G. C. Thomas (Lanham, Md.: Lexington Books, 2003), 293.

46. Joseph J. Eash III, "Harnessing Technology for Coalition Warfare," *NATO Review* (online edition) 48, no. 2 (2004): 32–33, http://www.nato.int/docu/review/2000/0002-11.htm.

47. Michael Ignatieff, *Empire Lite: Nation Building in Bosnia, Kosovo and Afghanistan* (London: Vintage, 2003), 24.

48. Ibid., 59.

49. Avery F. Gordon, *Ghostly Matters: Haunting and the Sociological Imagination* (Minneapolis: University of Minnesota Press, 1997), 12.

50. Stoker, *Dracula*, 41.

51. Ethan Bronner, "Historians Note Flaws in President's Speech," *New York Times,* March 26, 1999, A12, late edition, East Coast.

52. Clinton, "Statement on Kosovo," March 24, 1999, reprinted in *History, Policy, Impact,* Miller Center, University of Virginia, http://millercenter.org/president/speeches/detail/3932.

53. ABC *Nightly News*, March 27, 1999.

54. Ibid.

55. CBS *Evening News*, March 28, 1999.

56. CBS *Evening News*, March 29, 1999.

57. ABC *Nightly News*, April 11, 1999.

58. April 4, 1999.

59. CBS *Evening News*, April 10, 1999.

60. Ibid.

61. Walter Benjamin, "Theses on the Philosophy of History," in *Illuminations,* ed. Hannah Arendt, trans. Harry Zohn (New York: Schocken Books, 1968), 256.

62. Richard Cohen, "A Look into the Void," *Washington Post,* April 16, 1999, A29, final edition.

63. ABC, *Nightline*, April 12, 1999.
64. Rob Noland, "Vengeance of a Victim Race," *Newsweek*, April 12, 1999, 42.
65. Ibid.
66. Tony Blair, cited in Mick Hume, "Nazifying the Serbs, from Bosnia to Kosovo," in *Degraded Capability: The Media and the Kosovo Crisis*, ed. Philip Hammond and Edward S. Herman (Sterling, Va.: Pluto Press, 2000), 70.
67. Hume, "Nazifying the Serbs," 72.
68. Barnor Hesse, "Im/Plausible Deniability: Racism's Conceptual Double Bind," *Social Identities* 10, no. 1 (2004): 9–29.
69. Ibid., 14.
70. The conflation of "ethnicity" and "religion" has continued to frame post-9/11 coverage of U.S. interventionism in the Middle East, in which the figure of the "Muslim" stands for the ethnic, religious, and cultural difference that presents a fundamental threat to Western civilization.
71. See Marcus Banks and Monica Wolfe Murray's "Ethnicity and Reports of the 1992–95 Bosnian Conflict" on the media's use of the term "ethnic cleansing" in Bosnia in Allen, *Media of Conflict*, 147–61.
72. Jean Seaton, "The New 'Ethnic' Wars and the Media," in Allen and Seaton, *The Media of Conflict*, 43–63.
73. Ibid., 52.
74. See Stuart Allen and Barbie Zelizer, eds., "Rules of Engagement: Journalism and War," in *Reporting War: Journalism in War Time* (New York: Routledge, 2004), 3–21. Allen and Zelizer's introductory remarks demonstrate that the coverage of the U.S. war in Iraq, in which the practice of "embedding" journalists with combat troops made explicit the cooperation between the national media and the military is just the most recent example of how media images have been crucial for raising public support for military actions and intervention.
75. Society of Professional Journalists, "Reference Guide to the Geneva Conventions," http://www.genevaconventions.org/.
76. Piers Robinson, *The CNN Effect: The Myth of News, Foreign Policy, and Intervention* (New York: Routledge, 2002), 1.
77. Ibid., 128.
78. Mirjana Skoco and William Woodger, "The Military and the Media," in Hammond and Herman, *Degraded Capability*, 79–87.
79. Ibid., 81.
80. Howard Kurtz, "Serb Units Arrest, Interrogate, Expel Western Journalists," *Washington Post*, March 26, 1999, A26, final edition.
81. NATO Press Conference with Jamie Shea, April 23, 1999, http://www.nato.int/kosovo/press/p9904231.htm.
82. Amnesty International, *"Collateral Damage" or Unlawful Killings? Violations of the Laws of War by NATO during Operation Allied Force* (New York: Amnesty International USA, 2000), 41.
83. Cited in Amnesty International, *"Collateral Damage,"* 42.
84. CBS *Evening News*, April 21, 1999.

85. Shea, cited in Hammond and Herman, *Degraded Capability*, 85.

86. Goran Gocić, "NATO versus the Serbian Media," in Hammond and Herman, *Degraded Capability*, 88–93. Gocić cites examples of the "barbaric" regime's ironic MTV-style response to NATO. For instance, in the case of the shot-down stealth bomber, RTS broadcast images "captioned with a parody of the Windows '95 warning: 'This aircraft has performed an illegal operation and will be shot down,'" and people carried placards saying "Sorry, we did not know it was invisible" (89).

87. Tony Weymouth, "The Media: Information and Deformation," in *The Kosovo Crisis: The Last American War in Europe?*, ed. Tony Weymouth and Stanley Henig (London: Pearson Education, 2001), 143–62, 153.

88. Wendy Kozol, "Domesticating NATO's War in Kosovo/a: (In)Visible Bodies and the Dilemma of Photojournalism," *Meridians* 4, no. 2 (2004): 1–38, 14.

89. NATO Press Conference, March 25, 1999, http://www.nato.int/kosovo/press/p990325a.htm.

90. Lisa Parks, "Satellite Views of Srebrenica: Tele-visuality and the Politics of Witnessing," *Social Identities* 7, no. 4 (December 2001): 585–611, 589.

91. Ibid., 589.

92. ABC *Nightly News*, April 10, 1999.

93. Blaine Harden, "What It Would Take to Cleanse Serbia," *New York Times*, May 9, 1999, 4:1, late edition, East Coast.

94. NATO Press Conference, April 23, 1999.

95. Achille Mbembe, "Necropolitics," trans. Libby Meintjes, *Public Culture* 15, no. 1 (2003): 11–40, 30.

96. "Waging Peace," ABC, *Nightline*, June 14, 1999.

97. Skoco and Woodger, "War Crimes," in Hammond and Herman, *Degraded Capability*, 31–38, 37.

98. "Waging Peace," narrated by Ted Koppel, ABC, *Nightline*, June 16, 1999.

99. Giorgio Agamben, *Homo Sacer: Sovereign Power and Bare Life*, trans. Daniel Heller-Roazen (Stanford, Calif.: Stanford University Press, 1998), 19.

100. Giorgio Agamben, *State of Exception*, trans. Kevin Attell (Chicago: University of Chicago Press, 2005), 2.

101. Cited in William Glaberson, "Conflict in the Balkans: The Law," *New York Times*, March 27, 1999, A8, late edition.

102. Cited in Robert M. Hayden, "Biased Justice: 'Humanrightism' and the International Criminal Tribunal for the Former Yugoslavia," in *Yugoslavia Unraveled: Sovereignty, Self-Determination, Intervention*, ed. Raju G. C. Thomas, 259–85, 279.

103. Ivo H. Daalder and Michael E. O'Hanlon, *Winning Ugly: NATO's War to Save Kosovo* (Washington, D.C.: Brookings Institution Press, 2000), 11–12.

104. Even the political and media rhetorics that accompanied the post-9/11 U.S. aggression in Afghanistan and Iraq, which were much more explicit about U.S. national security as the foremost factor, continued to cite humanitarian ideals and universal values to justify intervention (for instance, spreading freedom, eliminating terrorism, liberating women, removing a rogue dictator, and installing democracy).

105. *Kosovo Report: Conflict, International Response, Lessons Learned* (New York: Oxford University Press, 2000), 164 (emphases in original).

106. "Address by Former President Nelson Mandela," in the *Kosovo Report*, 15.

107. Diana Johnstone, "Humanitarian War: Making the Crime Fit the Punishment," in *Masters of the Universe? NATO's Balkan Crusade*, ed. Tariq Ali (New York: Verso, 2000), 147–70.

108. Alex Callincos, "The Ideology of Humanitarian Intervention," in Ali, *Masters of the Universe*, 175–89.

109. Michael P. Scharf and William A. Schabas, *Slobodan Milošević on Trial: A Companion* (New York: Continuum, 2002), 3.

110. Roger Cohen, "From Bosnia to Berlin to the Hague, on a Road toward a Continent's Future," *New York Times*, July 15, 2001, 4:7, late edition, East Coast.

111. George Kennan, "Introduction: The Balkan Crises 1913 and 1993," in *The Other Balkan Wars: A 1913 Carnegie Endowment Inquiry*, International Commission to Inquire into the Causes and Conduct of the Balkan Wars (1912–1913) (Washington, D.C.: Carnegie Endowment for International Peace, 1993), 3.

5. The Feminist Politics of Secular Redemption at the International Criminal Tribunal for the Former Yugoslavia

1. Directed by Hans-Christian Schmid, 23/5 Filmproduktion GmbH and Zentropa Entertainment, 2009.

2. See, for instance, Wendy Hesford's chapter on Bosnia, "Witnessing Rape Warfare: Suspending the Spectacle," in *Spectacular Rhetorics: Human Rights Visions, Recognitions, Feminisms* (Durham, N.C.: Duke University Press, 2011), and Jasmina Husanović's article, "The Politics of Gender, Witnessing, and Postcolonial Trauma: Bosnian Feminist Trajectories," *Feminist Theory* 10, no. 99 (2009): 99–119.

3. Debra Bergoffen, "February 22, 2001: Toward a Politics of the Vulnerable Body," *Hypatia* 18, no. 1 (Winter 2003): 116–34, 116.

4. Ibid., 118.

5. Writing about British rule in Egypt, Samera Esmeir argues that with colonial rule, humanity ceased being a condition of birth, becoming instead a juridical category (3). In her incisive analysis of the colonial records, Esmeir finds that through colonial legal reforms aimed at taking Egyptians out of a state of lawlessness, conditions of excessive suffering, and inhumanity, "colonial powers carved out a space for their own intervention" (13). Moreover, as "modern law endows itself with the power of humanization, and declares that its absence signals dehumanization, modern law effectively binds the living to the powers of the state" (2). With what Esmeir terms the emergence of a juridical humanity, colonial rule produced "new men who would owe their 'being' and 'life' to the law" (2). Humanity thus became an "evolutionary narrative" that needed to distinguish between "humanity and its history" in a "chronological movement from the past to humanity (humanization, becoming human)" (86). See *Juridical Humanity* (Stanford, Calif.: Stanford University Press, 2012), 3.

6. From Resolution 827. Go to http://www.icty.org/sid/319.

7. As of 2012, it is not scheduled to close until 2016.

8. Scholars and commentators have often noted that the major distinction between the International Criminal Court (ICC) and Tribunals and Truth and Reconciliation Commissions (TRC) is the former's emphasis on identifying and prosecuting criminals as opposed to the latter's emphasis on establishing the truth while granting amnesty to perpetrators. Darryl Robinson, for instance, points out that during the ICC negotiations, truth commissions were regarded as an acceptable *supplement* to the proceedings of international courts, providing a forum for record keeping, education, reparations, and reconciliation, but not as an alternative, due to the contradictory aims of amnesty and prosecution. See "Serving the Interests of Justice: Amnesties, Truth Commissions, and the International Criminal Court," *European Journal of International Law* 14 (2003): 481–505. In Bosnia and Herzegovina there has been a movement for establishing a TRC, which is seen as providing a more comprehensive sense of justice for the victims than the ICTY. See Beyazit Akman, "Tribunal vs. Truth: ICTY and TRC in the Case of the Former Yugoslavia," *HUMSEC Journal* 2 (2008): 125–44. At the same time, the ICTY sees a TRC in the former Yugoslavia as taking away funds from its operations and, with its own emphasis on establishing the truth and a historical record, as largely redundant. Moreover, in spite of the idea that a TRC could lead to a more comprehensive sense of justice for the victims, as South Africa's TRC demonstrates, granting amnesty tends to be viewed as fundamentally unjust (that is, more in the service of reconciliation than justice).

9. "Inside the Tribunal," http://www.icty.org/sections/AbouttheICTY.

10. "About the ICTY," http://www.icty.org/sections/AbouttheICTY.

11. "Achievements," http://www.icty.org/sid/324#developing.

12. "Achievements," http://www.icty.org/sid/324#bringing. As of 2012, of the accused, sixty have been convicted of crimes, while thirty cases are in the process of being tried.

13. "The Cost of Justice," http://www.icty.org/sid/325.

14. As of 2012, 121 countries have ratified the treaty acknowledging the authority of the ICC as a permanent international criminal court. The United States, with concern over submitting its military actions to non-national juridical bodies, has not ratified the treaty.

15. Rachel Kerr, *The International Criminal Tribunal in the Former Yugoslavia: An Exercise in Law, Politics, and Democracy* (New York: Oxford University Press, 2004), 12.

16. Ibid., 12–13.

17. Isabelle Delpha, "In the Midst of Injustice: The ICTY from the Perspective of Some Victim Associations," in *The New Bosnian Mosaic: Identities, Memories and Moral Claims in a Post-War Society*, ed. Xavier Bougarel, Elissa Helms, and Ger Duijzings (Aldershot, UK: Ashgate Publishing, 2007), 219.

18. Ibid., 226. Delpha notes that many Bosnians blame the United Nations' "Blue Helmets" and the United States and Western Europe more broadly for the siege of Sarajevo and the massacre in Srebrenica and wonder why their leaders are not on trial at The Hague but are, rather, the ones sitting in judgment.

19. In a similar critique to Delpha's, Sanja Kutnjak Ivković argues that the structural preconditionality that pressed the nations of the former Yugoslavia to submit their domestic politics to the ICTY as the condition for entering into negotiations with the European Union and the primacy of the ICTY over the national courts point to a "democracy deficit" within the Tribunal and a new hierarchy of nations. See *Reclaiming Justice: The International Tribunal for the Former Yugoslavia and Local Courts* (New York: Oxford University Press, 2011), 84, 119, 153.

20. Ivković, *Reclaiming Justice*, 57. Rachel Kerr also argues that for the ICTY, the creation of a historical record has been important, especially since there are multiple versions of the "truth" on the ground. For Kerr, the supremacy of the ICTY's jurisdiction over war crimes accords it the authority to enact this important task of setting a unified history on record, as part of the reconciliation process (62).

21. "About the ICTY," http://www.icty.org/sections/AbouttheICTY.

22. Cynthia Enloe used the term "new feminist consciousness" to describe the relationship between the activism surrounding rape warfare and feminist progress. See "Afterword: Have the Bosnian Rapes Opened a New Era of Feminist Consciousness?," in *Mass Rape: The War against Women in Bosnia-Herzegovina*, ed. Alexandra Stiglmayer (Lincoln: University of Nebraska Press, 1994), 219–30.

23. Catharine MacKinnon's article "Turning Rape into Pornography: Postmodern Genocide," which was published in the July 1993 issue of *Ms.* magazine, spurred American feminists' interest in the Balkan Wars. MacKinnon argued that the availability of pornography in the former Yugoslavia led to what came to be known as the rape and death camps. This is an argument for which she came under much criticism, especially by feminists across the former Yugoslavia who contended that there was in fact much less pornography available there than in many Western European nations and in the United States. See, for instance, Dubravka Žarkov's *The Body of War: Media, Ethnicity, and Gender in the Break-up of Yugoslavia* (Durham, N.C.: Duke University Press, 2007).

24. Todd Salzman, "Rape Camps as a Means of Ethnic Cleansing: Religious, Cultural, and Ethical Responses to Rape Victims in the Former Yugoslavia," *Human Rights Quarterly* 20, no. 2 (1998): 348–78, 348.

25. A prominent example, the documentary *Calling the Ghosts*, one of the best-known portrayals of victims of rape in the former Yugoslavia, ends with Jadranka Cigelj, the main subject of the film, at The Hague, where she gives testimony. A number of feminist scholars have written compellingly about the ethics of representing rape in that film. See Wendy Hesford's "Witnessing Rape Warfare" in *Spectacular Rhetorics*; also see Katarzyna Marciniak, "Pedagogy of Anxiety," *Signs* 35, no. 4 (2010): 869–92.

26. Beverly Allen, *Rape Warfare: The Hidden Genocide in Bosnia-Herzegovina and Croatia* (Minneapolis: University of Minnesota Press, 1996), 108–9.

27. Ibid., 135.

28. Cynthia Enloe, "Afterword: Have the Bosnian Rapes Opened a New Era of Feminist Consciousness?," in Stiglmayer, *Mass Rape*, 219.

29. Ibid., 222.

30. Ibid.

31. Ibid., 221.

32. Even prior to the establishment of the ICTY, Tadeusz Mazowiecki's final report of the Special Rapporteur to the Commission of Experts, which established the need for an international tribunal for the former Yugoslavia, assessed that rape as a form of "contempt and hatred" is "one of the most tragic aspects of the plight of the Muslim population" in Bosnia. Cited in Sara Sharratt, *Gender, Shame, and Sexual Violence: The Voices of Witnesses and Court Members at War Crimes Tribunals* (Burlington, VT: Ashgate Publishing, 2011), 6.

33. "Crimes of Sexual Violence," http://www.icty.org/sid/10312.

34. Interview in *Sexual Violence and the Triumph of Justice*, DVD, ICTY Outreach Programme and ITSS Production, 2011.

35. Sharratt, *Gender, Shame, and Sexual Violence*, 20.

36. Cited in "International Justice Failing Rape Victims," Institute for War and Peace Reporting, Special Report, TRI Issue 483, February 15, 2010, http://iwpr.net/report-news/international-justice-failing-rape-victims.

37. Ibid.

38. Interview in *Sexual Violence and the Triumph of Justice*.

39. Sharratt, *Gender, Shame, and Sexual Violence*, 30.

40. Hesford, *Spectacular Rhetorics*, 96.

41. Debra Berghoffen, *Contesting the Politics of Genocidal Rape: Affirming the Dignity of the Vulnerable Body* (New York: Routledge, 2012), 67.

42. Ibid., 1.

43. Ibid., 2.

44. Ibid., 70.

45. MacKinnon compares the wars in the Balkans to the Holocaust, but for her, this time sex, and not religion or ethnicity, became the primary marker of the victims. She writes, "The world has never seen sex used this consciously, this cynically, this elaborately, this openly, this systematically, with this degree of technological and psychological sophistication, as a means of destroying a whole people. With this war, pornography emerges as a tool of genocide" (75). MacKinnon, in a sense, originated the idea that genocide in the former Yugoslavia was gendered. MacKinnon's article has been widely critiqued by feminist writers from Croatia, Bosnia, and Serbia, as well as from the United States and Western Europe, for its sensationalist and exploitative use of women's testimony, the unfair treatment of Balkan feminists, and the assumption that only women can be victims of rape. Of particular interest, however, is the question of what makes this genocide not just gendered but postmodern in MacKinnon's estimation. MacKinnon is particularly troubled that the Serbs, Croats, and Bosnian Muslims are not racially distinguishable. She claims that the Serbs used this in their favor. According to the article, Serb soldiers videotaped themselves while raping Muslim women, but because they placed crosses around the women's necks, they were able to claim the footage as evidence of Muslim soldiers raping Serbian women. MacKinnon writes, "Serbian propaganda moves cultural markers with postmodern alacrity, making ethnicity unreal and all too real at the same time" (76).

For MacKinnon, racial and religious identities in the Balkans are confusing and interchangeable; what is certain is the biological determinacy of sexual difference, and it is through this difference that the Muslim woman is visible as a victim of war crimes. Reprinted in Stiglmayer, *Mass Rape*.

46. MacKinnon, "Crimes of War, Crimes of Peace," in *Are Women Human? And Other International Dialogues* (Cambridge, Mass.: The Belknap Press of Harvard University Press, 2006), 153.

47. Ibid., 153.

48. Ibid., 154.

49. Tracy Fessenden, "Disappearances: Race, Religion, and the Progress Narrative of U.S. Feminism," in *Secularisms,* ed. Janet R. Jakobsen and Ann Pellegrini (Durham, N.C.: Duke University Press, 2008), 140.

50. Ibid., 139.

51. Ibid., 141.

52. Josip Broz Tito, Yugoslavia's president from the end of World War II through his death in 1980, gave the 40 percent majority Bosnian Muslim population the status of an ethnicity (*narod*) in the 1971 census. The republic also had large minority populations of Christian Orthodox Serbs (30 percent) and Catholic Croats (20 percent). After 1991, the division in Bosnia along ethnic and religious lines paralleled the nationalism in Croatia and Serbia.

53. Talal Asad, *Formations of the Secular: Christianity, Islam, Modernity* (Stanford, Calif.: Stanford University Press, 2003), 159.

54. Ibid., 171.

55. Ibid.

56. See Žarkov, *The Body of War*, 148; Tone Bringa, "Islam and the Quest for Identity in Post-Communist Bosnia-Herzegovina," in *Islam and Bosnia: Conflict Resolution and Foreign Policy in Multi-Ethnic States*, ed. Maya Shatzmiller (Montreal: McGill-Queen's University Press, 2002), 24–34.

57. Bringa, "Islam and the Quest for Identity," 33, 34.

58. For instance, Michael Sells, who has written extensively on religion in the former Yugoslavia, argues that during the war, "Serbian Orthodoxy [was] . . . the clearest and most obvious example of how religious myth and ritual were exploited" to create a homogeneous national conception of "Serbs" leading to ethnoreligious "cleansing" (212). See "Sacral Ruins in Bosnia-Herzegovina: Mapping Ethnoreligious Nationalism," in *Religion and the Creation of Race and Ethnicity*, ed. Craig R. Prentiss (New York: New York University Press, 2003), 211–34.

59. Ibid., 212. Sells thus ranks Serbian religious nationalism as the most genocidal, Catholic Croat nationalism as "reactively genocidal," and Islamic nationalism as not being indigenous to the region and, therefore, not genocidal.

60. Ibid.

61. Ibid., 217, 221.

62. For an excellent discussion on the kinds of legal claims enabled by emphasizing ethnic identity as opposed to religious identity within Europe, see Saba Mahmood, "Religious Reason and Secular Affect: An Incommensurable Divide?," *Critical*

Inquiry 35, no. 4 (Summer 2009): 836–62. As Mahmood argues within the context of the Dutch cartoon controversy, "Arguments about the racialization of Muslims provoke the fear among Europeans that if this premise is conceded or accorded legal recognition then European Muslims will resort to European hate-speech laws to unduly regulate forms of speech that they regard as injurious to their religious sensibilities" (851). The distinction between the treatment of race and religion in the law rests on the opposition between "immutable biological characteristic[s]" and matters of choice, with race falling into the former and religion into the latter category (852).

63. See, for instance, Swanee Hunt, *This Was Not Our War: Bosnian Women Reclaiming the Peace* (Durham, N.C.: Duke University Press, 2004).

64. Elizabeth Neuffer, *The Key to My Neighbor's House: Seeking Justice in Bosnia and Rwanda* (New York: Picador, 2001), 5.

65. Hunt, *This Was Not Our War,* 2.

66. Ibid., 137.

67. Ibid., xv.

68. Allen, *Rape Warfare,* 90.

69. Cited in Robert D. Kaplan, "A Reader's Guide to the Balkans," *New York Times,* April 18, 1993, BR1.

70. Swanee Hunt, *Worlds Apart: Bosnian Lessons for Global Security* (Durham, N.C.: Duke University Press, 2011), 50.

71. Ibid.

72. Ibid., 202.

73. Ibid., 157.

74. For instance, Roy Gutman, an American journalist who first broke the stories of the rape and death camps in the United States and Europe, proposed in his foreword to the most widely cited book on rape warfare in Bosnia, Stiglmayer's *Mass Rape,* that Muslim traditions facilitated the use of rape as a genocidal strategy on the part of the Serbs. He writes, "In the conservative society in which the Muslims of rural Bosnia grew up, women traditionally remain chaste until marriage. . . . [Victims of rape] have well-founded fears of rejection and ostracism and of lives without marriage or children. In this regard the pattern of rapes of unmarried women of childbearing age fulfills another definition of genocide—the attempt to block procreation of the group" (x). For a more detailed critique of such representations of Muslim traditionalism in scholarship on rape warfare, see Žarkov, *The Body of War,* 144–48.

75. Ruth Seifert, "War and Rape: A Preliminary Analysis," in Stiglmayer, *Mass Rape,* 56.

76. Alexandra Stiglmayer, the editor of *Mass Rape,* is clearest in her articulation of how "difficult" these women are to find: "It was not easy to find these women. In the refugee camps we visited, how frequently we were told: 'Of course we have cases of rape; I can show you the women, but they don't talk about it' " (83). Later in the chapter, Stiglmayer quotes a Muslim doctor, who seems to reaffirm that many more women were raped than spoke out because, according to him, " 'There's a psychological problem here. . . . Muslim society is patriarchal. A woman's honor is

important, and the men are jealous" (91). Cited in "The Rapes in Bosnia and Herze-govina," in Stiglmayer, *Mass Rape*.

77. According to Talal Asad, "The American secular language of redemption, for all its particularity, now works as a force in the field of foreign relations to globalize human rights. . . . Hence 'democracy,' 'human rights,' and 'being free' are integral to the universalizing moral project of the American nation state—the project of humaniz-ing the world." See Asad, *Formations of the Secular*, 147.

78. Ibid., 157 (emphasis in original).

79. "Statements of Guilt," http://www.icty.org/sid/203.

80. "Witness DD," http://www.icty.org/sid/10124.

81. "Habiba Hadžić," http://www.icty.org/sid/10123.

82. "Grozdana Ćećez," http://www.icty.org/sid/196.

83. Wendy Brown, "'The Most We Can Hope For . . .': Human Rights and the Politics of Fatalism," *South Atlantic Quarterly* 103, no. 2–3 (2004): 451–63, 453.

84. "About the ICTY," http://www.icty.org/sections/AbouttheICTY.

85. Giorgio Agamben, *Homo Sacer: Sovereign Power and Bare Life*, trans. Daniel Heller-Roazen (Stanford, Calif.: Stanford University Press, 1995), 4, 6, 10.

86. Ibid., 83.

87. Ibid., 176.

88. Ibid.

89. Ibid., 187.

90. Ibid.

91. Clea Koff, *The Bone Woman: A Forensic Anthropologist's Search for Truth in the Mass Graves of Rwanda, Bosnia, Croatia, and Kosovo* (New York: Random House, 2004), 152.

92. Ibid., 16–17.

93. The ownership of bodies, particularly those that have been reduced to the status of bare life, is the foundation for meaning making by distinct regimes of power. During the war, bodies in the camp were meant to signal the degradation of an entire ethnic or religious group. As Dubravka Žarkov argues, during the wars in the former Yugo-slavia, ethnicity was produced through the living and symbolic bodies of men and women. The wars themselves, and the technologies of war, became the modes of production of ethnicity and nationalism. According to Žarkov, the raped female body was always necessarily also an ethnic body. Through the production of femi-ninity as vulnerability, sexual violence against women was simultaneously vested with meanings of victimization and linked to territory. See Žarkov, *The Body of War*, 2, 153, 172.

94. "Stevan Todorović," http://www.icty.org/sid/225 (emphases added).

95. Brown, "'The Most We Can Hope For . . . ,'" 461.

96. Jasmina Husanović's excellent article, "The Politics of Gender, Witnessing, and Post-Colonial Trauma," discusses Žbanić's films as responding to the war in Bosnia through a creative approach to political loss as a politics of hope (101). Addressing culture as a site through which such critique can take place, she posits the importance of moving

away from thinking of Bosnia through the lens of survival and healing and moving on to a politics of reimagination and transformation that is based on a hopeful politics of witnessing. Here I am emphasizing a politics of refusal in place of a politics of hope in order to move away from a future-oriented temporality, which risks being engulfed in the messianic temporality of human rights, and toward a complex, heterogeneous temporality that emerges in Žbanić's films.

Epilogue

1. Swanee Hunt, *This Was Not Our War: Bosnian Women Reclaiming the Peace* (Durham, N.C.: Duke University Press, 2004), xv.
2. "Top Secret America," *Frontline*, PBS, http://video.pbs.org/video/2117159594/.
3. According to *Frontline*, the exact amount of money spent by the NSA in the years after 9/11 is one of the best-kept secrets of the new war.
4. For instance, during the 2009 protests in Iran following that country's controversial presidential election, the death of Neda Agha Soltan was captured on a camera phone, and the video quickly went viral. While many of the traditional news sources, which rebroadcasted her death in the United States, blurred out her face in a show of respect, on online platforms one was able to see the full horror of her lying in an alley, bleeding from the mouth after being shot by the government-sponsored patrol, which was attempting to squash the mass demonstrations. In this case, new technologies of communication were interpreted not just as changing the way in which the world reports the news but as disabling closed, antidemocratic, and nonsecular regimes, such as the one in Iran, from keeping their oppression hidden from the world's view. U.S. news sources framed Neda's death as the story of a young woman whose aspiration to leave the antidemocratic nation and live a secular, modern life with her boyfriend was quite literally killed by the Iranian state. Yet it is hardly an accident that a dying woman's body would come to elicit the West's humanitarian gaze by symbolizing the repressive nature of the regime—notions of Islamic terror have, after all, referenced sexual oppression as a foremost mark of illiberalism, especially after 9/11. The image of a Muslim woman's dying and injured body, whose sacrifice has come to emblematize the desire for democracy, gender equality, and sexual freedom in Iran, although seemingly disconnected from the ongoing occupation of Afghanistan and Iraq in fact circulates as the visible counterpoint justifying "top secret America" as being, fundamentally, about global human justice.
5. "Boston Explosions: 'Please Don't be Arabs or Muslims,'" *AlJazeera.com*, April 16, 2013, http://www.aljazeera.com/indepth/opinion/2013/04/201341681629153634.html, accessed on May 10, 2013.
6. "Tamerlan Tsarnaev and Dzhokhar Tsarnaev Were Refugees from Brutal Chechen Conflict," *Washington Post*, April 19, 2013, http://articles.washingtonpost.com/2013 -04-19/world/38660077_1_russian-caucasus-boston-marathon-chechnya.
7. "Boston Suspects: Immigrant Dream to American Nightmare," *CNN.com*, April 21, 2013, http://www.cnn.com/2013/04/19/us/massachusetts-bombers-profiles.
8. "The Wrong Kind of Caucasian," *AlJazeera.com*, April 21, 2013, http://www.aljazeera .com/indepth/opinion/2013/04/2013421145859380504.html.

9. "U.S. Senator Says 4,700 Killed in Drone Strikes," *Al Jazeera.com,* February 21, 2013, http://www.aljazeera.com/news/americas/2013/02/201322185240615179.html.

10. Jennifer Epstein, "White House: Dzhokhar Tsarnaev Not an 'Enemy Combatant,'" *Politico.com,* April 22, 2013, http://www.politico.com/politico44/2013/04/white -house-dzhokar-tsarnaev-not-an-enemy-combatant-162298.html.

11. Cited in "Boston Suspects," *CNN.com.*

INDEX

Davis, Peter, 95–96

Dayton Peace Accords, 130, 174, 185

decolonization, 20, 22, 26, 69, 106

Disuniting of America, The (Schlesinger), 33

diversity: and humanitarian militarism, 2, 4–5, 131–32; Islam on, 13; as liberty, 10, 134; and postsocialist imperialism, 180; promotion of, 41, 131–32; and prosperity, 137; and Sovietization, 22, 219n48. *See also* multiculturalism

Doney, Nick, 110

Dracula (Stoker), 128, 138, 140–43, 145

Dream Jungle (Hagedorn), 88, 91–94

Du Bois, W. E. B., 44, 214n14

Dudziak, Mary, 11, 20

Durschmied, Eric, 115–16

Eastern Europe: capitalism in, 24; as fledgling democracies, 42; immigration patterns from, 218–19n45; as other, 216n36; perpetual belatedness of, 40; transnational racialization of, 21

Ebony (magazine), 53

Eddie Adams: Vietnam, 98

El-Tayeb, Fatima, 216n35

Enlightenment ideologies, 5, 25, 68, 216n36

Enloe, Cynthia, 175, 176

Esmeir, Samera, 241n5

Essence (magazine), 53, 55

ethics: feminist, 185; of representation, 87–94, 198–99. *See also* humanitarianism

ethnic cleansing, 1, 188; in Balkans, 4–5, 61–62, 130–31, 145–47, 157; during Holocaust, 145–47; media documentation of, 153

ethnography, 26–27

ethnoreligious conflict, 1; travelogues on, 35, 39, 58–69. *See also* ethnic cleansing

European imperialism. *See* imperialism, European

exceptionalism, U.S., 4, 11, 17–18, 80–81, 94, 98, 144

exoticism, 45

Explorer (television program), 122–23

Fabian, Johannes, 38

Federal Republic of Yugoslavia. *See* Yugoslavia (former)

feminism: on Afghan girl image, 121; ethics, 185; and humanitarian imperialism, 179; on human rights, 168–69, 184; on juridical redemption, 174–78; Third World, 175; transnationalization of, 175. *See also* International Criminal Tribunal for the Former Yugoslavia (ICTY)

Fessenden, Tracy, 179–80

Foucault, Michel, 130

freedom: faith in, 105; racial, and capitalism, 40; rating classifications of, 58; in religion, 9–10, 40; religious, 3, 6, 9–10, 64, 67, 106, 109–10, 181; in travelogues, 38, 48–50

Freedom Rating classifications, 58

free world: vs. Communist ideology, 19, 88, 103–4, 106; and freedom to travel, 37–41; map of, 6, 19–20; redefined boundaries of, 71, 180; as U.S.-led, 6, 11, 19, 24, 40, 77, 133–34

frontier. *See* New Frontier concept

Frontline (television news program), 111–12, 201, 203–4

fundamentalism, 2, 13, 16, 205, 207; and women's rights, 235n56

Fukuyama, Francis, 34, 107

Geneva Conventions, 159

genocide, 5, 7, 100, 148–51, 157, 159, 162, 173; and foundations of U.S. nation, 9, 88, 134; and gender, 174–76, 189, 244n45, 246n74; postmodern, 243n23. *See also* Holocaust geopolitical imaginaries, 7, 15, 20–21; in travelogues, 42, 59, 61, 64, 70; and unveiling, 121–22

glasnost, 52, 53

globalization: of humanitarian imperialism, 10; and U.S. imperialism, 8

Gocić, Goran, 154–55

Golden, Lily, 53, 56

Golden, Oliver, 52–53, 57

Gorbachev, Mikhail, 52, 54

Gordon, Avery, 145

Gosser, David, 96

Greene, Graham, 125–28

Grewal, Inderpal, 36

guerilla groups: U.S. aid to, 101, 102–4, 107–8, 120

Gula, Sharbat, 124

Hadžić Habiba, 188

Hagedorn, Jessica, 88, 91–94. *See also Dream Jungle* (Hagedorn)

Hague, The, 149, 163, 166, 170, 188; and Peace Conferences, 164

Halberstam, David, 98, 99–100

Hapsburg Empire, 227n125

Hatch, Orrin, 115

Havel, Vlaclav, 161

Heart of Darkness (Conrad), 65, 75–77, 81–87; as critique of imperialism, 83–87; inspiration for film/writing, 87–89, 91, 93, 101, 102; storyline, 82–83

Hearts and Minds (Davis documentary), 95–96

Hearts of Darkness (E. Coppola documentary), 88–91

Herzegovina. *See* Bosnia and Herzegovina

Hesford, Wendy, 16, 177, 235n56

Hirsch, Francine, 22

Hochschild, Adam, 84

Holocaust, 146; as analogy, 133, 145–51, 244n45; and Soviet–Afghan War, 100, 114

homogeneity, 5, 6, 12, 13, 19, 22, 219n48, 245n58

Homo Sacer (Agamben), 189–90

Hong, Grace, 215n25

Hoover, J. Edgar, 19

Hoppe, E. O., 65

Hua, Julietta, 16

Huckleberry Finn (Twain), 50

Hughes, Langston, 44

humanitarian imperialism. *See* imperialism, humanitarian

humanitarian intervention, 1–2; and diversity, 131–32; emergence of, 163; justification for, 130, 133–34, 200–201; and perpetual warfare, 1, 14, 200–201; as postsocialist imperialism, 3, 22–23; rationalization of, 23; role of media, 151–59

humanitarianism: cultural critique of, 27; and diversity, 131–32; feeling of, 74–75, 81–82, 84–87, 95–99; foundations of, 3, 8, 15, 77; as global ethic, 14–15, 18, 26–27, 71; of ICTY, 170–74; ideals as hollow, 126–27; and international juridical governance, 167–68, 171; ironies of, 29, 76; militaristic, 15–16, 72, 103, 133, 135–36, 148, 152; of NATO, 156–57, 161–62; and otherness, 132; paradoxical concepts in, 16; racialization of, 81–87; redemption through, 14, 74, 104. *See also* imperialism, humanitarian

human rights, 1; vs. containment, 40; origin narratives of, 9; and postsocialist imperialism, 17–18; redemption through, 188, 194–95; revealing abuses, 7; sex equality as, 179; universality in, 16–17, 178; violations in Afghanistan, 113–14, 120

Hunt, Swanee, 183, 184, 200

Huntington, Samuel, 34, 107, 129

Hussein, Saddam, 163

Ibrahimefendić, Teufika, 186

ICC. *See* International Criminal Court (ICC)

ICTR. *See* International Criminal Tribunal for Rwanda (ICTR)

ICTY. *See* International Criminal Tribunal for the Former Yugoslavia (ICTY)

Ignatieff, Michael, 18, 137, 145

illiberalism, 12, 44, 56, 58, 248n4

"Image of Africa, An" (Achebe), 84

imperialism (generally): change in connotation, 70; fictions of, 93–94; racialization of bodies in, 3. *See also specific types*

imperialism, European: contribution to postsocialist imperialism, 5, 24, 27, 163; critique of, 83–87; moral darkness in, 81–82; and racialized colonies, 20; vs. Soviet imperialism, 22

imperialism, humanitarian: emergence of, 35, 163, 164; and Euro-American feminism, 168–69, 179; foundations of, 3; globalization of, 10; and racial/ religious difference, 10, 35–37, 70, 133, 150, 163; technologies of, 134, 137, 138–45, 151, 158, 201–2

imperialism, postsocialist: and diversity, 180; foundations of, 3, 5, 6–7, 33, 42; and human rights, 17–18; and international law, 159–65; justification for, 164–65, 201; technologies of, 14–18, 22–23, 137; U.S. imperialism as, 24, 132

imperialism, Soviet, 23, 43–44, 51, 70, 164; of Bolsheviks, 220n53; and religious minorities, 104, 115; in Third World, 43, 106, 217–18n42

imperialism, U.S.: endorsement of, 71; foundations of, 5; and globalization, 8, 137; and international law, 17; in Middle East, 103; as postsocialist, 24; rationalization of, 23; and social justice movements, 80; sovereignty of, 18, 160–61; in Third World, 144–45; in Vietnam War, 14–15; and women's

rights, 180; and world leadership, 6, 11–12

International Association for the Exploration and Civilization in Africa, 82

International Criminal Court (ICC), 171

International Criminal Tribunal for the Former Yugoslavia (ICTY), 1, 25, 152, 158, 163; digital archive, 186–88, 191–92; and feminist consciousness, 174–78, 243n22; film on, 166–68; humanitarianism of, 169, 170–74, 188–89; mission of, 173; reconciliation by, 193–94; statistics, 171; on wartime sexual violence, 176

International Criminal Tribunal for Rwanda (ICTR), 1, 171, 176

international law: ICTY influence on, 188–89; NATO violation of, 159–65; and U.S. imperialism, 17

intervention. *See* humanitarian intervention

intolerance, 12; circulation of images, 7; ethnic, 193–94; Islamic, 13, 30; racial, 10, 12, 56; religious, 13, 15, 19, 56, 193; Soviet, 48, 58; travelogues on, 36; in U.S. policies, 3, 15. *See also* tolerance

Iraq, war in, 202

Islam: Bosnian, 181–82, 184; Iranian, 184; journalistic portrayal of, 105; racialization of, 13; Saudi, 181, 184; and terrorism, 204–5. *See also* Bosnian Muslim women

Jacoby, Susan, 47–48. *See also Soul to Soul* (Khanga/Jacoby)

Jefferson, Thomas, 18

Jennings, Peter, 73

jihad, 110–12

Johnson, Lyndon B., 80

Johnstone, Diana, 162

justice: alternative visions of, 17, 195–99; and demise of communism, 172; effect of U.S. imperialism on, 17; just war

multiculturalism, 8–13; emergence of, 33–34, 44; and free market, 33–57; in postsocialist imperialism, 5, 37; on racial/religious difference, 6, 9, 37, 56; rhetoric of, 41; and secularism, 9, 194; in Soviet Union, 219n48; in travelogues, 52–58; and universal inclusion, 9; in U.S. militarism, 4, 133–34. *See also* diversity

Murnau, F. W., 140

My Lai massacre, images of, 80

National Geographic (magazine), 120–21

National Security Agency (NSA), 202

Native American peoples, 79–80

NATO. *See* North Atlantic Treaty Organization (NATO)

neoliberalism, 12, 214n19

New Frontier concept, 76–81, 96

New Imperialism, The (Seton-Watson), 22

new world order, 7, 12–13, 14, 59, 62, 129–30, 144, 162–64

New Yorker (magazine), 43

New York Public Library, 41

New York Times (newspaper), 18, 174

Nightline (television news program), 159

9/11 attacks. *See* September 11, 2001 terrorist attacks

North Atlantic Treaty Organization (NATO): in Afghanistan, 102; humanization of interventions, 151–59; international law violations, 159–65; and role of media, 151–59; in Serbia and Kosovo, 129, 130–31, 136–39, 143–45, 146, 147–65

Nosferatu (Murnau film), 140–41

Noyce, Phillip, 125–26

NSA. *See* National Security Agency (NSA)

Nuremberg Tribunal, 1, 170

Obama, Barack, 203

Operation Allied Force (1999), 59, 130–33, 137–38, 143–45, 146, 147–65

Operation Desert Storm, 140

Operation Horseshoe, 147

Orientalist discourse, 21, 60, 217–18n42

Orthodox Christianity, 63, 65–69, 129, 150; and Bosnian multiculturalism, 182; and the Serbs, 181, 245n52, 245n58

otherness: African, 85; Balkan, 60, 61, 69, 132, 133, 139; East European, 216n36; Islamic, 204–5; and new media technologies, 142, 152; racialization of, 71–72; in travelogues, 45, 60, 61, 69, 71–72

Ottoman Empire, 67–69, 70, 141, 180–81, 227n125

Pauli, Richard, 119–20

Peterson, Dale, 54

Pfaff, William, 43

photojournalistic images, 2, 15, 73–75, 77, 80, 94–100, 101

Pomegrenade, 139–40

Pond, Elizabeth, 47

postcolonialism, 22, 24, 26

postsocialism, 12; as analytic, 23–27; global conditions of, 23–27; and ICTY governance, 173–74; Vietnam War as first instance, 15

postsocialist imperialism. *See* imperialism, postsocialist

Pratt, Mary Louise, 36

Priest, Dana, 201–2

primitivism, 45

prisoners, treatment of, 1, 113, 203–4

Protestantism, 65; and notions of freedom 10, 68, 179; and Reagan, 104; and the Reformation, 62, 66–67; and U.S. imperialism, 214n13

Puritans, 10, 79–80

Quiet American, The (Greene novel), 125–26

Quiet American, The (Noyce film), 125–27

Quindlen, Anna, 174

racialization: and atrocities, 2; of bodies in imperialism, 3; of Communist unfreedom, 22; of continents, 7, 20, 64, 85–86, 217n38; and difference, 20; dualism in, 19; of Eastern Europe, 42; hierarchy in, 5–6; of humanitarianism, 81–87; of ideology and belief, 3–9; of labor, 10–11; of otherness, 71; of religious difference, 7, 8–13, 27, 37, 62, 132, 168–69; of seeing/feeling, 97; as transnational process, 10, 21, 41, 70

racism: institutionalized, 20, 217n39; against Native American peoples, 79–80; and totalitarianism, 46

Radio Television Serbia (RTS), 153–54, 157–58

rape warfare, 7, 30; against Bosnian Muslim women, 167, 168–69, 175, 178–85; camps, 167, 168–69, 174–78, 188–90; classified as torture, 168; collective shame on, 185; as crime against humanity, 174, 176, 177

Rather, Dan, 111, 117–18, 125

Reagan, Ronald, 40–41, 43, 54, 101, 103–4, 106, 115, 223n27

Reagan Doctrine, 101, 104, 106–12, 118, 125

redemption, 8; and atrocity, 2, 74, 195; humanitarian fantasies of, 14, 74, 104; juridical, 167, 169, 174–78, 185, 188, 190; religious, 110; role of tribunals in, 191; secular, 10, 178, 194, 247n77; in U.S. imperialism, 18, 24, 27, 151

Regarding the Pain of Others (Sontag), 97

religious difference: and atrocities, 2; and humanitarian imperialism, 10, 35–37, 70, 133, 150, 163; multiculturalism on, 6, 9, 37; racialization of, 7, 8–13, 27, 37, 62, 132, 168–69

religious freedom, 3, 6, 9–10, 64, 67, 106, 109–10, 181

Represent and Destroy (Melamed), 12

Revel, Jean-François, 113

Richards, Thomas, 142

Rights of Man, 17, 78

Robeson, Paul, 44

Robinson, Piers, 152–53

Romania: described, 64–65

Rome Statute of the International Criminal Court, 171

RTS. *See* Radio Television Serbia (RTS)

Russian Journal (Lee), 36, 41–52; freedom/unfreedom in, 48–50; reviews of, 46–48

Said, Edward, 25, 217n42

Sarah Phillips (Lee), 46

Schlesinger, Arthur, Jr., 33, 34

Schmitt, Carl, 160

Schwartz-DuPre, Rae Lynn, 121, 122, 124

Second World, 21, 60, 70

secularism: of Bosnian Muslim women, 168–69, 180, 181, 183–84; as ideology of human difference, 10; liberal principles of, 167, 179–80; and multiculturalism, 9, 194; and transcendence, 213–14n12

segregation, 20, 33, 40, 217n39

Seifert, Ruth, 185

Sellers, Patricia, 176–77

Sells, Michael, 181

September 11, 2001 terrorist attacks, 200, 201

Serbia, civil war in: media, role in, 147, 151–59; NATO military intervention, 129, 130–31, 133, 136–39, 143–45, 146, 147–65

Seton-Watson, Hugh, 22

Sharratt, Sara, 177

Shea, Jamie, 154

Shih, Shu-mei, 25–26, 69, 220n54

Shock and Awe campaign, 202

Silva, Denise Ferreira da, 20

Simmons, Alan, 83

Simmons, Cynthia, 60–61

Singh, Nikhil Pal, 11

60 Minutes (television news program), 111, 117, 125

Skoco, Mirjana, 153

slavery, 9, 18, 177

Slike sa ugla (Žbanić documentary), 195–99

Slotkin, Richard, 79–80

Sobchack, Vivian, 98

socialism: as alternative justice, 4, 11, 17; and self-governance in Yugoslavia, 194

Society of Professional Journalists, 152

Solana, Javier, 148

Soltan, Neda Agha, 248n4

Sonnenfeldt, Helmut, 107

Sontag, Susan, 97

Soul to Soul (Khanga/Jacoby), 37, 47, 52–58; review of, 55; title meaning, 54

Soviet-Afghan War (1979–1989), 70, 100–101; Afghan girl image, 120–24; atrocities, censorship on reporting, 112–16; comparison to Vietnam War, 105, 106–8, 115, 118; as hidden war, 113–15; human rights violations, 113–14, 120; journalists dressed as Afghans, 116–20, 121; mujahideen, depiction of, 110–11; Soviet Union, depiction of, 107, 112–13, 119; U.S. foreign policy, 102–3, 106–12, 125

Soviet Union: expansionism, 21–22, 43, 51; glasnost, 52, 53; Khanga travelogue on, 52–58; Lee travelogue on, 42–52; as multicultural entity, 219n47. *See also* imperialism, Soviet

Spanos, William, 80–81

spatial distance, 38

Spiegel, Der (magazine), 147

Srebrenica, mass murders, 173, 186

Starosta, Anita, 39–40

Stiglmayer, Alexandra, 175–76

Stoker, Bram, 128, 138, 140–41, 145

Storm (film), 166–68

Tanzania, 53, 56

temporality, 38–39, 46

terrorism: in Balkans, 64; religious intolerance as, 19; and securitization, 203–4; war on terror, 1, 23, 201–2

Terrorist Surveillance Program, 202

Third World: Balkans as part of, 64; and containment, 6; decolonization of, 20, 69; feminism in, 175; perpetual crisis in, 60, 70; racialization of, 21; Soviet imperialism in, 43, 106, 217–18n42; U.S. imperialism in, 144–45; U.S. liberal agenda for, 40, 43, 78, 80, 112. *See also specific countries*

This Was Not Our War (Hunt), 183

Thompson, Chad, 25

Three Worlds ideology, 20

Time and the Other (Fabian), 38–39

Tito, Josip Broz, 135, 173, 245n52

Todorova, Maria, 141, 216n36

Todorović, Stevan, 193–94

Tokyo Tribunal, 1, 170

tolerance: and ICTY, 167, 193–94; and multiculturalism, 4, 9, 23, 134, 207; and prosperity, 57, 137; religious, 10, 67–68, 181–84; and secularism, 179; and U.S. imperialism, 137–38, 148, 164–65; and women's rights, 200–201. *See also* intolerance

"Top Secret America" (television program), 203

Torov, Ivan, 134–35

transnationalization: of American dream, 110; of liberty/rights, 10; of racial logics, 10, 21

Transylvania: described, 64, 66, 128–29

travelogues, 37–41; on ethnoreligious conflict, 35, 39; on freedom/ unfreedom, 38, 48–50; and geopolitical imaginaries, 42, 59, 61, 64, 70; multicultural gaze in, 36, 52–58. *See also specific works*

tribalism, 33, 134, 136, 168, 188

Tsarnaev, Dzhokhar, 205–7

Tsarnaev, Tamerlan, 205–6

Tudjman, Franjo, 134

Turner, Frederick Jackson, 79

Twain, Mark, 50

20/20 (television news program), 54

UDHR. *See* Universal Declaration of Human Rights (UDHR)

Udovicki, Jasminka, 134–35

unfreedom: racialization of, 22; in religion, 6; in travelogues, 38, 48–50

United Nations, 130, 161, 168; Rome Statute, 171; Security Council, 1, 136, 170

Universal Declaration of Human Rights (UDHR), 17, 195

Unlikely Weapon, An (documentary), 73

USA PATRIOT Act (2001), 160, 201

U.S. imperialism. *See* imperialism, U.S.

U.S.S.R. *See* Soviet Union

Ut, Huynh Cong, 99

vampire: as political figure, 138, 162; rogue nations, 132

Van Helsing (film), 128–30

veiling/unveiling, 121–24, 184

Verdery, Katherine, 26

Vietnam War (1961–1975): failure of, 77, 94–95, 106, 126; images of atrocity, 2, 15, 73–75, 77, 80, 94–100, 101; loss in, 100–101; Soviet-Afghan War compared to, 105, 106–8, 115, 118; as U.S. imperialism, 14–15

Von Eschen, Penny, 21

Voting Rights Act (1965), 11, 80

Vukov, Tamara ("Pomegrenade"), 139–40

Vuković, Zoran, 176

warfare: just war rhetoric, 133–38, 146, 161; perpetual, 1, 23, 201–2, 204; war on terror, 1, 23, 201–2

Washington Post (newspaper), 53, 205

weapons of mass destruction, 202, 206

Weaver, Sigourney, 122–23

West, Rebecca, 69, 184

white supremacy, 5, 21–22, 44

Wiesel, Elie, 148

Williams, Randall, 17

Wilson, Charlie, 102–3, 125

Wired (magazine), 154

Wolff, Larry, 216n36

Woodger, William, 153

Worlds Apart (Hunt), 184, 200

Yugoslavia (former): Clinton on, 35; disintegration of, 134, 181; gendered genocide in, 174–75; humanitarian law violations, 170; postsocialist predicament in, 33; violent conflict in, 15, 23, 59–60, 63–64, 130, 134, 167, 173. *See also* Bosnia and Herzegovina; International Criminal Tribunal for the Former Yugoslavia (ICTY)

Žbanić, Jasmila, 195–96, 207–8

Neda Atanasoski is associate professor of feminist studies at the University of California, Santa Cruz.